CINEMAGOGUE

THE **MARVEL-US** ERA

by

James Harleman

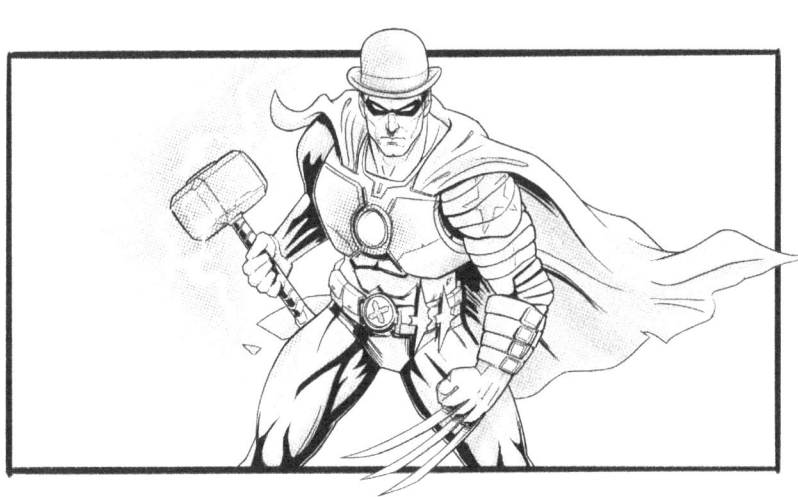

How **the 21st century** has **transformed storytelling**—for better and for worse—and how we can **use it for God's glory.**

First Edition
© 2025 by Cinemagogue Press

Published by Cinemagogue Press
16823 22nd Ave NE
Shoreline, WA 98155
http://cinemagogue.com

Cover and illustrations by Jeff Anderson.

Opening Credits

Thanks to

Kal, for the aspiration

Steve, for the perseverance

Peter, for the angst

John, for the existential crisis

Bruce (both of you) for the brooding

Tony, for the humility

Matt, for the faith

Danny, for the focus

Logan, for endurance

And as always, to

Kathryn…

my MJ,
my Lois,
my Pepper,
my Peggy,
my Selina,
my Felicia,
my gal in the chair

Chapter Menu

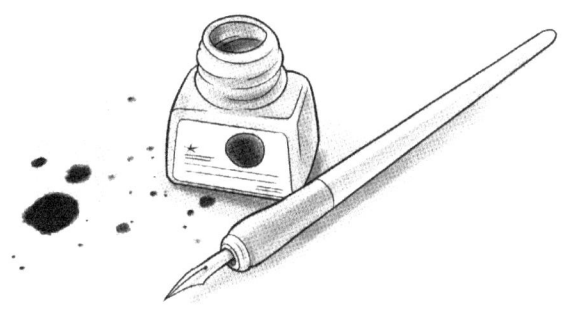

Foreword

By Jim Krueger, a fan

How do I talk about this book? How do I speak about the inherent spirituality and the insight? It's deep. So be prepared, gentle reader—as Stan Lee would often put it—to have your minds blown. There is no shortage of metaphorical Kirby dots here. No holding back on Ditko reality-challenging mind-expansions. What James Harleman does here is speak to the true nature of the Marvel Cinematic Universe. And more.

This is a book about the spirit of the MCU. The spirit of comic books. Of fantasy fiction. I usually never speak about my personal beliefs online or in intros, but James and I have a special friendship. A love for Marvel. A love for Horror. An appreciation for each other. A passion for the metaphorical. And metaphysical. As if the greatest stories of the most modern mythologies speak and instruct us about the oldest and most important stories of human history.

And human destiny.

While the book I wrote called *Justice* for DC, which was drawn by Doug Braithwaite and Alex Ross, won me an Eisner Award (and guaranteed forever that I could get friends into San Diego Comic Con) it's probably Marvel's *Earth X* that I am best known for.*

And best known to Kevin Fiege, miracle producer of the Marvel Cinematic Universe. I remember Kevin talking to me about his love for *Earth X* and his desire to make that into a movie. But so many characters, at the time, were not available for Marvel movies to use because of deals with Sony, Fox, etc. I told him he could do the big reveal of the series with Jack Kirby's unbelievable *Eternals*, which he did, maybe 25 years after our conversation. And I have also watched as the MCU used aspects of the *Earth X* mythology in everything, from Thor to Spider-Man to Moon Knight on.

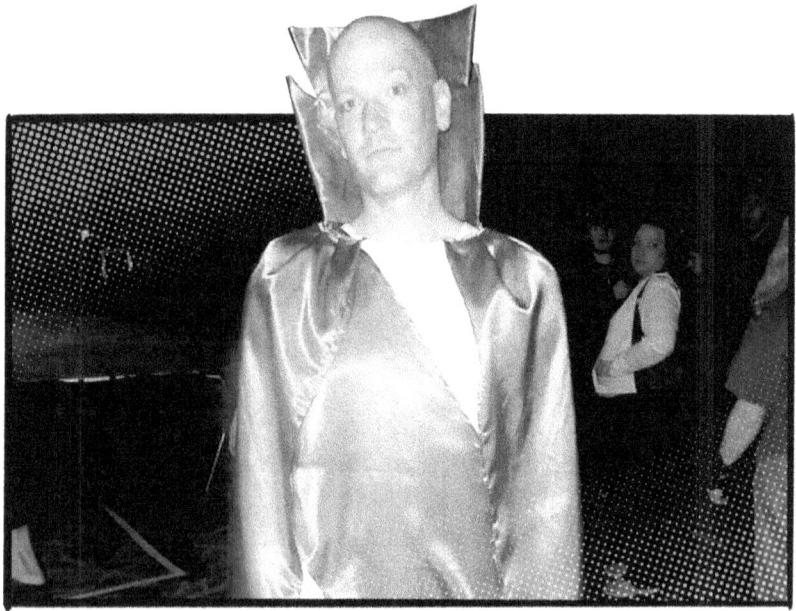

*Uatu know that *Earth X* was also a huge inspiration for this author (I reference it in the *Cinemagogue: Director's Cut*), and it's fair to say it punctuated my passion to pursue ministry, not to mention becoming a pastor. - James

None of this is to pat me on the back. What's most important is to talk about the *original* authors of the Marvel Universe. Artists like Jack Kirby, Steve Ditko, John Romita Sr., Gene Colan, Wally Wood and more created it, their work aided and honored and glorified by the scripts of Stan Lee.

They set the story, but more than anything they told stories that spoke to our humanity. And more.

> *"...for every story written in the Marvel Universe, just like our lives, there is another story, one beneath the stories. One that ties our own adventures all together... even "accidents" themselves are built into some sort of cosmic firmament. Like a blank page left open for our heroes to write upon in a book that's already been completed."* - from the *Earth X* Afterword

Some have said that the DC heroes are gods that walk among men, but the Marvel heroes are people. People with sniffles. People with bad hearts. With a damnable pride that only transforms them into monsters. People who needed something to lean on, to help them find the radioactive thunder, the gamma bomb of glory, the super serum, or the shining light of heaven itself to ignite the glory that was dormant within them. The glory of a renewed spirit.

If you only know the *cinematic* Marvel Universe, I implore you: seek out the printed comic book whimsy and wonder of the Fantastic Four. The pure pride and service of Captain America. The charm and bewilderment of being born different into the X-Men. And especially the greatness in being able to become someone else that is Spider-Man. Check them out. Please. You will be better for it.

But all of this brings us to this very special book. Stan Lee was Jewish. His wife was from a Christian tradition. But together, as a couple that dearly loved each other and loved this world, they created a universe that was uniquely human. Uniquely spiritual. There is no specific religion here, *yet there is.*

It's a faith, that speaks of sacrifice, or heroism, or a belief that it's far better to serve your fellow man (or mutant, for that matter) than to serve oneself.

Really, to be a fan of Marvel is to be a fan of miracles. To hope and defy the darkness that so often comes into our lives.

These heroes did not accept the status quo. They challenged it. Even if it meant their deaths. That was what made them heroes, these men and women and children with clayer-than-clay clay feet.

And that's why we cheered for them.

We saw ourselves in them, the very heroes we all hoped to be.

Is it any wonder that Stan, when he spoke to the readers and fans of these stories, called us "True Believers"? I know I am one. As is James Harleman. I can't wait for you to read what he did here. I can't wait to hear from him how this book made you watch and rewatch the miracle that Kevin and his team accomplished. I can't wait to hear from James how people who might never have read those original comics have dove (or diven, dived, I don't know, I'll be a real writer one day) deep into thousands of amazing comics from the past.

It was never just a modern mythology. It was deeper. *Better.*

Is there any wonder these stories haunt and inspire, like the holiest and greatest of ghosts, the very people who are making these movies?

Is it any wonder that James was compelled to write this book?

- JIM KRUEGER

Writer. *Earth X. Justice. Foot Soldiers. Hiroquest.*
The Frankincense Monster And Other Creepy Christmas Stories.
And friend and fan of James Harleman.

Editor's Note: *Like the Avengers, Jim and James first "assembled" in 2011 (as speakers at a creative conference). After the gig wrapped, they geeked out late into the night about their favorite comics, films and faith. And the world has never been the same…*

- James, friend and fan of Jim Krueger

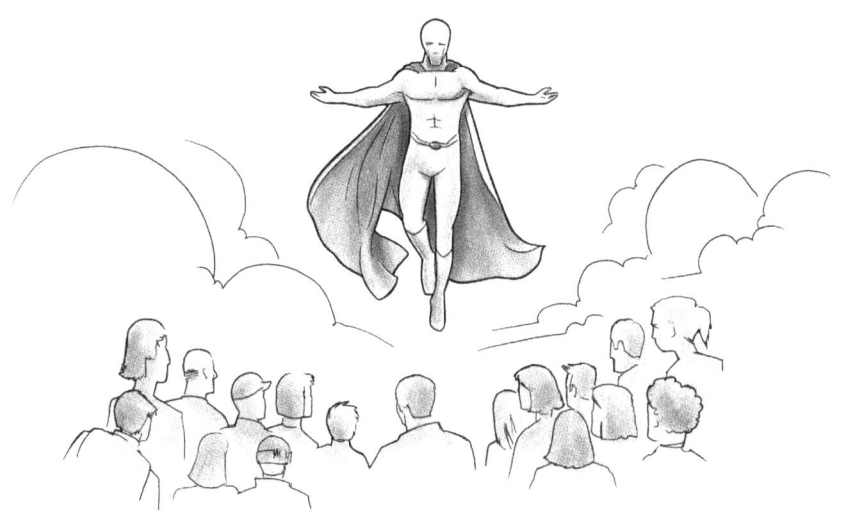

Prologue: **Hail Marvel, Full of Grace**

or

"Oh, when the capes go marching in…"

Scene 1: **The Geek Shall Inherit the Earth**

> *"The world has changed, and none of us can go back."*
> - Peggy Carter, *Captain America: The Winter Soldier*

We should have seen the signs. The portents.

In 1978, Christopher Reeve was our Adam.

In 1989, Michael Keaton appeared like a pointy-eared Moses, ready to lead us to the promised land. But a few years later the bat cave coughed out a golden calf and we were sentenced to the desert until the end of the century, with Wesley Snipes as our singular Joshua.

At the dawn of a new century, the prophets emerged… Hugh Jackman, Sir Patrick Stewart, Sir Ian McKellen and more, proclaiming a grand era to come. Like David with a webbed sling, Tobey Maguire swung in and killed the box office Goliath, heralding a time when his kind would sit on the throne forever… or at least a decade or so.

Finally, Christian Bale arrived like John the Baptist, beginning a story in 2005 that would hit a crucial intersection in 2008, the dawn of the golden age. The revitalized Robert Downey Jr. saw his star descend from heaven and a voice declared…

"This is my beloved Stark, and Hollywood is well pleased."

One might look back before 2008 and liken cinematic superhero storytelling to the Old Testament, but with the dawn of the Marvel Cinematic Universe we received the super-gospel, the good news of the comic book kingdom. Robert Downey Junior (or rather Tony Stark) gathered his disciples and after four years of movie ministry, *The Avengers* assembled in 2012. In that landmark year, commission would be comingled with ascension, as many would witness that *The Dark Knight Rises*. Andrew Garfield slipped on the Amazing Spider-man's mask and swung out to spread the good news. The comic combination would culminate in a commencement of disciple-making that would go to the four corners of the film world.

Even Cinemagogue, published in 2012, didn't see this coming.

Obviously, I'm having a bit of fun here, as any equivalency with the *true* gospel would be blasphemy, and the impact on the film industry isn't as world-altering as what Christ did over 2,000 years ago. However, it might be easy to miss the magnitude of change that has impacted Hollywood, fiction, and every area of entertainment. What built slowly since the turn of the century reached a crescendo in 2012, causing a flash flood of followers and franchises that has lasted longer than 40 days and 40 nights. And for any who aren't fans of the course cinema has taken, there is no rainbow in sight.

Of course, another stream has struck the storytelling industry in the last decade… or I should say streams, as the advent of streaming has changed the course of consuming entertainment. Add in a little pandemic—isolation mixed with fear, uncertainty, and hopelessness —and we've had a perfect storm of superheroes, superspreaders, and streaming services to shift where, why, when and how we engage narrative and fiction.

Then again, some things never change…

Scene 2: **You've GOTTA be KIDMAN me…**

An expensive, high-heeled shoe strikes a puddle on the pavement, the ripples revealing a reflection of neon light from above that forms the letters A-M-C. A beautiful actress beckons us back to the movie theater, to take off our masks and venture out of our homes to a place that—like many churches—has been vacant for far too long. Will we respond to her invitation? Will we heed the siren song of cinema?

In September 2021 theaters were struggling to stay afloat following pandemic closures and a still-present culture of fear, or at least timidity, toward the large group gatherings that came screeching to a halt in 2020. AMC theaters launched a campaign to regain their audiences, and as I watched actress Nicole Kidman define our purpose in moviegoing I was frozen, stunned, and thought to myself: *Skynet just became self-aware!*

While that movie-referencing logic leap might not make sense to everyone's synapses at first, it was my way of processing that Hollywood had become aware of itself, or at least a stone's throw away from understanding the heart and soul of Cinemagogue. If anyone thought my musings about cinema being worship, movie theaters being church, and narrative immersion like a baptism were a bit far-fetched or hyperbolic, I had just received a confirmation and validation that couldn't be more on the nose.

Consider the content of Kidman's short soliloquy:

"We come to this place… for magic.
We come to AMC theaters to laugh, to cry, to care."

"Because we need that, all of us, that indescribable feeling
we get when the lights begin to dim."

*"And we go somewhere we've never been before;
not just entertained, but somehow reborn."*

"Together."

*"Dazzling images, on a huge silver screen.
Sound that I can feel."*

"Somehow, heartbreak feels good in a place like this."

*"Our heroes feel like the best part of us,
and stories feel perfect and powerful."*

"Because here… they are."

When we look at the key elements of this filmgoing description, it is nothing short of a religious epiphany. Consider:

- The **reason** for our attendance? *Magic…* the hope of an experience that is transcendent and supernatural.

- The **hope** of our emotions? Catharsis… that like the Greek theater's dichotomy of comedy and tragedy we will *laugh, cry*, and be so deeply immersed that we *care*.

- The **depth** of its offering? Not just want or desire, it's a *need* for a *feeling* beyond human description.

- The **lengths** to which it takes us? *Somewhere we've never been.*

- The **emphasis** of its effect? Not just fleeting entertainment, but an experience in which we are *reborn*.

- The **scope** of this rebirth? Not simply an individual experience of being born again, but communal experience that brings us *together*.

- The **focus** that brings us together? Heroes that are the *best…* showing us who we ought to be and how we should live.

- The **authority** of this gathering? A story that is *perfect…* a narrative that has *power*.

Christians gather *together* every Sunday to elevate the greatest *story* ever told, to recognize the *perfect hero* who holds all *power* and authority, to herald good news that His life and work have tended to our deepest *need*. In Him we are *born again…* we live, *laugh, cry,* and *care*. And we await the day when we will be with him in a place *we've never been before*, his *transcendent* and eternal kingdom.

Simply put, this is worship.

Even more fascinating, and punctuating, is the subsequent phenomenon that emerged in response to the AMC anthem, inspiring in-theater audience participation ranging from recitation to standing salutes (not to mention memes, merchandise and parodies). When theaters initially began to pull the ad, or reduce the 60-second version with a truncated 30-second spot, audiences actually complained. Even though it was played for camp and often enjoyed with a wink, the commercial had universally struck a chord.

One goal of the first Cinemagogue book was to shake Christians out of the idea that their moviegoing is "mindless entertainment." That for many, it is a surrogate form of worship, a placebo. In fact, even for many Christians it's a form of idolatry, the biblical Rachel's "household idols" but made of story, venerated as much (or more) in their hearts as the Savior they say they serve. If anyone doubted me in 2012, they need only look and see what the industry perceives itself to be. Movie-houses are our churches, and the movies are our baptisms… though the immersion offered us is as shallow as the puddle we see Nicole Kidman ripple with a well-placed heel.

Movies offer a superficial reflection of rebirth, and that's all. Rinse and repeat, bring on the sequel. The question is, what happens to Hollywood when it becomes aware of the power it wields, the fervent fealty of its film followers? The last decade subsequently served up a stunning change in the impetus and agenda behind storytelling and it's important to address this as well. The messaging has become increasingly overt and confrontational, creating a more toxic environment in both the industry and its corresponding fandom. Should Christians still be engaged? Of course, but they also need to understand that the rules of engagement have changed.

Scene 3: **IP (not so) freely**

"…but we're not IN a sequel, because nobody just makes sequels anymore. We're in a franchise! And there are certain rules to a continuing franchise…" - Mindy Meeks-Martin, *Scream VI*

Growing up, my friends and I didn't have conversations about intellectual property or IP. Well, I suppose technically we did, but those words never featured in the conversation. Today it's not uncommon to hear college students or even high schoolers talking about the future of their favorite IPs, how they're being handled, and even who's guiding it and what they think about the future of franchise. Because *everything's* a franchise. Everything's a *universe*.

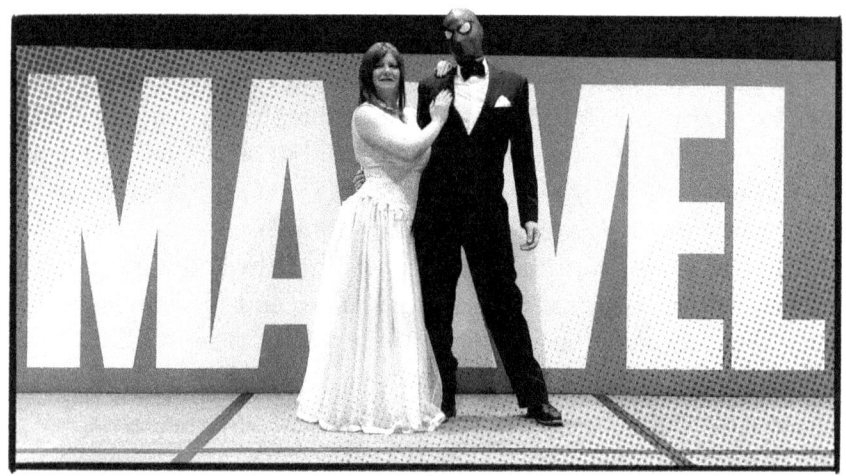

The wife and I renewed our vows at C2E2, cosplay-style. She's MY universe.

When *The Avengers* came out mid-year in May 2012, I was finishing my first draft of the original Cinemagogue book. There's a moment in that film, when the third act alien incursion has begun in earnest, led by a sneering, horned Tom Hiddleston. I'm sure you remember it; it's been replayed and copied extensively. The six founding Avengers circle and stand against their foes, the camera spinning around them wildly as arrows are nocked, repulsors are readied, shields are slung and guns are cocked, hammers spinning and muscles flexing. It's an iconic moment that commemorates more than the coming together of the MCU's icons, because while audiences saw Avengers assembled, an industry saw something else: *potential*. If Iron Man and the Dark Knight lit the fuse, this was the explosion, catalyzing a Hollywood-wide passion to combine, connect, and capitalize on movies and their narratives… in what has turned out to be both a betterment and detriment to the medium.

And lo, the "MARVEL Us Era" began… named for the brand that started this last decade-plus of ever-expanding (or in some cases, contracting) universes, far from limited to Marvel alone. The Marvel Cinematic Universe was only the tip (or maybe we should specify top) of the IP iceberg. We have the Sonyverse, the DC Extended Universe, (or was that Snyderverse?) the Monsterverse, the LEGOverse, the Star Wars universe, the Conjuring-verse, the Potterverse or "Wizarding World", the Wickverse, the Star Trek universe, the Fast and Furious-verse… the list goes on and on, even with failed franchises like the Dark Universe. Scrolling through Netflix, I discovered that the scary shows by director Mike Flanagan apparently co-exist in the same "world" and now the term "Flanaverse" has been coined. Flanaverse? Seriously?

At some point it all begins to sound convoluted (and a bit silly), but Hollywood has embraced it with gusto… or perhaps a whiff of desperation? Interconnecting stories and characters are a ploy to keep consumers focused on one ever-expanding brand in a world where competing content offerings are growing exponentially. This forces audiences to seek out and view content they might otherwise skip. Consumption becomes work, takes effort, requires investment and devotion. Gone is the idea of casual engagement or the notion that it's just "mindless" entertainment. Distraction? No, your attentiveness is compulsory!

One might think the writer of Cinemagogue would appreciate a culture shift toward entertainment that demands *mindfulness*. Sadly though, it's not a mindfulness that lends itself to biblical thinking, but rather a total immersion into fictional worlds that don't exist or ultimately satisfy (and often push unbiblical agendas). We even see this inability to satisfy having a present-day effect, as fans divide over the handling of their favorite IP with a zealot's fervor, a verbal ferocity that reveals the sacred place it holds in their heart. And so it goes… every sacred cow salvaged from Hollywood's IP vault and slapped with a slate of sequels becomes a religious icon which followers then judge as blessing or blasphemy.

Again, this is worship... and the caped crusaders and other franchise characters have become our demigods of the decade. And they're everywhere, aren't they? In 2008 two rich guys in armored suits spawned a host of heroic protagonist progeny from every corner of fiction to fill the last decade and more, from comics and video games to classic literature and myth... and at some point, with such a rush and volume... they all started to blur together. How many specials and supers can we have before it all gets a bit tired?

"I'll sell my invention so that EVERYONE can be superheroes, everyone can be super! And when everyone's super [laughs maniacally] NO ONE will be." - Syndrome, *The Incredibles*

What happens when the sheer glut of larger-than-life heroes becomes a flurry of fleeting, unsatisfactory sameness? When "franchise fatigue" kicks in and the silver screen worship wanes? When the fictional fails to fortify in any truly fulfilling fashion? This is not a time for a Christian to complain, but the time and place to practice Peter's call to readiness in holy scripture:

"...but in your hearts honor Christ the Lord as holy, always being prepared to make a defense to anyone who asks you for a reason for the hope that is in you; yet do it with gentleness and respect..." - 1 Peter 3:15

Christians have the answer to the felt fatigue coming in the wake of a decade of ultra-heroic, larger than life fantasy figures. The goal of this book is to journey through the major shared universes, the modern mythologies of our 21st century media, with a goal of finding the redemptive through-lines, the narrative talking points that nudge us—and perhaps others—toward the best story and greatest storyteller. It is also a warning and wake-up call to the changing face of secular storytelling, perhaps some changes in how we gird and guard ourselves and look out for others.

When the cape and cowl era starts to look a bit tattered, when the IPs feel less intellectual and more like property to move merchandise, when the favored franchise flatlines or our favorite artists are replaced with activists, we can point to something beyond all these stories, born of the most creative mind of all, who declares:

> *"Before all your people I will do MARVELS, such as have not been created in all the earth or in any nation. And all the people among whom you are shall see the work of the Lord, for it is an awesome thing that I will do with you."* - God, *Exodus 34:10*

Hollywood has marveled us for a decade, but Christians know—and can share—the one who is *truly* marvelous.

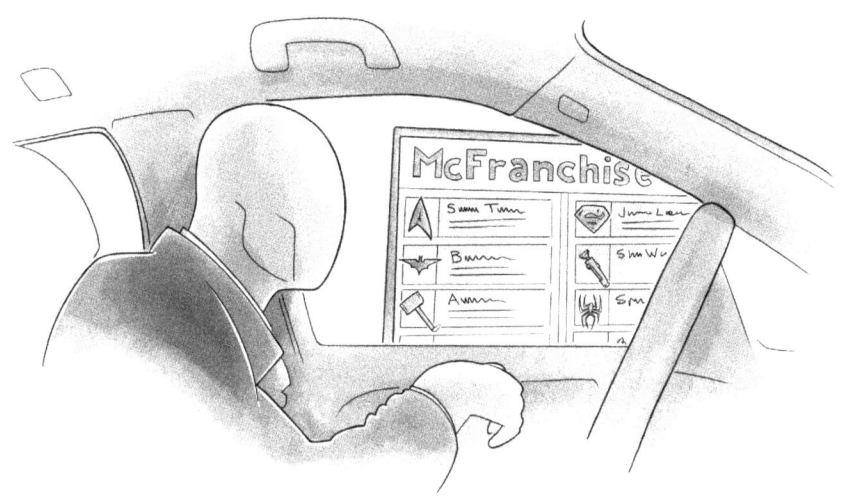

Act 1: **RISK A 'VERSE**

or

"Can I get a franchise with that?"

Scene 1: **Confessions of a Lying Author**

> *"I can remember everything. That's my curse, young man. It's the greatest curse that's ever been inflicted on the human race: memory."* - Charles Foster Kane, *Citizen Kane*

Forgive me reader, for I have sinned.

It's true. I lied in my first book. Not intentionally, mind you. Do you remember the first book? First chapter? First question? *Whose hand am I holding?* That's the one. It's followed by a vivid recounting of my earliest childhood recollection, consisting of X-Wing Fighters and drive-in theaters, building up to a big, bold question for all of us to ponder: **what is your first memory?**

Well as it turns out, Star Wars wasn't mine. Sorry about that.

"Sometimes I remember it one way, sometimes another. If I'm going to have a past, I prefer it to be multiple choice."
 - Joker, *The Killing Joke*

A few years ago, I was explaining another franchise-adjacent experience I had as a youngster: an adrenaline-fueled night when I was desperate to get home after my swim lesson at our local YMCA. The car wouldn't start, my mother was calling my dad to come help, and I was sobbing and shrieking that I was going to miss the premiere of a television show I was—from all the noise I was making—apparently dying to see. *Note*: there was no streaming yet, no DVRs, no pausing, not even VHS recording. Miss it and it's gone, unless you catch a rerun months later (and that's if you're lucky).

Like a superhero, my father seemed to fly down to the Y in record time, give my mom's car a much-needed jumpstart, then had me jump in his car as he prefigured *The Fast and the Furious* to whisk me home. I remember that wild ride… my pulse pounding, eyes wide, angry at God and the world for trying to deny me this moment, my mind bursting at the seams, blood boiling with anticipation… until finally we're in the driveway, I'm exploding through the door, racing to the living room, turning on the television just in time… to see the main character experiencing car problems? Man, talk about art imitating life.

The driver—David—is trying to change a tire, but everything is going wrong. It's pouring down rain, the lug nuts won't budge, and the whole experience is making him flash back to a prior car accident that caused the death of someone he loved. His pulse is pounding, his eyes not just wide but pupils turning white, and he's angry at God and the world, his mind bursting at the seams as his body bursts through the seams of his clothing. His flesh turns green as he overturns the car in an unbridled rage. And a young James is no longer sobbing, he's speechless, trying not even to blink as David Bruce Banner transforms into the Incredible Hulk.

You've felt that moment, haven't you? True, the days of "date and time" event viewing have certainly changed in the 21st century, but there's still that streaming release date, or that Thursday night movie premiere, that day the new season of your show drops and you can binge-watch all weekend, the anticipation and adrenaline coalescing into an unforgettable moment! Of course, it's not just you… or me. For our media-saturated generation, it's Universal. The need feels Paramount. You get the idea.

As I was relating my nearly-tragic tale to someone, they noted that the CBS Bill Bixby/Lou Ferrigno TV series premiered in 1977. Although Star Wars came out in May that year, I knew my father didn't introduce us to the adventures of Luke Skywalker and friends until 1978. So that meant… crap. My memory of the not-so-jolly jade giant preceded my hyperspace jump to a galaxy far, far away. That makes my earliest memory, well… simply MARVELous.

So there you have it: before I was a Star Wars fan, I was a Marvel Zombie, which for the purposes of this book works surprisingly well. But in retrospect, I unknowingly lied in my first book and stand humbly corrected. Please don't be angry with me.

> *"Don't make me angry. You wouldn't like me when I'm angry."*
> - David Bruce Banner, *The Incredible Hulk*

Now, it's a good bet that I'd gotten my hands on some comics featuring the green gamma guy and his web-spinning, mutant-powered, universe-sharing compatriots… otherwise I'm not sure why I would have been so excited for the Hulk's television debut. Comics were like literary desserts in my formative years; my parents encouraged us to read mostly prose; comic books were treated like sweets and doled out sparingly (which, of course, framed them as the most desirable). Thus, seeing these candy-coated characters transcend the still-frame comics page to even a small screen was like a dream come true.

I say "like a dream" because even five-year old James could see this Hulk wasn't as big or strong as his comic counterpart. There was always some lament that Stan Lee's creations were simply impossible to adapt to live action… at least until the 2000s. Those of you who've grown up in the 21st century can't fully appreciate the superhero Shangri-La you've been living in. Seeing the Hulk standing next to his fellow Avengers in 2012, I shed a tear that my dad couldn't be there with me. We'd watched that television premiere side-by-side, (and all the episodes that followed) read comics together for years, and in 2003, health failing, he joined me for a midnight premiere of the underrated Ang Lee *Hulk* film. I'm sad my dad missed the MARVEL-us era… but where everything's headed now? Maybe not so much.

Scene 2: **Who's On First?**

"There was an idea… the idea was to bring together a group of remarkable people to see if they could become something more. To see if they could work together when we needed them to…"
  - Nick Fury, *The Avengers*

It turns out the eye-patch sporting, card-bloodying man with a plan played by Samuel L. Jackson wasn't just talking about grouping together a bunch of special heroes to fight the battles that we never could. This quote would become Hollywood's central idea, to bring together groups of marketable products to see if they could become something more. More profitable, that is… to see if they could work together, to fight the box office battles in a new race for cinematic supremacy. The idea appeared like Loki did at the beginning of that first *Avengers* film—a stunning singularity—but just a few years later the shared universes would start raining down on us like Chitauri from a hole in the sky over New York City, only this time it would be over Tinseltown… again.

"There's nothing new in human experience, Mr. Tully. Each generation thinks it invented debauchery or suffering or rebellion, but man's every impulse and appetite… is on display right here, all around you… if you truly want to understand the present—or yourself—you must begin in the past. You see, history is not simply the study of the past, it is the explanation of the present." - Paul Hunham, *The Holdovers*

Let's clear something up really quick: *shared universes aren't new.* Just because you've never been in a hurricane doesn't mean you haven't experienced a storm, and Hollywood has certainly had some of these brainstorms over the years. The difference now is simply the size of the deluge. My personal introduction to the first cinematic shared universe was by way of my father's favorite comedians,

Abbott and Costello. The family-friendly duo danced with the denizens of Universal's original Monsterverse in 1948 in the hilarious *Abbott and Costello meet Frankenstein*, featuring classic characters and actors that had been portraying Dracula, The Wolfman and more in films since 1931.

Like Phase One of the Marvel Cinematic Universe, several standalone films and even some sequels happened before anyone crossed over into the other's films. We see the official "shared" moment arrive in 1943 when—as the title explains—*Frankenstein meets The Wolfman:* essentially a sequel for the hairy guy and Frank's fifth outing. *House of Frankenstein* followed in 1944, pairing multiple characters and classic actors, and then *House of Dracula* did it again one year later. Many would then complain that the Abbott and Costello film in '48 put a stake in the franchise's heart by turning the characters into caricatures and jokes. (*Thor: Love and Thunder* anyone?) All told, the classic Universal Monsterverse legacy would span about 15 years before running out of steam (i.e. interesting stories and audience interest). One might contend that the MCU in the 2020s appears to be on a similar trajectory…

Of course, a tangled web of characters co-mingled together isn't the only way to expand one's intellectual property profitability. Shared universes aren't the only way to grow a franchise; the ongoing film series is far from new. As of this book's publishing James Bond has been a continuing character in 27 films and counting. Godzilla has 38 films, the longest running franchise of all time (and the big guy finally won his first Oscar). Those two, however, have always felt free to play fast and loose with continuity (or reboot, jettison, ret-con as desired). They embody the traditional form of rinse/repeat we've seen with Batman, Spider-man, Apes movies, and others over the years. After all: continuity is hard! Just ask Star Trek.

That's right, Star Trek has been world-building since 1966, mostly in television, yet still building a shared universe with continuity across 12 television series (more than 900 episodes over 47 seasons) and 12 films, plus 500 novels, 800 comics, 200 video games and more. Next to the massive cross-comics continuities of Marvel and DC, Trek probably comprises the largest attempt at maintaining a "canon". I even mention in my first book the many fans who maligned the J.J. Abrams Star Trek trilogy for essentially being a reboot (or "timeline adjacent"). They lamented that now this means certain previous events "never happened" (to which I must point out that—with or without the reboot—*it's all fiction: none of it happened!*) But these fans want their canon, they want a fully formed universe: what used to be a somewhat fringe, fanatical expectation by Trekkers and a few other fanbases has become more and more the norm for movie-goers in the 21st century. Naturally, media-makers are scrambling to bait the hook and give them what they want. They want their escapism designed so meticulously that it isn't just a temporary, fictional escape, but a plausible, potential reality.

A natural question emerges here: why?

Scene 3: **Welcome to the Hotel California**

"I don't want to GO." - The Doctor, *Doctor Who: The End of Time*

I remember watching the final moments of *Star Wars: Return of the Jedi* for the first time in 1983, feeling a peculiar sensation sweeping over me. The Rebel Alliance had won, Ewoks were dancing, the core heroes were gathered together, and everyone— even the force ghosts, including Anakin—were smiling. I was filled with a ten-year old's childlike wonder… and yet, at the same time, there was a growing pit in my stomach. I was flushed, short of breath. Maybe I had my first panic attack? Whatever the case, I felt wonderful and sick all at the same time, because this was it. Any second now the credits would roll, and this story… the Star Wars… would be over. Forever.

Ah, how wondrously naive in retrospect (although consider: sixteen years passed before another film. Sure, there were books and comics, but one was never totally clear about them in terms of "canon"). The ones I'd been reading would soon be swept aside for a new batch, that would be in turn swept aside by Disney decades later. In that era, *Return of the Jedi* truly did feel like a finale. The end. Thanks for playing, but playtime's over kid. You had a swim in our immersive entertainment; now it's time to get out of the pool.

See before, I could check out any time I wanted… but now I had to leave. It's not that Star Wars was my only fantasy, right? As mentioned, I was already a Marvel kid (and I loved Superman and Batman too). I'd take breaks from the Star Wars universe and swim in other pools, but now the "Closed" sign was on the New Republic's door—closed forever—and I'd never wanted to leave.

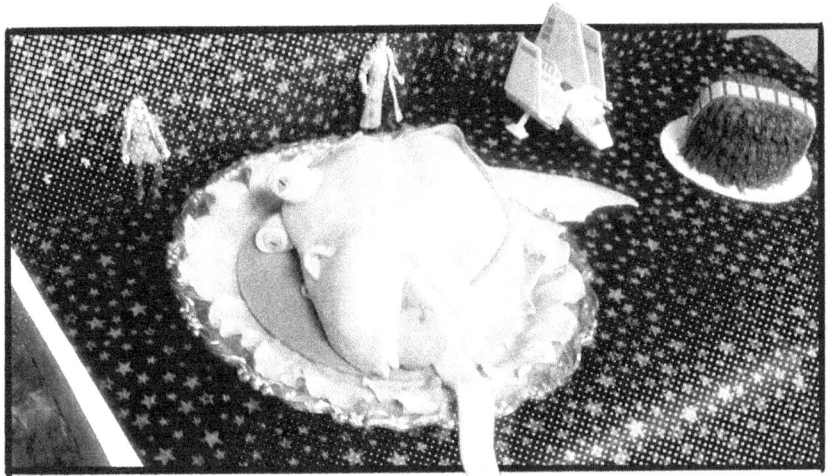

The prequels would give me another fantasy…   …for Jar Jar's head on a platter.

Fortunately, Transformers came along to fill the fantasy void at that point in my life, and I had a similarly surly Harrison Ford character to glom onto for the rest of the 80s in the form of Indiana Jones. But what would happen to Han Solo? To Chewbacca? Or the others? Well of course the answer was that nothing was going to happen to them *because they weren't real*. The story stops, they stop. They don't go on. Nothing was "happening" to them that I was missing out on, but this tells you something about my psyche in the midst of a franchise's end, and others too in this modern, magnified craving for immersive, shared universes.

These worlds aren't just shared by the multiple crossover characters that round out the universe. Part of us believes we exist there alongside them… sharing their struggles, preferring their world to ours, and perhaps even taking up spiritual residence there.

One year after *The Dark Knight* and *Iron Man* lit the fuse that would become the MARVEL-us Era, James Cameron blew up the box office and audience's minds with *Avatar*, still the highest grossing film of all time. Naysayers will write it off as *Ferngully* meets *Pocahontas* with a dose of *Dances with Wolves*, but I already covered the reality that no narratives are original in my first book. It's not about making something new, but rather something fresh, and *Avatar* was a fresh reinvention of FAR more than just those three films. With a sprinkle of Burroughs' *John Carter of Mars*, a dash of the creature-riding, messianic foreigner Paul Atreides from *Dune*, a scantily clad gal on a flying bird by way of *Heavy Metal,* and a healthy remix of other James Cameron films from *Aliens* to the *Abyss*, what *Avatar* offered was a fantasy-science fiction stew, topped with a special effects sauce we'd only dreamt of up 'til then. On top of that, we also got something else even more unexpected.

"The Pandora Blues" is what I remember hearing it called back in 2010, but now—in the wake of the watery sequel—the symptoms are referred to as "Post-Avatar Depression (P.A.D.) Syndrome. According to Ana Peres on MovieWeb, P.A.D. *"causes suicidal thoughts and depression in some viewers."* These feelings *"are evoked by how dark and depressing the real earth we live in is when compared to the gorgeous views of Pandora."* Some might read this and assume it's fake, or satire, or rare, but no: this wasn't a Babylon Bee article.

The story's protagonist, Jake Sully, leaves his broken and empty life behind to find himself on a world where the environment seems like paradise. Surrounded by the glorious 3-D world James Cameron and a team of visionaries designed as a feast for the senses, Jake finds a new life… and then the credits roll, causing some people to leave the theater with a reality-crashing sense of withdrawal, dissatisfaction and loss. And why? It's true the film depicts an alien style "mother-earth" worship that Christians naturally reject, but wait: back up. Before we address the pagan portion is there a felt loss that makes sense, an instinctual wonder that both Jake—and movie viewers—are keying into?

> *"And the Lord God planted a garden in Eden, in the east, and there he put the man whom he had formed. And out of the ground the Lord God made to spring up every tree that is pleasant to the sight and good for food. The tree of life was in the midst of the garden…"* - Genesis 2:8-9

At a base level, humans DO connect with a garden paradise existence and a big sustaining tree at its center. Such images may turn up in pagan traditions, but they don't own the origin, and there is also a sense of loss and brokenness over the real fact that sin— human evil—shattered this reality a long time ago. Although *Avatar* may layer wild sci-fi ideas with touches of Hinduism and other religions, this essential basis echoes a sobering truth that—if not for sin—we could be living in a completely wondrous world.

Now, this brings us back to that overarching question about franchises, universes, meticulous world-building, and our obsession with "canon". Here's the deal: we want the immersion so deep, the universe so large, the franchise so filling, the canon so convincing that we've all but ushered in our own chosen new Eden. People are longing for Pandora, and when the credits roll, the canon breaks, or the franchise fails, the fictional formation of our ethereal Eden falls apart. We're waking up from the dream of our hand-picked new earth (whether we call it Pandora, Endor, Hogwarts or The Shire) and we are simply not there. We're reminded that we're still in the "grey town".

> *"I believe, to be sure, that any man who reaches Heaven will find that what he abandoned… has not been lost: that the kernel of what he was really seeking even in his most depraved wishes will be there, beyond expectation, waiting for him in 'the High Countries'."* - C.S. Lewis, *the Great Divorce*

For those who don't know this classic work of fiction, *The Great Divorce* was the C.S Lewis' allegorical stab at heaven and hell. In the story, Lewis' character leaves the "grey town" with other travelers and wind up in the foothills of heaven. Although the landscape is the most gorgeous panorama they've ever seen, every inch of its geography—the ground, blades of grass, etc.—is unbearably more solid, more real, than they are. A single leaf is too heavy to lift, and traversing the terrain gives them immense pain. The visitors can't endure the world as they are, because they are ill-suited for paradise. This reminded me of Cameron's Pandora, which is toxic and hostile to humans. So… does it surprise me when the film *Avatar* ends, and theatergoers are similarly "exiled" back to old planet earth, that they suffer a unique form of the blues? That their lives feel "meaningless"? Not at all.

The first film didn't initially leave a large cultural footprint either. Disney World had a Pandora section, but there weren't movie tie-ins, books, comics or lasting toy lines. Until *The Way of Water* Pandora lovers were effectively adrift without a franchise, without continuing "canon", without ever-expanding escapism by which fans could keep world-building a new earth—or a new heaven—of their own desire. In other words, P.A.D. was partially due to a decided lack of IP… whereas in most other entertainment arenas, that content is exploding. And that, dear reader, explains what I believe is happening with the postmodern era of myth-making.

> *"For behold, I create new heavens and a new earth, and the former things shall not be remembered or come to mind. But be glad and rejoice forever in that which I create…"* - Isaiah 65:17

Scene 4: **Fictional World, Real Religion**

"Building Better Worlds"
   - The Weyland-Yutani corporate slogan, *Aliens* Franchise

If someone offered to transport you to a very real Shire from *The Lord of the Rings*, would you say yes? Even some Christians might answer in the affirmative… or they might choose Rivendell, or the white city of Gondor shortly after the climactic events of *The Return of the King*. If Christ-followers were offered Tolkien's fantasy world this very night—though it meant leaving their current "fellowship" of believers—how many might say yes? How many would be tempted, like Boromir was tempted by the Ring of Power? If we might trade a fictional new world for the reality of the eternal kingdom of the scriptures, it tells us something of the multiple compartments in which we've placed portions of our heart.

This side of heaven, one might consider a diversified portfolio to be a good thing. To have one's monetary plans and hopes spread across a variety of funds might be a safe way to invest. But placing some of our deep emotional stock in human storytelling is questionable at best and potentially damaging. I compared this earlier to keeping the "household gods" like Rachel did in the Bible. She kept her father's idols (stole them, to be precise) when she left with her husband Jacob, and subsequently denied it. When Christians embrace the meganarrative of God's sovereign story, we must be careful that we don't cling to human stories (earthly treasures) in a way that makes God's story anything less than supreme in our lives. Otherwise, we find ourselves storing up myths, stockpiling dreams and preferences in surrogate stories. In the passage below, let's replace the word treasures with "stories".

> *"Do not lay up for yourselves [stories] on earth, where moth and rust destroy and where thieves break in and steal, but lay up for yourselves [stories] in heaven, where neither moth nor rust destroys and where thieves do not break in and steal. For where your [story] is, there your heart will be also." -* Matthew 6:19-21

You can see the problem here: when a piece of us dies inside at the end of a fictional series, franchise, what have you, it might indicate we were over-invested. When the end of a story (often not even one told by a believer) makes our heart ache at the passing, something might be amiss. To be clear, I'm not talking about when a narrative is simply moving by way of the story it's telling. A story's power to evoke thought and emotions is a potent, real and often wonderful thing. It's part of what defines storytelling. But if it's just the fact of the fiction's finale that fills me with a profound sense of loss, including despair and an emptiness that feels like a piece of my identity is now missing, it suggests I have my emotional and spiritual financing in the wrong place. Or, if a new creative team takes my fictional favorites in a direction I don't like, my level of vitriol might suggest an imbalance of investment.

Is my negative attitude implying a complete rejection of fiction? Certainly not! I emphasized the value of engaging culture— including pop culture—quite adamantly in my first book. But we must always be on guard about how much we're *investigating* versus *investing*; how much we're enjoying without ensnaring ourselves. If we give too much of ourselves to these passions, we may lose our way, like an undercover cop who gets compromised. Like a culture-infiltrating spy, we "go native". Not only does that hurt us, it also means we're less effective in terms of helping others find The Way:

"For the time is coming when people will not endure sound teaching, but having itching ears they will accumulate for themselves teachers to suit their own passions, and will turn away from listening to the truth and wander off into myths. As for you, always be sober-minded, endure suffering, do the work of an evangelist, fulfill your ministry." - 2 Timothy 4:3-5

When we think of wandering into myths, we usually think about false religion. Who would have thought those myths might be Supermen, Skywalkers or Star Lords? Living in the postmodern West, the usual Christian outcry is that we've culturally forsaken objective truth and any form of organized religion… but I don't think that's entirely true! In some ways, people have never been more religious. Have you seen Marvel fans extolling the virtues of their shared universe and how superior it is to DC? They engage in comic book apologetics with the opposition. Fans of the now-ended DCEU are literally called "Snyder apologists". Have you seen the devotion of franchise fans proving how much they know? They revel in their knowledge of canon, treating fictional history and lore like theologians nit-picking each other, conversations fraught with endless interjections of *"Um, actually…"*

As more and more franchises divide fans, we may not see *actual* burning at the stake… but we see cancel culture as certain fans (and even creators) are virtually labelled heretics. Have you seen the hatred for J.J. Abrams? J.K. Rowling? Have you seen the vitriol between factions of Star Wars fans online? It's not hyperbole to call it a religious schism: the prequel trilogy split fans like the Catholics and Eastern Orthodox, and now the sequel trilogy has shattered things again like the Reformation. It's no longer popular to argue about "What Would Jesus Do" but hey, you can scream and shout about what Luke Skywalker would or wouldn't have done. More on that later, I promise.

Do people "believe in" their neo-religious franchise figures? Well, yes and no. They don't believe Tony Stark, Bruce Wayne, or Harry Potter are "real" in terms of existence, but they obviously DO put stock in some levels of transcendence of their characters and what they represent: their ideals and what they appeal to, what they make us aspire to. Many Greeks and Romans didn't believe in a literal Zeus or Hercules either, and many of our founding fathers didn't believe in a literal Jesus (or at least not His divinity). They worshiped the teachings and ideals, not the man, and in this we see a symmetry between man-made religion and the zealousness of modern-day movie fandom.

Instead of religious leaders, these movie-going masses have living inspirations as well (or enemies, depending) like Pope Whedon, or Prophet Feige, or perhaps for Warner Brothers and the DC Universe they're looking to James Gunn to be their Moses… to lead their franchise from Snyder's Pharaoh to the promised land. The sad thing is, these people have chosen their new earth, or new heaven, but it hasn't been brought down out of the clouds like we see God doing in Revelation 21. It's not majestic, it's a movie set, manufactured by a media machine that has no care for their soul. Hollywood views them mostly like humans plugged into the Matrix —as power sources for their machines—batteries to fuel the "lights, cameras and action" that line their pockets with money. And while a subset of Hollywood admittedly does care, it seems only in terms of a highly specific, message-laden agenda they wish to indoctrinate viewers with (we'll explore that more fully in chapter eight).

Bottom line? Franchises and shared universes have exploded because of customer desire, not Hollywood engineering… at least initially. Studios have been reacting and seeking to give the customers what they want, while at the same time realizing the increased power this era gives them and trying to harness it. The more immersive their entertainment, the more they maintain and expand their followers. The deeper and more intertwined the offerings are, the harder it is for viewers to simply cherry-pick a few from one studio while sampling another. Like Pokémon, you gotta catch 'em all. Trap your consumers in the labyrinth of your universe and make sure they never want to leave. Make them feel wholly satisfied. Let the House of Mouse be their religion. And all Mickey's people said? Amen.

For over-entangled Christians, a good litmus test is listening to yourself when you're passionately arguing for your favorite IP. Are you more animated, vociferous, and knowledgeable than when you make a case for Christ? Which actually gets more emotional energy in terms of articulation from you: God, or [insert-favorite-IP]? There may be room for growth here... or repentance. If you're spending more time noodling on nerd stuff than God stuff, you probably have some priorities to sort. It's safe to say that where we spend the lion's share of our time reveals how much we love The Lamb.

Our spiritual residence is not Narnia, Cybertron, Middle-Earth, Oz, Azeroth or Arrakis. It is the kingdom of God. We should not settle—we need not settle—for anything less. And like the extraction team from *Inception* needed a "kick" out of the dreamscape, we should be similarly seeking to wake others up. These lesser, cinematic passions invented by men may point to something real, but we must not be overly satisfied with dreams and shades when we know the true substance.

> *"You're the best I can do; but I'm sorry, you are just not good enough."* - Cobb, *Inception*

For dedicated Christians, our mission is still the same; that's why we'll kick off with the era's reigning champion—Mighty Marvel—and deep dive into the decade-plus of expansive themes for exploration and discussion. For the sake of space I'm generally going to avoid writing synopses for each film; this leaves the reader with three choices:

1. If you're like me, you've watched these movies many times and don't need a plot point refresher.

2. If you're more of a casual fan, we live in an era where a summary is just a smartphone search or Marvel wiki away.

3. Third, (and maybe the best option) you could turn your reading experience into a multi-media adventure and engage each movie again as you enjoy this book.

After tackling the Marvel major league, we'll tackle the Justice League... and throw in some pickup games for other franchises and future contenders to the cinematic throne. For any curious non-Christian readers, I hope you can appreciate the perspective sifted from this latest era of storytelling and perhaps consider the consistency of the tune it is playing on our hearts.

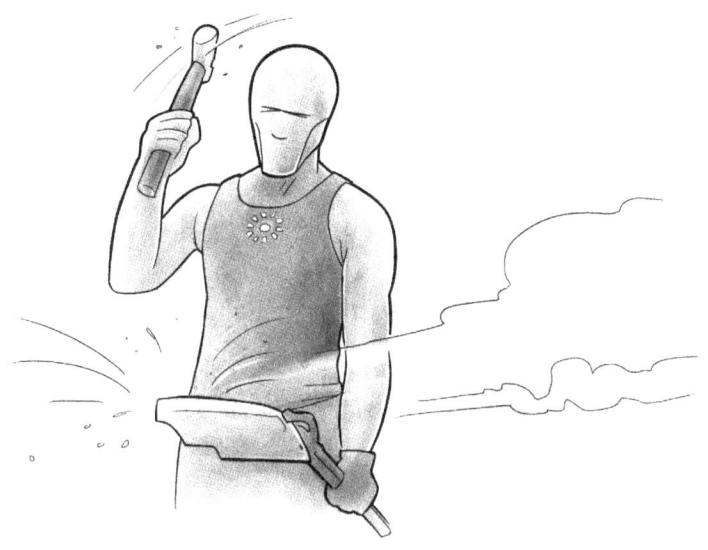

Act 2: **To Infinity...**

or

"The STARK reality of the box office"

Scene 1: **We Love Marvel 3000**

"I can do this all day..." - Steve Rogers, *Captain America*

...or maybe he should have said "decade".

It's not speculative to say that the 2010s, cinematically speaking, will always be remembered as the film era fueled and dominated by Marvel. No matter where this still-unparalleled cinematic universe goes, or how it fares in years to come, it monopolized this decade with an unprecedented experiment that paid off beyond expectations, spawning much imitation and changing the landscape of moviemaking... and perhaps mythmaking.

Quickly climbing to become one of the highest grossing movie franchises of all time with 32 billion and counting, and claiming the coveted "highest grossing film of all time" slot with *Avengers: Endgame,* (until *Avatar's* rerelease snuck Cameron's epic back on top) it's clear that—overall—the first three "phases" of Marvel films have been embraced and beloved by the majority of the world. Now, one might try to dismiss this triumph as the flash and bang of noisy, "mindless" crowd-pleasing blockbusters and negate anything deeper at work here. Indeed, even great filmmakers like Martin Scorsese have disparaged this genre, saying that superheroes aren't even true cinema. *"Honestly,"* he opined, *"the closest I can think of them—as well made as they are, with actors doing the best they can under the circumstances—is theme parks."*

First of all, theme parks are awesome, so… not even a criticism! But even if Scorsese is right about certain film entries, it isn't fair to lump a whole cinematic universe, or superhero genre, into one dismissive lump when that "lump" includes directors like Jon Favreau, Kenneth Branagh, Joss Whedon, James Gunn, Ryan Coogler, the Russo Brothers, etc. (and Scorsese pilloried the whole genre, which means he's throwing in Christopher Nolan, Matt Reeves, James Mangold, Richard Donner and more). But that's not the main issue here: I hope by now Cinemagogue readers know better than to dismiss *any* genre as mindless, and I elaborated at length in the first book just what this style of modern myth-making mimics, what Joseph Campbell elaborates on in terms of "monomyth" in his book *The Hero with a Thousand Faces*. I don't like to quibble with creatives like Scorsese or Tarantino, but it seems as though—if Homer had lived and created today—they'd write off his Iliad and Odyssey as the stuff of theme parks. *Hey kids, get ready for the Scylla and Charybdis coaster!*

This kind of heroic fantasy epic in modern culture mirrors Greco-Roman myths that captivated people in their age, as well as the same sword-wielding and planetary romance heroes that left radio listeners spellbound in the early 20th century. Larger than life, fantastical heroes have garnered an audience in every era, and part of that is because it's tapping into more than myth: it's scratching the itch of the felt "meganarrative" in which we all share a part (whether we believe it or not). This is another reason the Marvel Cinematic saga deserves a look, because Feige and the team bravely grappled with the concept of "meganarrative" on a level that hadn't been attempted with film. Instead of separate franchises, each with their own character's metanarrative, they tried—and succeeded—to make Marvel next level, to weave what would have traditionally been individual franchises into one grand story, in which all the characters play a part. What they attempted is beyond traditional, it's practically *biblical*.

Seriously, Christians enjoy God's true meganarrative contained in 66 books by around 40 different authors spanning 1,500 years. Each author also brings their own unique literary style and tone, but they all tie together (by one guiding Spirit) to illuminate one story with many players, ultimately revealing a central character and monumental climax. By this standard, Phases One to Three of the MCU—the "Infinity Saga"—should seem much lesser. But hey, let's give credit where credit is due: tying together 23 films by 14 different directors across 11 years (with one guiding guru) is nothing to sneeze at, and most of these entries were undisputed hits. Also, like the Bible, each story—and the overarching story—is filled with mindful moments for understanding and life application.

I want to journey with you from *Iron Man* to his *Endgame*, highlighting the major themes along this well-traveled road. I'll also cherry-pick a few films that have followed as we ponder where the shared universe is headed now. I've covered many of these movies in depth with text and audio reviews for *Cinemagogue* and *Popcorn Theology*, and there is more meaning and nuance to the heroes, villains, and circumstances of each MCU entry than we can fully unpack here. But sometimes looking at the whole, from a higher view, provides a unique perspective versus putting each individual story under the microscope. Here, we have a chance to see how the Marvel Narrative measures up to the Meganarrative that Christians love the most.

Fire up the boot jets and let's do a fly-by, shall we?

"...suit up... I'm bringing the party to you."
 - Tony Stark, *The Avengers*

Scene 2: **Avengers, Ecclesia!**

"Big man in his suit of armor. Take that off, and what are you?"
  - Steve Rogers, *The Avengers*

In chapter four of the first *Cinemagogue* book, I laid out a framework for the two primary stories humans keep telling: **life under the sun** stories and **life transcendent** stories. Within the latter, there are two variants of that transcendent tale: *the transformed life* and *the redeeming savior*.   Tony Stark's first film outing is a classic *transformed life* tale, which I covered extensively, citing parallels with Ezekiel 11 and Ephesians 6 as Tony essentially "gets a new heart" and then puts on armor to stand against evil. It's not just a new outlook on life, but also a form of repentance for his former sin and folly. I won't repeat that full analysis here, but the theme of the first **Iron Man** film is **mankind's dire need of a transformed heart**. Subsequent to that, the rest of Phase One's pre-Avenger films each serve up well-paced, individual character studies before any assembling can happen; as a result, we get to explore archetypal variations on the brokenness of the human condition. And when we think of brokenness, we often think of…

THE INCREDIBLE HULK: *Slaves to our Nature*

Soldier #2: *How are you feeling, man?*

Emil Blonsky: *Like a monster.*

It's easy to wag our finger at Tony Stark's behavior with a bit of a wink, and maybe even a hint of salacious and vicarious enjoyment. We know we shouldn't, but his wit and manner almost make his actions charming. It's the softer side of sin, the allure that draws us in. However, when we consider the damaging behavior that Bruce Banner can't seem to shake, all the glamour of an inherently destructive nature is sloughed off—like torn shirts and trousers—to reveal the beast beneath.

Bruce Banner knows that there is something dangerous, something deadly, something devastating inside him. It ruins his life, spoils relationships, and ensures harm to anyone who gets too close. There's a monkey on his back that demolishes everything he touches. Worse yet, what he has inside might be useful to others with ill intentions; his bottled-up traits could be weaponized. Though he attempts to control the behemoth with chemicals and even the power of his mind—at one point he even uses super glue to keep the danger in—it lurks, it waits, it bides its time… and invariably bubbles to the surface.

As the Hulk mythos obviously borrows from the classic tale of Jekyll and Hyde, the story of Banner's struggle strikes a chord of mankind dealing with its own evil—our sin nature—and the attempt to use every human means to rid ourselves of that which leads to destruction.

"I don't want to control it, I want to KILL it!" - Bruce Banner

Banner desires to do good, but the "other guy" seems to invariably cause problems that ruin his plans and jeopardize his situation. While the fact that Banner is never quite able to rid himself of his dark, emerald alter ego probably owes more to a franchise's desire for sequels, it inevitably captures the stark reality that the physician cannot heal himself. We cannot cure our own sin or put it to death. The apostle Paul illustrates this poignantly in Romans 7:

"For I do not understand my own actions. For I do not do what I want, but I do the very thing I hate… For I know that nothing good dwells in me, that is, in my flesh. For I have the desire to do what is right, but not the ability to carry it out. For I do not do the good I want, but the evil I do not want is what I keep on doing. Now if I do what I do not want, it is no longer I who do it, but sin that dwells within me… I see in my members another law waging war against the law of my mind and making me captive to the law of sin that dwells in my members. Wretched man that I am! Who will deliver me from this body of death?"

The Hulk is a decent illustration of our sin nature, to be sure: sin corrupts, sin destroys, sin lurks in our hearts and often manifests when we least expect. Part of us doesn't want it, though part of us enjoys what it sometimes does for us. It can be weaponized; sinful talents may be useful to us, and others around us may encourage it or exploit it. Ultimately, however, it's an albatross around our neck.

But wait… the Hulk isn't all bad, is he? The film depicts him saving Betty, fighting abominations. One might look at this and say the Hulk falls short of being an analogy for sin. And that's fine. He certainly does: unlike sin, the green Goliath isn't all bad… and Banner isn't all good. While this 2008 film doesn't dive as deep into Banner's psyche, the 2003 Ang Lee film *Hulk* (though not part of the MCU canon) has a quote that's endemic to every incarnation of the character. Banner confesses to Betty:

> *"Even now, I can feel it. Buried somewhere deep inside. Watching me. Waiting. But you know what scares me the most? When I can't fight it anymore, when it takes over, when I totally lose control… I like it."*

We can't really divide ourselves from our sin nature any more than Jekyll could remove Hyde, or Bruce Banner can separate the Hulk's actions from his own. That part of us we'd like to blame as something "other" is, in fact, us. We can't say the "other guy did it" any more than we can say the devil made me do it. The Hulk and Banner are a tangled web of brokenness, both at times lamenting the hurt and damage their fractious nature causes.

Others, however, don't seem to care at all. Emil Blonsky is shown here in contrast to Banner (who is unable to fix his condition but at least laments it). Tim Roth's character in the film embraces this nature and revels in it. Here we have a nice contrast of how people deal with their sin nature. Some of us, like the apostle Paul described in Romans 7, recognize and wrestle with it in agony, crying out for a solution. Some however, reflect more of what Paul describes in Romans 1:29…

> *"God gave them over to a debased mind to do what ought not be done. They were filled with all manner of unrighteousness, evil, covetousness, malice. They are full of envy, murder, strife, deceit, maliciousness."*

Instead of finding Bruce's condition tragic or terrible, Blonsky covets that power. When he gets it, we see him more and more given over to it, truly deserving the name Abomination. In 1 Timothy 4:2 Paul describes people like this whose *"consciences are seared,"* their soul cauterized to the point of dulling any sense of right and wrong.

However, it's important to note that neither Bruce nor Blonsky seem to have any power to remedy their condition (until later Marvel phases, perhaps, but let's not get ahead of ourselves). While Blonsky might embrace it, both men are stuck with it. Again, whereas Tony Stark seemed to indulge in his depraved nature, Bruce is more clearly depicted as being shackled to it.

Speaking of Tony, that brings us to…

IRON MAN 2: *Wisdom and Self-Insufficiency*

"All I can give you is my knowledge."
  - Howard Stark, *Iron Man 2*

As the man inside Iron Man wrestles with the government, personal relationships, a poisoned body, the sting of Mickey Rourke's Whiplash and the bludgeoning of Sam Rockwell's Justin Hammer, he realizes at a pivotal moment in the film that his late father is "still taking him to school". However, by Howard's own proclamation he has only left his son with "knowledge" when what Tony's discombobulated life desperately needs is wisdom.

"Science is organized knowledge. Wisdom is organized life."
  - Immanuel Kant

Conversion can happen in a day, but as most Christians know: *sanctification* is ongoing. In the first film of the franchise, Tony had an awakening, a life-transforming event that manifests as both physical and spiritual. Here, we see that old habits die hard; he's burning the candle at both ends, bootstrapping his way along, relying on knowledge and moment-by-moment intuition. No one would describe Tony as "organized". He's blessed in many ways because his natural talents DO propel him down life's racetrack, but he's delusional enough to believe (like many of us) that this will get him across the finish line. Whiplash's fierce introduction on a racetrack in Monaco is a metaphor for the inevitable life-crash Tony was headed for anyway.

Making matters worse, Tony's manic manner is due in part to the fact that he's slowly being poisoned by the arc reactor in his chest. He's frantically trying to find solutions and/or settle his affairs to establish a legacy... or perhaps more accurately continue and further his father's legacy. It sounds well-intentioned, but again, there's something lacking here: *wisdom*.

> *"We know that all of us possess knowledge. This knowledge puffs up, but love builds up. If anyone imagines that he knows something, he does not yet know as he ought to know."*
> - 1 Corinthians 8:1-3

Iron Man's empire—Stark Industries—brings to mind the historical King Solomon before his older, wiser ecclesiastical lament. The son of Israel's King David was handed the keys to a kingdom—and even given wisdom by the one true God—but he let these resources go to his head much like our fictional Tony. As Stark rebuilt his father's Expo, King Solomon built the temple in Jerusalem; it all looked like legacy building, but personal appetites compromised what could have been triumphant. Stark's cheerleaders parade in the film like Solomon's harem, and Tony's wandering eye keeps delaying his commitment to an obvious helper suitable (Gwyneth Paltrow's long-suffering Pepper Potts).

> *"By wisdom a house is built, and by understanding it is established; by knowledge the rooms are filled with all precious and pleasant riches. A wise man is full of strength, and a man of knowledge enhances his might, for by wise guidance you can wage your war, and in an abundance of counselors there is victory."* - Proverbs 24:3-6

Proverbs so perfectly captures Tony Stark's flaws. The billionaire playboy has filled his rooms with precious and pleasant riches, capitalizing on his impressive knowledge. We even see him giving away his art collection and trying to do something with his accumulation as the film begins... but the Stark legacy isn't built on a solid foundation. His brilliance has certainly "enhanced his might" in red and gold arc-reacting glory, but his war is found wanting because his only counsel has been his own. When he stops jabbering for 30 seconds and actually listens to Rhodey, Pepper, and Fury in this sequel... he begins to discover some keys to victory.

> *"You can solve the riddle of your heart."* - Nick Fury

The reformed theologian in me initially choked on this fortune cookie wisdom, but after thoughtful reflection on Nick's encouraging sentiment I realized that to solve the problem, Tony needed to listen to Nick. He can only solve the riddle by leveraging the wise people in his life that are speaking to his heart. The first voice—in the first *Iron Man* film—was Yinsen; not only did he perform Tony's initial heart work, he also laid down his life for Stark; later in that film, Pepper's love and tangible gift—*"proof that Tony Stark has a heart"*—provided the strength he needed to survive. This "you can solve it" mantra isn't about the answer being inside you, as you pull yourself up by your bootstraps. Tony has loving extra hands on each bootstrap, which implies he continually needs help for ongoing wisdom and heart change. The film reinforces this again with Tony's need for intervention and aid from Rhodey, who becomes War Machine, fighting impossible odds by his side.

This notion goes even deeper for the discerning viewer. Once again, Tony can't remedy his condition. Even when he explores his father's belongings, he finds himself at a loss. It's only when he's broken, feeling defeated, hitting bottom—and the bottle—that the last bit of his dad's film plays, and a message he didn't expect comes from a transcendent patron from beyond. Father Stark essentially destined a solution for his son's heart, a new element that pre-dated his actual condition! Tony experiences some reconciliation with his dad, understanding precisely how his father provided for him, so he might be a blessing to the world.

Many times, our story is like Tony's. When we seem to have exhausted all options and have nowhere else to turn, our heavenly Father shows up and reveals the design that's been there all along, that we simply weren't paying attention to: steps laid out in advance for us to walk in that renew our hearts and restore a faith not possible without His intervention. All the knowledge Tony possesses can't compensate for a lack of wisdom… not to mention a love and trust that extends delegation to others. The sanctifying road in *Iron Man 2* teaches him valuable lessons about opening up this closely guarded part of his heart. No man is an island, and he cannot hold it all together by himself. This, of course, will lead to further team-ups down the road, including the man who doth wear his mother's drapes…

THOR: *The Transforming Power of Discipline*

> *"Therefore pride is their necklace; violence covers them as a garment."* - Psalm 73:6

When we first meet Thor, he is sure of himself, FULL of himself, and—goaded by his devious brother Loki—disobeys his father in an inter-realm incident that puts the kingdom at risk and nearly gets people killed. It's fair to say pride is one of Tony Stark's problems, but he has a multitude of vices. Thor's introduction shows a much more pointed and singular character flaw in urgent need of correction. His Father swiftly deals out a severe consequence for his son, taking away the armor, the hammer, and the power, pronouncing sentence:

> *"You are a vain, greedy, cruel boy… you're unworthy of these realms, you're unworthy of your title, you're unworthy of the loved ones you've betrayed. I, Odin Allfather, cast you out!"*

Now, forget what you know about where they take the character of Odin in sequels and the saga under different storytellers; take this story framework as its own narrative communication device. Is Odin being harsh here, or is he being biblical? We're talking about the God of the Bible who justly cast Satan out of heaven for pride; we have precedent. But that isn't even what Odin is doing here, is it? This isn't a life sentence, it is fatherly discipline, and he even sets the stage for Thor's learning, sanctification, redemption and restoration. It shouldn't surprise us that the initial humbling is an intense tough love. After all:

> *"The haughty looks of man shall be brought low, and the lofty pride of men shall be humbled, and the Lord alone will be exalted in that day."* - Isaiah 2:11

A disheartened Thor walks among men and women of the world and sees that he is no better or more worthy than them. He begins to learn the lessons his father intended him to learn. This should remind us of yet another verse about our heavenly father:

"My son, do not despise the LORD's discipline or be weary of his reproof, for the LORD reproves him whom he loves, as a father the son in whom he delights." - Proverbs 3:11-12

Thor suffers, he feels alone—even abandoned—but through this he learns humility. He leans into help from newfound friends, and cares for the "mere mortals" he once felt so far above. We see these things begin to build in him a better character and disposition. Again with the verses…

"…we rejoice in our sufferings, knowing that suffering produces endurance, and endurance produces character, and character produces hope…" - Romans 5:3-4

Seriously, this movie is a masterclass on the value of discipline and invites comparison with a wealth of scripture. Thor is schooled by his time on earth: sculpted, shaped. He tells a friend he was wrong, and that his father was right.

"Whoever exalts himself will be humbled, and whoever humbles himself will be exalted." - Matthew 23:12

When an unstoppable force threatens new and old friends, Thor offers himself as sacrifice to save them. He asks his enemy, his brother Loki, what he's done to wrong him, and he asks forgiveness. Once again, the transformed life story is delivered, this time with a very active "heavenly father" guiding that transformation.

And let's not forget Loki, Odin's adopted son, who feels second best and in the shadow of his brother. He's jealous, he covets Thor's status and wants to merit Odin's favor instead of accepting a father's grace. He wants to prove he can rule better than Thor, or his father, or anyone. Effectively, Loki wants to be his own god, and wants everyone to bow to him. He has all of Thor's pride and none of his repentance. He's a cautionary tale: the Christian's story is not to be the central hero, and yet we want to be the favored son or daughter; we want to be the center of the story. We want the Father's kingdom and all its rewards… but we want the throne, and we want to define the relationship. We certainly don't want to stand in the shadow of a superior saving son (like Jesus). But the reality is—like Loki—we are adopted:

> *"For those who are led by the Spirit of God are the children of God. The Spirit you received... brought about your adoption to sonship. And by him we cry, "Abba, Father." The Spirit himself testifies with our spirit that we are God's children. Now if we are children, then we are heirs—heirs of God and co-heirs with Christ..."* - Romans 8:14-17

Like Thor and Loki, we have pride, self-centeredness, and a lack of humility before our father God. We need to receive correction, and that's what much of this life is about. Someone already took up the mantle of savior for us: someone worthy, someone sacrificial, someone who laid down their life for us. Jesus paid it all, extending his hand on behalf of the father. Will we take his hand, or choose to fall into the pit in our own stubbornness and rebellion? Will we be humble, repentant, adopted sons and daughters of God?

> *"It is for discipline that you have to endure. God is treating you as sons. For what son is there whom his father does not discipline? If you are left without discipline, in which all have participated, then you are illegitimate children and not sons... he disciplines us for our good, that we may share his holiness. For the moment all discipline seems painful rather than pleasant, but later it yields the peaceful fruit of righteousness to those who have been trained by it."* - Hebrews 12:7-11

CAPTAIN AMERICA: *Strength in Weakness*

Unlike Tony Stark's story of a transformed life—changing from self-absorbed sinner to a seeking, struggling saint—the origin story of Steve Rogers is that of a man enduring in his weakness and finding himself equipped with the strength to reflect the character of his heart. The fact that this movie takes a chaste, determined, stalwart man and doesn't treat him like a joke, or boy scout, but instead lifts up his honorable (and even shy) traits as respectable was refreshing when it was released. The viewer sees scrawny Steve as someone to admire long before he manifests Chris Evans' true muscles, perhaps most dramatically modeled when he jumps on what he thinks is a live grenade to shield others. He's someone who Peggy Carter admires and likes for who he is, before how he looks *outside* matches the strength of spirit he possesses *inside*.

> *"(God) said to me, 'My grace is sufficient for you, for my power is made perfect in weakness.' Therefore I will boast all the more gladly of my weaknesses, so that the power of Christ may rest upon me."* - 2 Corinthians 12:9

It's a biblical parallel that God often takes the weak (even the foolish) and equips them to shame the strong, willful lovers of self who seek to oppress and conquer. The reason we like the underdog may often be due to selfish reasons—we want to conquer like they do—but at its core this narrative roots itself in a scriptural reality: God reveals Himself by working miracles through the seemingly incapable: a long-haired blind man can literally bring the house down on Philistines, a scrawny boy can take out a giant with a slingshot, a dozen traveling men—mostly uneducated fishermen—can virally spread Christianity throughout Rome and eventually the globe. Most importantly, a meek and seemingly helpless man nailed to a wooden cross can overcome sin and death.

> *"God chose what is weak in the world to shame the strong"*
> - 1 Corinthians 1:27

Steve Rogers' heart holds true when strength is gifted to him. He gathers a diverse team of men in the first film, helps free the enslaved, and is ultimately willing to lay down his life for those friends and the world. Cap is chosen by Professor Erskine, who understands and explains one of the things that makes Steve the best choice for the super soldier serum:

> *"A weak man knows the value of strength. And knows compassion."* - Abraham Erskine, *Captain America*

Erskine also explains that the film's nemesis Johann Schmidt, the Red Skull, represents the opposing nature in mankind, exposing what happens when power comes to those whose heart is tainted and amplifies the negatives inherent in our nature.

"For out of the heart come evil thoughts, murder, adultery, sexual immorality, theft, false witness, slander."
- Matthew 15:19

Can any of us say we were born as "pure of heart" as Steve Rogers is depicted in this film? Not really. The reason we likely resonate more with Tony Stark is because we know we've never been inherently upstanding like Steve. Power might not tempt us to be as flamboyantly wicked as the Skull, but we'd still have a struggle against abusing that power in lesser ways that deserve similar admonishment, even punishment. Captain America represents an archetype we desire to emulate, a kind of suffering servant we aspire to be, who properly applies the power he's been given and recognizes it as a gift not for himself, but for those around him. His heart is something we wish we had, not something we inherently possess.

Today, many of us have lost faith in that spirit related to "America", but what the Captain emulates is something that transcends national identity: a Christ-like sacrificial servant that (at the end of the day) is perfectly portrayed only by the gospel story. The kind of heart we see in Steve Rogers only finds a perfect correlation in this life by looking to Jesus Christ.

"By this we know love, that he laid down his life for us, and we ought to lay down our lives for the brothers." - 1 John 3:16

Steve will reveal some flaws as the Infinity Saga progresses, so we know he isn't a Christ figure, but if you look at Cap and Tony as the two most pivotal personages in the MCU, there are lesser biblical figures to compare them to. The dramatic conversion of Iron Man is quite Pauline in parallel, even down to having their lives rocked while literally traveling "on the road" (and both headed down the wrong direction in life). Tony's life does a complete 180 from self-serving to sacrificial... although he's still far from perfect. Meanwhile, the flawed-but-earnest Steve Rogers looks more like a post-resurrection Peter. Like Peter—the rock upon which Jesus says he will build the church—Cap is rocksteady and ready to serve.

Also, just as Paul and Peter had occasion in Acts to get in each other's faces, Tony and Steve will too… but I'm getting ahead of myself. Let's look more deeply at Tony's journey in…

THE AVENGERS:
Assembling, Kneeling, and Dealing with Debt

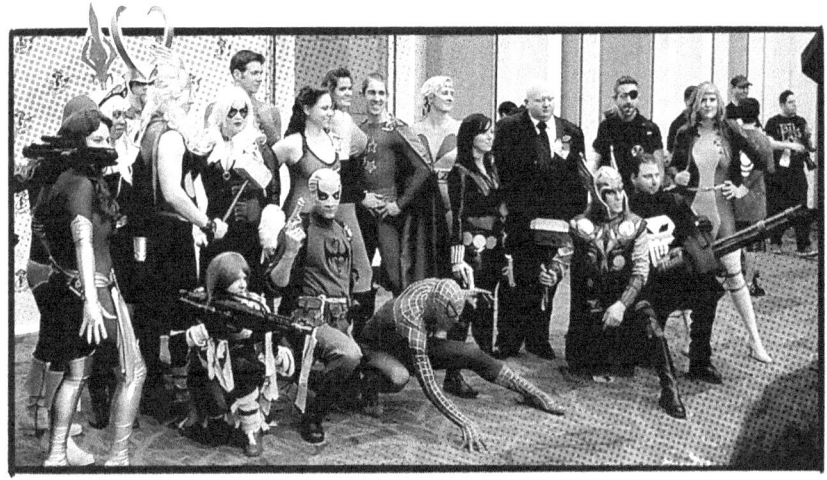

"And there came a day unlike any other, when earth's mightiest heroes were united…"

We're here! The crazy experiment of the MCU comes to its first merging of multiple franchises into one superhero stew. And yet… most of our heroes have been explored and developed individually in preceding films. It's the film's horned antagonist that brings the most theological pondering and parallels this time.

> *"Kneel before me. I said… KNEEL! Is not this simpler? Is this not your natural state? It's the unspoken truth of humanity that you crave subjugation. The bright lure of freedom diminishes your life's joy in a mad scramble for power. For identity. You were made to be ruled. In the end, you will always kneel."* - Loki

Guess what? Loki is right.

And Loki is wrong.

And we are Loki.

Those are the first three (of five lessons) to learn from The Avengers first film, so without further ado…

1. Loki is Right…

Born to kneel? It's not a particularly American sentiment, certainly. We don't generally think of bowing to a monarch or pledging subservience to be in line with having freedom (whereas other cultures have and do). Our first response to Loki's statement is probably one that looks less like a bended knee and more like a particularly raised finger. One might imagine there were rowdy cries of "hell, no!" in the theaters in response to Loki's assertion.

The problem is… there's truth in his words.

Even a lot of professing Christians live life as if God exists as an accompaniment to our self-centered universe, a force that exists to serve our needs, and although we'd never dare say it, the way we picture the relationship actually looks more like *he's* kneeling to serve *us*. He's like the genie from Aladdin. We forget a basic part of who we are, and how we were made, and it doesn't get any clearer than in the psalmist King David's words:

"Oh come, let us worship and bow down; let us kneel before the LORD, our Maker!" - Psalm 95:6

Now, what of Loki's accusation that we crave subjugation? Do we willingly shackle ourselves and lose our joy? Scripture is clear that the proper posture before the true Creator brings joy, not the other way around. Still, that same scriptural source tells us exactly how we enslave ourselves to oppressive people and things:

"… they exchanged the truth about God for a lie and worshiped and served the creature rather than the Creator…"
- Romans 1:25

We lose our joy in a "mad scramble for identity" by attaching it to something lesser, binding our hopes and dreams to a celebrity, a politician, a spouse, a fictional universe or hero, a national identity, a sexual identity, a gender identity, a career, a co-dependent relationship, or vicarious achievements through our children. We "freely" soil our knees on these shifting foundations hoping these will satisfy, give us purpose and worth. Worst of all, we effectively see ourselves as "god"—the center of our own life and universe—and find ourselves kneeling to an identity that is certain to let us down, shackled to our own fallibility and finitude.

Loki is right again: we crave subjugation and lose our joy, chasing a "freedom" (that is actually slavery) and declaring it as our identity. It is our "natural state", and we need help. And what about our identity? It's not just about dusting off our knees and rejecting the wrong identities, we need to know our *actual* identity. Scripture suggests we all—and each—have a job description:

> *"For we are his workmanship, created in Christ Jesus for good works, which God prepared beforehand, that we should walk in them."* - Ephesians 2:10

That job description for all mankind makes us subject to the one true God, but also offers amazing freedom and responsibility. We're not meant to be subjugated by anyone else. We have a dominion to wisely oversee and steward (and protect):

> *"Let us make man in our image, after our likeness. And let them have dominion… over all the earth and over every creeping thing that creeps on the earth."* - Genesis 1:26-28

So, Loki is right: we don't need to scramble for identity. We just need to submit to—and embrace—the one we've been given by God.

2. …but Loki is Wrong.

There IS one worldview that offers perfect relationship held in tension, that offers both freedom and servitude. The creator and God we obey humbly and bow before utters this unique command:

> *"For freedom Christ has set us free; stand firm therefore, and do not submit again to a yoke of slavery."* - Galatians 5:1

Loki is wrong: we were made to be free. The power-hungry, adopted Asgardian son in the Avengers movie offers a subjugation without freedom, a cruel rule of oppression and tyranny. He is no benevolent dictator. Conversely, the God of the Bible proclaims that we receive true freedom through Jesus, that our subjugation to lesser things is broken forever as we give our lives to a life-giving God.

This seems dichotomous, right? We're "free" only by becoming God's "bondservants"? It runs counter to our notion of freedom which—if we stop and think about it—often seems nebulous and undefined. What is freedom, anyway? Simply to do whatever we want? What if our own "wants" are corrupted? What if you and I are flawed creatures that even deceive ourselves, slaves to bad programming and predispositions? How can we truly transcend and experience REAL freedom?

Consider: if we were created and crafted to have a most glorious function, and things exist that inhibit that function (including our own hearts and minds) then *true* freedom would be objective release from those restricting shackles. Only then would our external direction and internal desires finally be freed to operate as originally intended. In other words, we're freed from all the things that enslave us in this life—including our own passions—by becoming a servant to the one who knows us better than we know ourselves.

"Live as people who are free, not using your freedom as a cover-up for evil, but living as servants of God." - 1 Peter 2:16

Loki is wrong: freedom is not a "disease" to which servitude is the "cure". Rather, placing our lives under the truly all-knowing, all-powerful rule of our Maker brings us freedom to know ourselves and the empowerment to live freely.

In the end, we WILL kneel… but not to a Loki.

Loki is wrong, because he knows the outcome but believes he's the answer. When the term god is used to describe Loki and Thor, Captain America has an earnest reply: *"Ma'am, there's only one God, and I'm pretty sure he doesn't dress like that."* Steve Rogers knows full well that this tyrant is not someone he or anyone should bow to. As a man growing up 70 years ago and likely raised in a Christian home, he was probably taught the message of the gospel, in which God's good news to all men culminates with those bended knees being loved, exalted as siblings and co-heirs with Jesus.

Freedom in Christ is rooted in the reality that God doesn't treat his bondservants as slaves… he treats us as his own children.

> *"So you are no longer a slave, but a son… an heir through God. Formerly, when you did not know God, you were enslaved to those that by nature are not gods."* - Galatians 4:7-8

As the Hulk so aptly puts it (in the crowning moment of the film) Loki is indeed a *"puny god"* (by nature, NOT God at all) and only offers the rule of a tyrant… whereas the God of the bible offers adoption, family, inheritance, and eternity. Would you not kneel for the savior who sacrificed for you? In *The Lord of the Rings: The Return of the King*, Middle Earth kneels to honor even the little hobbits, while they willingly submit themselves to the rule of Aragorn. It's not that we weren't created to kneel; we should just bend our knee to the one who deserves it.

> *"God has highly exalted him and… at the name of Jesus every knee should bow… and every tongue confess that Jesus Christ is Lord, to the glory of God the Father"* - Philippians 2:8-11

Of course, before we scoff and spit at Loki in all of his vainglorious folly, there is one more important thing (perhaps the most essential thing) you should realize about this man, his mind, and methods.

3. We are Loki

Tom Hiddleston's nuanced acting gives audiences one of the best performances in the MCU, period. The character of Loki—albeit flawed, and perhaps not as formidable as other villains—is simply the most interesting. And one of the reasons I believe it's so interesting is because it most closely resembles each of us at one time or another. No, that doesn't mean we've all had that day where we got upset and assembled alien armies to take over Manhattan. (Although we've all been there, am I right?) I'm referring to our pride, jealousy, rebellion and obstinance.

> *"I remember a shadow, living in the shade of your greatness."*
> - Loki

This bitter son of Asgard still burns from the understanding of his life and status: he's adopted. Although he has a father who loves him, he can't accept it. His rebellion and rage make him act on desires for destructive dominion, rather than enjoying a healthy place in his father's kingdom. The quintessential "prodigal son", he proclaims himself king and god even though it's so clear how much he's found lacking.

Consider this: have we not all been here at one time or another? Are some of us here now? The Bible describes God as our heavenly father, and despite our sinful nature he offers us more than simply a service role in his kingdom… he offers adoption as full siblings:

> *"But when the fullness of time had come, God sent forth his Son, born of woman, born under the law, to redeem those who were under the law, so that we might receive adoption as sons."*
> - Galatians 4:4-5

There IS something humbling about this, however. Although the Odin/Thor/Loki relationship is an imperfect mimicry, it's entirely true that part of our relationship with the God of the universe means we are in the shadow of the one true son. We are co-heirs, but he's the preeminent child, the true and perfect Son of God, our savior and hence the one to whom we kneel.

> *"Therefore God has highly exalted him and bestowed on him the name that is above every name, so that at the name of Jesus every knee should bow, in heaven and on earth and under the earth, and every tongue confess that Jesus Christ is Lord, to the glory of God the Father."* - Philippians 2:9-11

We don't really like this. Even professing Christians are guilty of recasting Jesus as the co-pilot to their story, the helpful Robin to their Batman (or Rick Jones to the Hulk). We see living in the shadow of the perfect Son as something negative, humiliating instead of humbling, chafing at the shadow instead of resting in the shade of his salvation. We can't be happy to have a big brother that loves us, protects us, rescues us, equips us, empowers us and offers us friendship and eternal relationship in our father's kingdom. We want to be the center of the story, the one who slays the dragon… we want the movie to be called "The Amazing Loki" instead of Thor.

The truth is, it's Christ's story in which we're a part. Even the Soundgarden song that ends the film hints at such a reality: *"what if all you understand, could fit into the center of our hand? Then you found it wasn't you, who held the sum of everything you knew."*

> *"So you take the world I love as recompense for your imagined slights?"* - Thor

We see our pride and sinful self-worship bear itself out in the way we dominate our planet. Collectively, (if not individually) have we not done more damage to God's world (its people, its riches, its environment) than even Loki does in the movie? We haven't needed Chitauri or giant flying worms to wreak devastation on hearts and hearths. We have our own "imagined slights" and reject God, we spit on the grace and love offered by our father because it doesn't suit our warped desires.

> *"You give up this poisonous dream! You come home!"* - Thor

Thor's passionate cry is filled with love in *The Avengers*. He has no desire to punish his brother, and continues offering reconciliation, seeking to win his fallen brother back all the way to the film's end. Loki's response? He pierces his brother in the side, bitter to the finish, and in the final moments of the movie we see Thor taking him back for judgment instead of reconciliation.

We all will stand someday before our heavenly father. If we don't give up our own poisonous dreams, if we don't turn from our bitter rebellion, scripture tells us our future will look like a courtroom. If we accept the saving shadow of the Son, it looks like home: devoid of strife and woe, and brighter than Asgard. But that also means salvation—the cancelling of our debt due to sin—comes from the Son, and not our merit. Which brings us to…

4. Dealing with our Debt

> *"I've got red in my ledger; I'd like to wipe it out."* - Black Widow

This intriguing confession and self-reflection comes from Natasha Romanoff, admitting that she's done bad things in her past and desires to "settle her accounts". Our deeds might not be as heinous as Natasha's work for the mysterious Red Room, or others, but her conundrum is a common thread in our existence: we know we've done wrong, and we often harbor some vague hope that we can add weight to some kind of cosmic scale and tip it once more to the favorable side. Call it balance, call it karma, but as Loki points out: call it elusive:

> *"Can you? Can you wipe out that much red? Dreykov's daughter? Sao Paulo? The hospital fire? Barton told me everything. Your ledger is DRIPPING—it's gushing red—and you think saving a man no more virtuous than yourself will change anything? This is the basest sentimentality. This is a child at prayer. Pathetic... you pretend to be separate, to have your own code, something that makes up for the horrors. But they are a part of you, and they will NEVER go away."* - Loki

While it's true that Natasha Romanoff gets to play a part in literally saving the world during the course of *The Avengers* film—or at least millions of lives in New York City—Loki raises a valid point. Does moving forward and doing good deeds heal all the pain for the people she's hurt in the past? Do her valiant efforts for others comfort the families of the lives this "Black Widow" previously snuffed out? Does fighting to stop Loki now bring those dead persons back to life?

> *"Saving someone doesn't UNKILL someone else"*. - Jessica Jones, *Jessica Jones Season One*

People aren't numbers in a ledger, and atonement isn't simple math. Forgiveness isn't just doing better next time, and although Natasha might be "paying it forward" now, how does that possibly pay anything backward? Loki doesn't just mock her numbers and totals; he calls her whole worldview into question. Like a serpent in the garden, he spits out quite a few true statements... but then twists the ending, concluding that because she has NO way of truly addressing the "red"—atoning for her sins—that they can "never" go away.

It's the answer we've all sought at one time or another (if we have any conscience left at all). We've all hurt others in some way—practically, physically, emotionally, financially, spiritually—and may be trapped in the same vicious circle as Natasha Romanoff, trying to reconcile our own life accounts and downplaying or justifying how we're dealing with the red in our ledgers. Natasha sees her problem, and Loki rightly points out she'll never settle her OWN accounts... but neither has an answer, and the film leaves it for contemplation.

"Blessed are those whose lawless deeds are forgiven, and whose sins are covered; blessed is the man against whom the Lord will not count his sin." - Romans 4:7-8

Red in the ledger would equal debt, and this is exactly why Jesus Christ taught his followers to pray to his Father God in heaven, the famous "Lord's prayer" in which we ask him to "forgive our debt, as we forgive our debtors". A life of grace walks in the reality that Jesus died to forgive the red in our ledgers, to cancel the debt of sin and offer freedom and reconciliation not by our own merit. We don't balance cosmic scales. True heroes are those not desperately seeking their own reconciliation, but rather walking in confidence and mirroring that God-initiated love and forgiveness by forgiving our debtors, by emulating that offering (as God has redeemed and forgiven us).

"Is anyone among you suffering? Let him pray... And if he has committed sins, he will be forgiven." - James 5:13-15

It's great to see a heroic and even powerful character wrestling (as we do) with just how her accumulated sin might be dealt with and how redemption works out... to realize her shortcomings, suffer the doubts we all share at one time or another, squirm under that gut-wrenching guilt and shame that pervades even as she tries to conceal it, bury it, or take comfort in imminent victories to offset the gnawing reality at the back of her brain.

While the Black Widow is fiction, here's hoping those presently struggling like her don't spend the rest of their lives caught in that never-ending battle. We've got red in our ledgers; the blood of Jesus can wipe it out. And a life in Jesus also calls us to relationship not just with him, but with others.

5. Some Assembly Required

"The Avengers. That's what we call ourselves; we're sort of like a team... takes us a while to get any traction, I'll give you that one. But let's do a headcount here..." - Tony Stark

Finally, the moment arrived; this motley multi-movie crew of colorful characters pulled together in the inaugural attempt of Marvel franchise-mashing that proved a smashing success. At its heart, we have a very familiar trope that—conveniently enough—turns up in a lot of television and movies handled by *Avengers* director Joss Whedon. His specialty seems to involve stories about *made family*: families born not of blood, but of something common that forces and/or forges them together. They're uniquely comprised of people with a variety of complementary abilities. This made family often bickers, argues, even breaks up only to be brought together again, and sometimes it seems like they stumble more than they succeed. And yet, it seems they're used by the narrative (and the storyteller) to pull off something that seems amazing, unbelievable, even miraculous: remind you of anything?

"For as in one body we have many members, and the members do not all have the same function, so we, though many, are one body in Christ, and individually members one of another."
- Romans 12:4-5

The armored avenger, the star-spangled man, the hammer wielding hunk, the spy and the archer all come together to be one unit on mission together. Oh, and don't forget: they have a Hulk. Coming from different backgrounds, countries—even planets—this disparate group assembles and does the work they were called and commissioned to do by Nick Fury, banding together as brothers and sisters with a common goal to stop Loki.

"For whoever does the will of my Father in heaven is my brother and sister and mother." - Matthew 12:48-50

Nick Fury isn't a worthy stand-in for our heavenly Father, and ultimately even Odin will fall short, but this idea of becoming family is a fuzzy portrait of the called and commissioned church. Even the word church in the Bible is the Greek word *ecclesia*, which literally means "to call" and/or "assembly". The *"Avengers, assemble!"* rally cry is not unlike the church's call and command to gather together. There's only one element missing in comparison with the common bonds that bring believers together into what we call the church. In order of priority, these would be:

- **Common God**
- **Common Goals**
- **Common Enemies**

The Avengers come together based only on the first two commonalities (as they likely wouldn't agree on God) but the parallel still works as an encouragement toward why Christians strive to maintain an assemblage despite differences and bickering. We stand together in Christ against the enemies of Satan, sin and death. And there are days where we feel much like the Avengers do, locked in an insurmountable battle. The comforting thing is, we already know the outcome of the war.

Tony, Bruce, Thor and Steve have—in their preceding stories—already been refined, tempered, and primed to make the sacrifice play individually. Although Tony gets the ball (or nuke, technically) and has the most dramatic moment in this film, they're all willing to lay it down collectively, together. Their main inspiration in the film comes from the death of Phil Coulson. The bonding agent for these Avengers was blood—a sacrifice—and they become an effective and solidified team in the wake of his sacrificial example.

The goals of a Christian aren't avenging Phil Coulson, and our enemies aren't the Chitauri; our goals are living out God's commands and commission, which can only be done together. But what a wonderful twist that reminds mindful Christians that the church comes together around the example of Christ and His sacrifice (and yet more than that: our victory is assured through his completed work on the cross and resurrection, which is the miracle that makes us family).

As we wrap up Phase One of the MCU's great experiment, it seems prudent to distill and bullet point the simplest way we might understand the inaugural arc of Marvel's cinematic gospel:

1. **We're in desperate need of a transformed heart** (*Iron Man*)
2. **We're shackled to a destructive nature** (*The Incredible Hulk*)
3. **We will not solve this problem by ourselves** (*Iron Man 2*)
4. **Our pride needs humbling and divine discipline** (*Thor*)
5. **In our weakness, we are gifted w/strength** (*Captain America*)
6. **Those strengths are fully realized together** (*The Avengers*)

Do you see it? The incomplete understanding, the intuitive yearning, the felt need only those who are truly born again understand is fully realized by kneeling to the gospel of Jesus Christ? Not all the ingredients are detailed in this comic-to-film narrative, certainly, but enough pieces are there to make the believer rejoice and the seeker curious. The subtext is practically a six-point sermon. We should pray in God's providence that we stand before Him in the kingdom to come one day, and rejoice that Marvel's cinematic experiment yielded a fruit that Hollywood likely never anticipated: a provocation of spirit that led some to seek the true solution to our malady, and the kingdom family at which that these fictions feebly grasp.

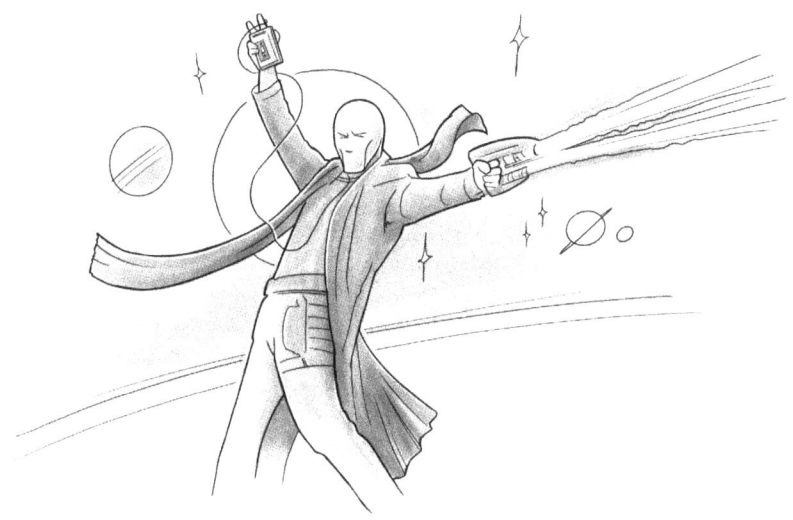

Act 3: **It's Just a Phase**

or

"Admit it. You NEED me. We're connected"

Scene 1: **Where do we go from the top?**

Art imitates life, and as the Avengers achieved world-saving success on the screen, Marvel achieved worldwide success at the box office. The question emerged: after the victory (and the shawarma) and the groundbreaking event that Phase One represented… where would they go from here?

> *"I offer you the chance of a far richer sacrament…"*
>   - Thor, *The Dark World*

> *"So… you got detention. You screwed up…"*
>   - Captain America PSA, *Spider-man: Homecoming*

The movies in Phase Two gave us what many think are the best, and worst, of the Infinity Saga. Fortunately, there were still plenty of points and parallels to be gleaned by the mindful consumer as Marvel's cinematic universe continued to expand…

IRON MAN 3: *How then, shall we live?*

After being tormented by his past and fearing for his future, Tony's greatest foe turns out to be… *today?*

Tony Stark has been introduced to a world that is bigger than his brain (and ego) and must face the fact that he can't create a suit for every possible contingency. At the beginning of the film, he's putting the finishing touches on suit #42—perhaps a nod to *The Hitchhiker's Guide to the Galaxy*, wherein 42 is the answer to life, the universe, and everything—but this Mark 42 prototype doesn't work as it should (which is also fitting). Tony Stark can't create a solution for all the universe's problems, and this vexes him: anxiety attacks and insomnia plague Tony and hamper his relationships. Even little things manifest as part of Tony's anxiety; he obsesses about whether he got Pepper the right Christmas present. Bigger, better, more impressive: Stark keeps facing the need to one-up himself, to keep ahead of the game. His suits have become externalized expressions of his anxiety, a desire to prove he can solve anything, stop anything, cover himself and others in any given situation… that he can save everyone. But he knows the reality is… he can't.

> *"And which of you by being anxious can add a single hour to his span of life? Therefore do not be anxious about tomorrow, for tomorrow will be anxious for itself. Sufficient for the day is its own trouble."* - Matthew 6:27,34

Ultimately, Tony Stark knows his present condition is dysfunctional and confesses to Pepper what a "hot mess" he is, lamenting that *"I'm just a man in a can."* He writes a goodbye note to a lover in the opening flashback of the film, flippantly saying *"you know who I am,"* but the narrative proceeds to make Tony face the fact that he's forgotten who he is.

Even those who find themselves with a transformed life still fall back into misunderstanding their identity. The world sees Tony as a suit of armor and he's correspondingly bought into this, forgetting that Iron man is the person inside, the heart and renewed life given to him by the sacrifice of Yinsen in the first film. Tony's misplaced identity is further confused by two ghosts from his past who come back to haunt him… but thankfully these are outnumbered by three people who help Tony remember his true identity and place in the greater scheme of things. These three are best described as:

1. The Helper Suitable

Iron Man's story winks and jokes about his carousing days, but ultimately treats Tony's playboy life as something to be turned away from. Pepper Potts served as Stark's "helper" long before he chose to love her, even cleaning up his indiscretions. It took two films for him to commit, and as the story unfolds Tony admits she's the only thing keeping him sane in his current predicament.

> *"Then the Lord God said, 'It is not good that the man should be alone; I will make him a helper fit for him.'"* - Genesis 2

The Iron Man trilogy makes it clear there is no one else who can keep up with him (or stand up to him) except this smart and vivacious woman. She manages the "household" of Stark Industries and it's clear that she is his equal. Tony has been losing sleep and having panic attacks, primarily that he can't protect the thing he cares about the most (her) but as events unfold, we see a reciprocal relationship; Pepper's also saving him. The final blow that takes down Killian comes from her hand, so it's fitting that Tony finally puts a ring on it.

2. The Faithful Friend

James Rhodes has been Tony's friend for a long time, but it's clear that Stark doesn't think of "Rhodey" as his equal. He doesn't think he wants or needs help, and only reluctantly receives it in the back half of the second film. He isn't even sure he wants Rhodes to keep the suit! But in the final act of Iron Man 3, James Rhodes is clearly skilled and adept without a metal suit, and even shoots better than Tony. In fact, while Stark runs around diving in and out of his 30+ armors for protection, who saves the POTUS (and takes out Extremis operatives) without armor?

> *"A man of many companions may come to ruin, but there is a friend who sticks closer than a brother."* - Proverbs 18:24

Not only does Pepper Potts defeat the "big bad," the big rescue of the U.S. Commander-in-chief is not by Iron Man, but Rhodey. If everything was contingent upon a lone, self-capable Tony Stark, that's two strikes. And while we're at it…

3. The (Faith of a) Child

"Truly, I say to you, whoever does not receive the kingdom of God like a child shall not enter it." - Luke 18:17

Jesus wasn't talking about defeating Extremis-enhanced bad guys when he explained this, but he was making a point about how growing older can retard our understanding of God, each other, and ourselves. Knowledge puffs up, pride corrupts, and wisdom becomes worldly; we lose our identity and our place in the universe. Tony finds himself in Hicksville, USA, suffering more panic attacks and questioning his ability, but pep talks with a spunky kid named Harley refuel his hope, rekindle his imagination, and make Stark face his fears, reminding him who he is. Not only that, when he faces operatives in the bar and down the street it takes this child's snowball to stop Tony from being gunned down (not to mention the boy's later intervention with a flash grenade). A child becomes as essential to the fight as the billionaire, genius Avenger.

Whereas he needed some assists from others in prior films, this time Tony's life, the President's life, and "the day" is clearly saved by others. The weight of the world doesn't rest on Stark alone.

Tony describes his armor as a *"cocoon"*, the idea that he'd been reborn, but protected… transforming over time. It's not a bad analogy for the "now and not yet" aspect of Christian transformation, that we're being protected and conformed to the image and likeness of our savior. At the end, Stark is appropriately dressed in white, his old home and all the symbols of his prior life cast down, his healed heart ready to start a new life. It's a great epilogue to Phase One and could have been a fitting end to Tony's story… but as we know by now, it isn't.

THOR, THE DARK WORLD: Growth & Role Reversal

Oh, it started out so well…

"And God said, "Let there be light," and there was light. And God saw that the light was good. And God separated the light from the darkness." - Genesis 1:3-4

Beginning with a formative battle between light and darkness—Odin's father and Asgard versus Malekith and his dark elves—Thor's sophomore film was perfectly set up to give us something deep and biblical. Sadly, this film turned out to be a sophomore slump with an undercooked antagonist and his weapon, the Aether. At least in biblical fashion, the enemy does not succeed:

"The light shines in the darkness, and the darkness has not overcome it." - John 1:5

While Asgard has a host of characters they might have chosen to contrast with Thor's sanctification since the first film, they sadly decided to showcase his growth at the expense of the formerly honorable Odin. First, they make the strange choice of having the Allfather act with gross prejudice toward Jane. Then, more understandably, he's emotionally compromised by the loss of his wife. It's disappointing on one hand, since the first film made him a great parallel with the biblical God, but at the end of the day Odin isn't the one true God (*Dark World* even has Odin confirm in conversation with Loki that Asgardians aren't gods at all, just long-lived). So, a flawed Odin who gives in to anger and hate—ready to employ the destructive methods of his foe and sacrifice his own people to achieve his goals—is understandable. In the first film he reflected our *heavenly* father, but any mortal father may do that one day yet stumble the next.

Thor's maturation is thus placed center stage as he opposes his fallible father and is forced to disobey, not only to do what's right but to save multiple worlds. Of course, he makes the questionable choice to employ his brother Loki, and the film initially seems to suggest a change in the former trickster villain. The adopted brother's willingness to help, his subsequent sacrifice and "death" feel genuine (and Hiddleston's performance sells it) but we find out, again, it's simply another move in Loki's long game to take the throne. Oh, what a third Thor film might have been if this sibling rivalry had truly come to a head, instead of turning into a joke... but I digress.

It's also notable how, despite Loki's pride and self-serving nature, he truly is fond of his mother Frigga, and emotionally devastated when she is killed. Some Marvel villains, like The Red Skull, are portrayed as completely "*EEEEEEEvil*"—at all times and in every way—when the reality for most of us is that we're inherently compromised by our sin. The term *total depravity* is used to describe the biblical condition of the sin nature, but this differs from *utter* depravity. "Total" means we are totally compromised, but not utterly given over to every worst thing we might do or say all the time. You can be a slave to sin and still care about your family; it's historically documented that Hitler loved his mother and grieved when she died. Guess he wasn't so bad then, right?

We can't let an understandable sympathy or empathy in these cases allow us to justify or lessen the severity of wickedness in Loki, or in ourselves and others. Sadly, this is where many fans began to reinterpret Loki (particularly women who just found Tom Hiddleston to be hot) and began to view him as simply "misunderstood", or a good guy just acting out. Some defend or justify his wicked actions when what he really needs is humbling, confession, repentance, and a complete heart change (like we see Thor and Tony Stark undergo in their narratives).

Odin: *All this because Loki desires a throne.*

Loki: *It is my birthright!*

Odin: *Your birthright was to die as a child! Cast out on a frozen rock. If I had not taken you in, you would not be here now to hate me.*

Like Loki, we want to be on the throne of our own lives. We act like royalty is our birthright instead of recognizing the one who is truly on the throne, and our rebellious state against Him. Even as Christians, we gloss over the fact that our familial status is only because of God's mercy and grace, despite our otherwise pitiable and damnable state. When we begin to justify our own inner Loki, or downplay the severity of our sin, it truly does become a dark world.

After Thor's well-meant but somewhat disappointing sequel, we find ourselves in the year 2014, and what I consider the apex year of the MARVEL-Us Era (both for the MCU and surrounding superhero films in general). These next two films may comprise the best this shared universe has to offer, at opposing ends in terms of tone and genre, but at the top of their game in terms of expressing those forms. So…

"Before we get started… does anyone want to get out?"
     - Steve Rogers

CAPTAIN AMERICA, THE WINTER SOLDIER: Trust

"For as long as I can remember I just wanted to do what was right. I guess I'm not quite sure what that is anymore."
     - Steve Rogers

Here we have my favorite "solo" Marvel Cinematic film, courtesy of the Russo Brothers, and a movie that shifts the familiar Phase One tone to that of a taut, political action thriller. As with many thrillers and political dramas, the tension comes from betrayal and a sudden inability to know whom to trust. Natasha is seemingly off mission: can Captain America trust her? Nick Fury hides things from him. Director Pierce also seems to be hiding something. Is S.H.I.E.L.D. really the organization he thought it was? Who is he really working for? Oh, and an old friend seems to be back from the dead: can he trust his own senses?

Like a narrative sniper, this focused story is an exploration of who we trust, why we trust, and how we trust. The sheer number of quotes about trust in the film stack up quickly:

"Grandad loved people. But he didn't trust them very much."

"Soldiers trust each other."

"Truth is a matter of circumstances…"

"...it's kind of hard to trust someone when you don't know who that someone really is."

"Last time I trusted someone, I lost an eye."

"If... it was down to me to save your life—and you be honest with me—would you trust me to do it?"

"Don't. Trust. Anyone."

Steve Rogers is the kind of upfront, forthright guy who wears his personality and character on his sleeve: what you see is what you get. He's trustworthy, and when he extends that trust he expects it in return. This movie splashes water in the earnest hero's face with the cold reality that real trust is hard to come by. While Steve's frustrations involve world-shaking stakes and specific persons, the traits that challenge Steve's ability to trust are quite applicable to our own relationships, such as:

- **Compartmentalization:** Nick Fury only tells people the information that he determines they *need to know*. While it's understandable in certain positions of authority and chain-of-command (even parenting) it doesn't translate well to adult, peer-to-peer relationships in terms of trust; it makes you wonder what they're hiding and why.

- **Conspiracy:** Hydra has infiltrated S.H.I.E.L.D. from within, employing manipulation, lies and deceit to cover up their true actions and intentions. This can translate to a cheating spouse covering up adultery, a corporate takeover, or some heretical church members getting on the church board and building a team to take the church in a new direction.

- **Chameleon:** Natasha Romanoff freely admits to Steve that her "truth"—indeed, her identity—is malleable, asking him *"Who do you want me to be?"* People like this may not have nefarious intent or be covering up a big secret, but they're still technically deceitful, presenting externally only what they know people want to see. When we know that's what a person is doing it's difficult to trust them, or even know who they are.

- **Comfort**: Arnim Zola explains that *"HYDRA created a world so chaotic that humanity is finally ready to sacrifice its freedom to gain its security."* Sometimes people will compromise their ethics and principles for their ease, to feel safe. If people are willing to sacrifice the morals they claim in the name of comfort, how can they be trusted?

- **Conscription:** Steve struggles to believe his friend Bucky could be turned into a cold-blooded killer and soldier of Hydra. While most situations in our lives won't include *actual* brainwashing, our trust may be tested when a friend falls in with a bad crowd or even a cult, no longer resembling the person we knew. For the Christian, this might be when a person is seduced away from the faith. If someone we trusted so deeply can be turned, how can we trust anyone?

Of course, there's a sixth challenge to trust in the film that warrants honest scrutiny. On the one hand, Hydra's actions in the film are wrong, but what of their guiding principle?

"Hydra was founded on the belief that humanity could not be trusted with its own freedom…" - Arnim Zola

Uh-oh. As a Christian in the 21st century, it's difficult to look around and argue with them, and the Bible doesn't speak well of humanity either when it comes to trust, whether it's individuals or institutions:

"Put no trust in a neighbor; have no confidence in a friend…"
   - Micah 7:5

"Cursed is the man who trusts in man and makes flesh his strength…" - Jeremiah 17:5

I can appreciate Captain America's ability to look for the best in people, but biblically we're forced to share Nick Fury's outlook when we consider humanity. As he explains to a naive Steve:

"S.H.I.E.L.D. takes the world as it IS, not as we'd like it to be."

Steve Rogers is probably one of those guys who'd say humans are "basically good" (though this film rattles his worldview a bit).

Christians know man is inherently sinful, and we've abused our freedom since the garden. Our trust is never to be sourced or built upon a belief in humanity. That's why Arnim Zola's answer is equally flawed; turning to someone like Pierce or Hydra isn't the biblical answer either.

> *"Put not your trust in princes, in a son of man, in whom there is no salvation. When his breath departs, he returns to the earth; on that day his very plans perish."* - Psalms 146:3-4

In the end, Hydra is taken down… but so is S.H.I.E.L.D. There's no clear answer about how we can really trust anyone in life, though it seems that many are intrinsically able to trust Steve and act according to *"Captain's orders"*. They can rely on this unique and special man, one who exists as the peak of human potential physically (thanks to the first film) and now morally in the sequel. He's even willing to take a beating, willing to lay down his life to redeem his broken friend. Is that perhaps what we really need? A Captain who is the perfect specimen of mankind in every way that we fall short? A Captain whose judgment is above all human institutions? A Captain to command us, one whom we'll salute and follow his orders over our own will?

> *"Trust in the LORD with all your heart, and do not lean on your own understanding. In all your ways acknowledge him, and he will make straight your paths."* - Proverbs 3:5-6

> *"It is better to take refuge in the LORD than to trust in man."* - Psalm 118:8

Steve Rogers is far from a perfect parallel for Christ, but it's a good reminder of the wellspring from which our trust should come. Even when we extend trust to family, friends, churches or institutions, we know these will all be imperfect, and we need our primary trust to comfort and guide us through mishaps, both when they fail us… and when we fail them. Remember, it won't always be others breaking trust with us. None of us are Jesus, and few of us are Steve Rogers… and even Steve may be breaking trust with someone in the near future.

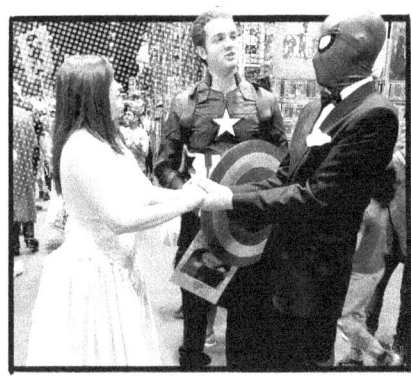 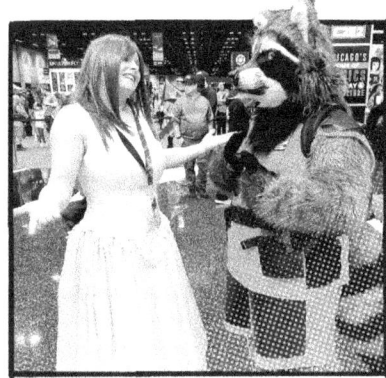

Choosing an officiant: sorry Rocket, but Cap said he could do this all day…

GUARDIANS OF THE GALAXY: Unlikely Allies

"I am going to die surrounded by the biggest idiots in the galaxy." - Gamora

A long time ago in a century far, far away, the famous creator of Tarzan—Edgar Rice Burroughs—also introduced the world to John Carter and his adventures on Mars. Since 1912, this character has informed many science fiction/fantasy stories in terms of the hero's journey, from *Superman* to *Avatar*. Usually, a man is removed in some amazing fashion from his normal environment (often earth) and finds himself in a new and troubled world (or galaxy) where he accrues alien friends—and enemies—and a love interest, effectively becoming the savior of this strange corner of the universe.

In 1999, Hallmark Entertainment and The Jim Henson Company produced a groundbreaking television show that unashamedly copied this formula. John *Carter* became John *Crichton*, ripped from a modern-day earth and armed with lots of pop culture references, finds himself in a galaxy far away amidst a bunch of escaped convicts including: a strong-willed, highly skilled warrior woman, a hulking alien brute, a humanoid plant, and a pint-sized alien with an enormous chip on his shoulder. Hopefully the similarities here haven't gone over your head.

"Nothing goes over my head! My reflexes are too fast, I would catch it." - Drax

It turns out *Guardians* director James Gunn was indeed a huge *Farscape* fan, unashamedly retooling a lot of Marvel characters that weren't original Guardians of the Galaxy to fit this familiar formula. He even gave Ben Browder (the actor who played John) a cameo in Guardians Vol. 2. The reason I note the recurring tropes and themes is to highlight an older narrative recurrence we see with Peter Quill, beyond even the John Carter template. Both Carter and Crichton are simply humans who "incarnate" their fantasy corners of the universe and become saviors, but Peter Quill unashamedly plays with an even deeper biblical archetype by nature of his origin. The opening scene portrays his birth by a human mother, but an unseen father who was *"an angel... composed of pure light"*. Quill seems human, yet possesses a heritage that makes his lineage unique, a birth that hints at a more specific incarnation like that of Christ: truly God and truly man. A "Star-Lord" indeed. All the ingredients are here to outdo even Superman in terms of the savior motif: after all, Clark Kent was 100% Kryptonian and only *appeared* human.

Now, the Guardian sequel will both confirm, and greatly diminish, this idea of Peter's "godhood". But it shouldn't go without note that it's what empowers Quill to endure the destructive nature of the power stone in this film. The savior HAD to be more than mere human, which is part of many a classic Christian catechism and a key element of biblical doctrine; it's notably curious that our central "Guardian" showcases this facet. However, if Steve Rogers was lacking in terms of a parallel for Christ, Peter Quill fails to reach even a parallel with Captain America! When we first meet Peter, he's worse than Tony Stark, because for all of Stark's depravity and selfishness he was at least *competent*. The self-professed "Star-Lord's" rap sheet calls out minor assault, public drunkenness, fraud and more.

Upon examination, the lives of Drax, Rocket, Gamora and even Groot don't fare much better. Star-Lord and most of his soon-to-be guardians are not only criminals, but fools, undisciplined or flawed in ways that make them the polar opposite of the Avengers, who were fairly accomplished when they united. The most competent Guardian is Gamora, yet she also carries the most grievous sins from her time with Thanos, a lot of "red in her ledger" like The Black

Widow. Drax is consumed by his desire for vengeance, while Rocket harbors a deep well of bitterness; he and Groot are just living for personal gain.

"When I look around, you know what I see? Losers."
  - Peter Quill

So, despite a premise that might have provided a central saving figure reminiscent of Christ, Guardians pivots to spotlight a group of ignoble losers languishing in a far more wayward, wicked state than the Avengers, and yet thrust together into that same made-family model that *The Avengers* did so well. The main difference is that these characters were the zeroes, not the heroes… and in this way might Guardians provide a more accurate depiction of the church?

"For consider your calling, brothers: not many of you were wise according to worldly standards, not many were powerful, not many were of noble birth. But God chose what is foolish in the world to shame the wise; God chose what is weak in the world to shame the strong; God chose what is low and despised in the world…" - 1 Corinthians 1:26-28

The film's antagonist, Ronan, is certainly brought to nothing by our problem-laden protagonists; the proud Kree warrior is shamed and laid low by a bunch of nobodies… with a dance-off, no less! The fools make a fool of one who thought himself wise, who considered himself equal or superior to the titan Thanos. It's also interesting that Ronan's title is The Accuser: he accuses Xandar and condemns the planet, then openly mocks the Guardians and discredits the fruit of their labors… only to summarily have his alien hoodie handed to him. As Peter's birth shares some eerie similarities with Jesus, it's equally interesting that Ronan's title is shared by Satan as well, who seeks to accuse and discredit the children of God.

"Now the salvation and the power and the kingdom of our God and the authority of his Christ have come, for the accuser of our brothers has been thrown down, who accuses them day and night…" - Revelation 12:10

It's easy to take pride in our calling and consider ourselves like Captain America or Iron Man, Hawkeye or Thor, admitting some flaws but considering ourselves pretty impressive in our own minds (as if God was lucky to have us in his family, downplaying our faults and upselling our gifts). The Guardians better reflect the seemingly awkward hodgepodge of people from every tribe and tongue that compose Christ's bride, the church, filled with frailties in need of much growth and sanctification. Christians today weren't actually there at the Great Commission; we don't literally have Jesus (or Nick Fury) calling us together and giving us a mission face-to-face. Our congregations can sometimes feel more like the Guardians, a haphazard or even happenstance assemblage. However, just as this MCU story has a screenwriter that intentionally brought this alien family together through "circumstance" we know that our Christian congregating is no accident and providentially planned as well. After all:

"We are Groot." - Groot

As we reflect on Groot's sacrifice near the film's climax, it's a poignant moment with a parallel that points us away from individuality to the plural focus we're called to as the church. *"I am Groot"* becomes *"WE are Groot,"* suggesting a sublime *oneness* for this motley crew, much like the church transcends worldly notions of family and is described as one *body*. We should always remember that most of the time the Bible uses the term "you" it is the *plural* you. Scripture is not speaking to "me" but rather "us". Our call is not individual, but communal. We are not individually called brides of Christ, but together the bride of Christ.

> *"There is one body and one Spirit—just as you were called to the one hope that belongs to your call—one Lord, one faith, one baptism, one God and Father of all, who is over all and through all and in all." -* Ephesians 4:4-6

The Guardians stand, hand-in-hand, enduring the furious onslaught of the power stone together, a fitting image of how God has called us to walk by faith and follow him. They still have a long way to go, and grow, as we see in their compromised to-do list at film's end: *"Something bad? something good?"* Peter determines they'll do a *"bit of both!"* That should humbly remind us that— individually and together—the church is often stumbling along, similarly compromised and ever-reliant on our Lord (not Star-Lord) to take the helm and steer us from the bad to the good, changing our outlook as dramatically as we see Gamora, Drax and Rocket change, willing to die for what they believe in and what they share together.

"Well now I'm standing. Happy? We're all standing now... standing in a circle." - Rocket

AVENGERS, AGE OF ULTRON:
Regression & Judgment Bringer

"And on this rock I will build my church." - Ultron

The maniacal artificial intelligence in the Avengers sequel quotes Jesus Christ as he obtains a significant amount of precious vibranium. While he refers to the metal as his prize, and part of his world-changing solution, the verse takes on another relevance when we consider the context of that scripture in Matthew 16:18. Christ is speaking to Peter: a disciple we see growing in faith, walking briefly on water, and chosen to be a founding member of the church in the first century. Yet not long after Peter has been told of his important role, he regresses to cowardice and denies Christ three times.

Regression, stumbling back into old fears and habits, is something we see happen to one of the founding Avengers in this film (and it won't be the last time). As the film opens, we enjoy an amazing scene of "Earth's Mightiest Heroes" working together as a team, pausing in slow-motion for a perfect shot of synchronized motion. As mentioned, they can hold a pose and give us a super-heroic glimpse of the church as depicted in Romans 12 and 1 Corinthians 12, using their gifts in gracious harmony. But Romans also gives us a warning as preamble to that priestly portrait.

"For by the grace given to me I say to everyone among you not to think of himself more highly than he ought to think, but to think with sober judgment, each according to the measure of faith that God has assigned." - Romans 12:3

Tony Stark—with his fears exacerbated by Wanda Maximoff—falls prey to a cocktail of fear and hubris, admittedly not the leader of the Avengers and yet intentionally choosing to act without their counsel. He arm-twists Bruce Banner into an executive decision to tamper with alien technology for good intentions… and from this rash maneuver Ultron is born (to devastating effect). Once again "Tony knows best," avoids consulting others, and falls into the same pitfalls we see in *Iron Man 2*. His goal is to protect the planet, but scripture warns us that seemingly noble aims don't always justify our behavior.

> *"There is a way that seems right to a man, but its end is the way of death."* - Proverbs 14:12

Ultron, voiced with unique gravelly gusto by James Spader, plays off familiar fears that have appeared in movies for decades and—as of this book's publication—are at renewed heights of concern and conversation. The dangers of artificial intelligence have surfaced many times in film, from *The Terminator*'s Skynet in the 1980s to *The Matrix*'s Agents in 1999. Just as Tony Stark thought he knew better than his compatriots, his artificial offspring decides it knows better than the entire human race, and like many of his aforementioned cinematic brethren Ultron sees the best way to achieve world peace:

> *"There's only one path to peace… your extinction."*

What's fascinating is that, for the Christian, we shouldn't be surprised at Ultron's summary judgment. Just as his cinematic cousin Skynet determined the world was better off without mankind, and Agent Smith tells Neo that—where this planet is concerned—we're more virus than symbiotic creature, these accusers share a point that is undeniably biblical. The world is under a curse because of human sin, and our nature has led to a host of devastating consequences for our world and for one another. When Wanda questions Ultron's methods in the film, as to whether they're absolutely necessary, his reply is ***"Ask Noah."*** Ultron has essentially declared himself God and decided to bring about judgment day… or at least a meteor-sized restart event akin to the Great Flood in Genesis 9.

If Christians are consistent in their theology, we can't argue such a fate isn't deserved. But we CAN counter that Ultron (or anyone besides God) lacks the authority to bring about that fateful day or pronounce that sentence. Biblically there has been a flood, and there will be a judgment day, but only by God's hand and plan. Ultron, then, appears more like Satan than God; another accuser who hasn't been given the role of judge, jury or executioner. Additionally, the crazed robot's plan lacks any allowance for grace or any path of redemption. And so, our protagonists must team up once again to overcome the villain that Tony created.

Later, Stark (and Banner) seem to make the same character mistake again, acting hastily and unilaterally to use a synthetic body and upload Tony's "Jarvis" AI. This sparks another argument with their fellows, yet this time the venture becomes more of a team effort as Thor appears, freshly returned from receiving a "vision" and using his hammer Mjolnir and lightning to give this second creation life. The Avengers are wary of this new presence—uncertain what to make of this "vision" before them—but he adds a critical turning point for the narrative that gels them together and gets them refocused on their common goal. This new Vision demonstrates the ability to wield Thor's hammer and earns the team's trust, and when asked exactly what he is, he replies *"I am."*

Astute viewers will catch the Christ-like implications of this incarnation that is part human creation and partially "divine," imbued with the power of an Infinity Stone that will have more dramatic repercussions later. Ultron's flawed, destructive existence is followed by this second Ultron—or second Adam?—who is ultimately better, decisive yet compassionate, very human yet something beyond. In a film franchise that loves to toy with biblical savior imagery, this one is hard to miss. When the film reaches its climax, he delivers the crushing blow that ends the accuser Ultron.

Ultron: *Stark asked for a savior, and settled for a slave.*

Vision: *I suppose we're both disappointments.*

Ultron's accusation that Vision is a slave is laden with differing layers of metaphor. On one hand, Stark is Ultron's creator, and we witness how much Ultron loathes and lashes out against that connection. From one angle, his hatred of Stark and disgust of Vision remind us of Adam, and our own subsequent sin nature; we rebel against our Creator and want to be our own God; we're prodigal sons who look on the dutiful and serving son with disdain. Indeed, Jesus came to do the will of His Father in heaven, as well as humbling himself and taking the *"form of a servant"* according to the book of Hebrews. Scripture even calls Christ the "second Adam" who achieves what the first failed to do. Likewise, the second "incarnate AI" in this Avengers film is the hero the first failed to be.

From another angle, we could also read the Ultron/Vision quote above and see Stark as a parallel for the people of Israel when the Savior came in scripture. They expected a warrior, savior king who would bring earthbound changes: war and victory against their enemies, and judgment on everyone outside the family of God. The religious leaders and many others found the humble servant form of Christ to be a "disappointment" compared to their expectation. But of course, Christ—even more than the Vision—was neither slave nor disappointment, but rather exactly what God's narrative intended him to be.

Ultron: *How do you hope to stop me?*

Tony: *Like the old man said, together.*

As for the other Avengers, they give us another mirror of the church throughout history; Christians strive for the imagery, artistry, and God-honoring chemistry of acting together as one, even as we fall into pride like Tony, as we bicker and argue. We still struggle to image it better, together. Whether it's Tony and Cap's wood-splitting conversation, the encouragement Barton gets from his wife, Bruce and Natasha's conversations as they work through insecurity and shame, or Clint's mid-battle pep talk to encourage Wanda, we see that team parallel of the church seeking to encourage, equip, and build each other up.

> *"...let us consider how to stir up one another to love and good works, not neglecting to meet together, as is the habit of some, but encouraging one another, and all the more as you see the Day drawing near."* - Hebrews 10:24-25

After the battle is won, we see Tony wisely step back from the front line, along with Clint. This again mirrors the church over the course of generations, whether people step back for spiritual growth (like Tony) or leave a mission field to focus on their family (Clint). That mission, however, goes on, whether it's the work of the gospel or the Avengers, as Cap and Black Widow tend to the discipling and preparing of Wanda, Falcon, Rhodey and Vision for the next season. We also see the growing Avengers complex and a glimpse of the multitude of participants in this massive assembly. But as the credits roll on this film, it's worth a final note about Tony's hubris, in conjunction with Nick Fury's final words to Natasha:

"Trouble, Ms. Romanoff. No matter who wins or loses, trouble still comes around."

Ultron wanted to be the one who brought about judgment day; Tony truly thought he could put a shield around the world and bring full protection and peace. Both suffered from the same "playing-God" overreach, and even Christians must be realistic about their role in God's plan. We seek to win battles, but none of us —or even us collectively as the church—will be the one who wins the war. Christ alone fills those shoes, as he tells the disciples. Poverty, war, and more will be with us until He comes again. Our peace is an inner peace, in that we *participate* in his plan, but He will bring that ultimate victory and reconcile all things.

"…in me you will have peace. In the world you will have trouble. But take heart; I have overcome the world." - John 16:33

ANT-MAN: Shame & Second Chances

"Scott, I've been watching you for a while now…" - Hank Pym

Let's be honest, most of the MCU's main characters aren't what we'd call the "everyman". Tony is a billionaire and tech genius, Steve is remarkably tenacious and forthright from day one, Bruce is a scientist beyond compare, Thor is otherworldly and godlike, etc. The closest we've gotten so far is Peter Quill, but he's ripped from the earth at an early age and lives in a galaxy far, far away. With Scott Lang, we finally get what may be for most moviegoers the most relatable character yet: certainly someone an average American can relate to. The struggle to hold down a job, juggle relationships, be a parent, and keep a good attitude while facing everyday adversity… we know it's not easy. And he also suffers from another relatable element: guilt.

"Therefore a curse devours the earth, and its inhabitants suffer for their guilt…" - Isaiah 24:6

The Ant-Man story provides two forms of guilt for us to ponder: *real* guilt and *felt* guilt. Both perpetuate brokenness, but only one is true. Scott is suffering for his very real crime and what it has cost him in terms of marriage and daughter. Meanwhile, Hank Pym suffers from the guilt he harbors over the loss of his wife, though it clearly wasn't his fault (it was her choice). In the same way, we often suffer for our sins while also taking on guilt and shame for things in this world that weren't of our causing. The problem is, letting these things fester only creates *more* problems for which we *are* culpable; Hank's unresolved shame has caused the relationship with his daughter to suffer. Real and felt shame left without resolution tend to snowball and further compromise the choices we make. Even our most ardent fans—who may think the world of us —may start to see the flaws, like Scott's daughter.

"Is daddy a bad man?" - Cassie

As Scott suffers for his former sins and criminal record, his struggle to find employment and desire to impress Cassie make him return to a life of crime. Fortunately, Hank's plans overlap and intercede in a way that changes Scott's life forever.

"Second chances don't come around all that often. I suggest you take a really close look at it." - Hank Pym

By all means, let's look at the beautiful parallel in Hank's intercession that looks a bit like God revealing "the gospel," good news in the lives of those whom He's redeeming and adopting as His own. Hank's been watching over Lang's life for a while, and becomes something of a father figure to Scott. Now factor in that it's a father figure whom Scott has stolen from, literally trespassed against! Instead of having Scott locked up, Hank gives him grace; in fact, he reveals it has all been part of a plan. The original Ant-Man literally dubs his offer to Scott "a shot at redemption." Scott has a choice before him—an invitation to a special calling—and takes it.

A curious aspect of this redemption is that it doesn't reject Scott's accrued talents, it redeems them. To be clear, someone who's good at sinning (in Scott's case, stealing) doesn't become a Christian and start "stealing for God", but in many cases our talents aren't evil in-and-of themselves; they're often just being used in the wrong direction. On top of that, Scott receives equipping for his new mission in the form of a suit and helmet. Much like Iron Man, we see Scott's new life and redeemed talents are further equipped and shielded, much like the spiritual "armor of God" the Christian receives in Ephesians 6. It's an even better metaphor than Tony Stark's story because Scott does *nothing* to build it; it's entirely a gift. He also gets a veritable "army" to work with in the form of ants, a collective working together, moving and shaping and achieving the goal as one, much like the form and function of the church. It doesn't get much more coordinated than an anthill!

As a comedy/heist film, we get a hilarious montage of Scott's training with the suit, then with the ants, and then for the specific mission he's been assigned. It's a helpful reminder that though we may have talents and be given gifts (as Christians, spiritual gifts) they must be exercised. Just as Scott receives physical and mental training, we need discipleship, spiritual training and persistence.

> *"...train yourself for godliness; for while body training is of some value, godliness is of value in every way, as it holds promise for the present life and also for the life to come. The saying is trustworthy and deserving of true acceptance. For to this end we toil and strive..."* - 1 Timothy 4:7-10

There's a funny-yet-serious subplot about Hope, Hank's daughter, being far more capable and trained than Scott, yet being passed over for the mission (and of course in this film part of that is due to an overprotective father). But as with *Guardians of the Galaxy*, this narrative brings in the familiar trope of "foolish" things being used to "shame the wise" from 1 Corinthians 1. By this we don't mean Hope is being shamed, but rather silly Scott Lang is being used to humble and take down "Yellowjacket" Darren Cross and all his trained cronies. This is even further exemplified by Scott's use of the three wombats: Luis, Kurt and Dave (not to mention a little wounded pride for Sam Wilson/The Falcon mid-movie). Just like the walls of Jericho, the unlikely ones—here represented by the everyman and his goofy buddies— topple what seems like the most impregnable stronghold. And just as David took down Goliath, the formidable villain in the story is taken down by an Ant-sized man.

The story culminates by giving us hope of reconciliation and restoration of relationship, primarily in two portraits of father/daughter relationships and their various states of brokenness. And rather than make it a self-focused catharsis for Scott, at a critical moment Hank tells Scott the purpose of his salvation:

"It's not about saving OUR world; it's about saving THEIRS."

We can often forget that our salvation, and subsequent sacrifice and serving, are not primarily to be focused on self-redemption, or even just out of gratitude for the grace we've been given for that second chance. We were saved for a purpose beyond ourselves, and we live and perhaps even lay down our lives for others, from our children to neighbors and even strangers.

"Let each of you look not only to his own interests, but also to the interests of others. Have this mind among yourselves, which is yours in Christ Jesus…" - Philippians 2:4-5

Scene 2: **Let us leave the elementary doctrine…**

As we wrap up Phase Two of the MCU's great experiment, we see it moves past a cinematic gospel to give us examples of cinematic growth in our transformed lives. To wit:

7. **We must accept our limitations and invite help** (*Iron Man 3*)

8. **We must be mature when others are not** (*Thor: Dark World*)

9. **Trust is difficult to find, and easily lost** (CA: *Winter Soldier*)

10. **We may find ourselves paired with odd allies** (*Guardians*)

11. **Shunning counsel brings bad consequences** (*Age of Ultron*)

12. **We should listen to the elders who will teach us** (*Ant-Man*)

At this point, we prepare to enter a new phase with Paul Rudd levels of enthusiasm, playfulness and fun. Onward and upward now, right? Right?

Uh-oh…

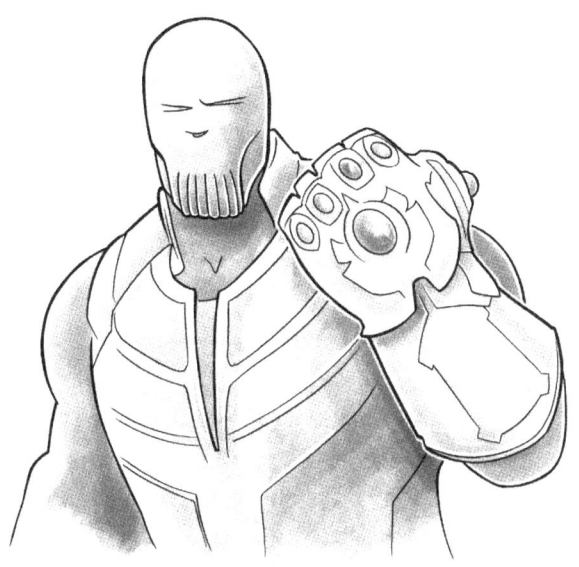

Act 4: **Ashes to Ashes**

or

"Mr. Stark, I don't feel so well…"

Scene 1: **Play Time's over, kids**

Two phases of the MCU took moviegoers through stories that were building things: *world*-building, *character*-building and *team*-building. The final phase of the Infinity Saga puts all this building to the test, beginning and ending with a gritty-but-honest look at the impermanence of these relationships, the worlds they reside in, and even life itself. Two entries in particular require the most scrutiny, reflecting the doomsaying words of Irish poet W.B. Yeats:

> *"Things fall apart; the centre cannot hold;*
> *Mere anarchy is loosed upon the world,*
> *the blood-dimmed tide is loosed, and everywhere*
> *The ceremony of innocence is drowned;*
> *The best lack all conviction, while the worst*
> *Are full of passionate intensity."* - The Second Coming

On that happy note, we'll slide right into the first one…

CAPTAIN AMERICA, CIVIL WAR: Religious Schism

"Compromise where you can. But where you can't... DON'T. Even if everyone is telling you that something wrong is something right. Even if the whole world is telling you to move. It is your duty to plant yourself like a tree, look them in the eye and say, 'No. YOU move.'" - Sharon (quoting Peggy) Carter

Being religious about someone or something isn't a term wholly relegated to organized religion; it can be the zeal of patriotism or ardent franchise fandom. We can be religious about a LOT of things, and find ourselves at critical junctures of disagreement that divide families, friends, nations, churches, and denominations. The fracture of the Avengers in this film resounds just as deeply, and on several of those levels at once. And thus—at the risk of alienating half of the readers of this book—I'm going to plant myself like a tree and say whether the Christian should be "Team Iron Man" or "Team Cap", who divide in this movie over the signing of the Sokovia Accords.

TEAM IRON MAN motivations

Guilt - We already saw Tony Stark confronted with the inherent problems of doing everything himself in *Iron Man 2* and *3*. Though he learned to take other people's counsel, he regressed in *Avengers: Age of Ultron* by acting unilaterally, and the world suffered a terrible cost; he even took himself off the Avengers roster as a result. Tony has been plagued by guilt over what Stark weapons have done—what his former life caused—and now what his creation of Ultron has wrought. So, when a woman confronts him after a technology presentation and shows him her son, who died in Sokovia, Tony projects his admittedly real need for oversight onto all the other Avengers, easily swayed by the Accords through an emotional, anecdotal argument.

Truth be told, the situation is Sokovia and what happens in Lagos at the beginning of this film are worlds apart. Tony created Ultron, which led to the battle of Sokovia. The Avengers *intervention* in Sokovia didn't kill the woman's son, and others; Tony's *creation* of Ultron did. In his guilt, he conflates these aspects. And stopping

Rumlow in Lagos at this film's beginning was not a situation caused by the Avengers at all; in fact, it saved far more lives than were lost. While tragic, collateral damage is a reality of almost any conflict. Tony's insistence on oversight seems a lot like…

Legalism - When the alcoholic realizes they have a substance abuse problem, they often have to give up alcohol entirely. But an error occurs when they start making that a necessary response for everyone, declaring drinking to be inherently evil or sinful. They don't believe anyone can practice moderation. Similarly, Tony realizes he needs oversight and control because he's prone to act rashly, but he insists that same mandate be shackled on every other Avenger. When Natasha notices Tony hasn't spoken much in their argument over the Accords, Cap sees it's evident he's already made up his mind. Tony's not open to real debate. Again, he's regressed; without even really scrutinizing or considering the nuances or consequences of the Accords, he's barreling ahead without listening to counsel. Because of his past sins, everyone needs what he needs.

Pragmatism - Tony argues *"If we don't do this now, it's gonna be done to us later. That's a fact."* Later, he argues with Steve that *"I'm doing what has to be done, to save us from something worse."* Natasha, with a history of flexible morality, agrees with him. *"I'm just reading the terrain,"* she says (not leaning into principles or ethics, but purely thinking in terms of survival). Later in the film Tony presses Steve to sign the Accords, admitting they are flawed but arguing that they can be amended; in other words, sign them now even though you don't agree and we'll "massage" them later. Rhodey argues the pragmatic notion that "the majority" or "seniority" inherently validates the Accords. Ross has a medal of honor, 117 countries have signed… okay, but does majority agreement, or a compelling authority figure, automatically make something ethically right?

Logic - Vision makes the most compelling case… not for the Accords, but for oversight in general. He thoughtfully cites statistics and events since the dawn of super heroics in 2008 and concludes that *"oversight is not an idea that can be dismissed out of hand."* He presents the best argument out of all of Team Iron Man. The only issue here is that, as we look at Team Cap, they aren't rejecting oversight *conceptually* but critiquing the *actual* Accords. In fact, the only one we see actually reading the document is Steve. He's also critiquing it for *content* more than *concept*, the "who" and "how" of implementation, and later admits he's willing to sign if changes are made. Sadly, Tony has exacerbated things to a point where that's no longer possible.

Hypocrisy - Later in the film, when Natasha has the humility to admit *"we played this wrong"* Tony insults her and accuses her of lapsing into her past as a double agent. *"Are you incapable of letting go of your ego for one g—d— second?"* She retorts. It's true; he's regressed yet again. We see this clearly, because for two-thirds of the film he chastises and chases Cap and crew for breaking the Accords, and then… when it suits his own personal judgment in the third act, he does exactly what he's mad at Steve for doing: he breaks the Accords, disobeys Ross, and goes off without approval to intercept Rogers, Bucky and Zemo. Apparently "everyone needed oversight" actually meant "except when Tony disagrees with it." Even while a Team Cap fan might be glad Stark disagrees at this point, it doesn't change the fact that his actions refute his own argument.

Emotionalism - Late in the film, two men face difficult truths and have decisions to make. T'Challa (the Black Panther, given a spectacular introduction to the MCU) learns that Bucky Barnes did not kill his father. He sees that they've all been manipulated by Zemo, a man driven to a horrible and devastating vengeance by his emotions, and watches Captain America, Iron Man and Bucky Barnes locked in combat. The thoughtful, calculating Wakandan hero refuses to give in to the same sin, declaring:

> *"Vengeance has consumed you. It's consuming them. I'm done letting it consume me. Justice will come soon enough."*

Tony Stark also faces some difficult truths. One is that Steve was right: Bucky was not to blame for current events, and the nefarious Zemo was the mastermind behind a more insidious plot. The other is that, while The Winter Soldier killed his parents, it was a brainwashed, manipulated, and exploited Bucky Barnes. Hydra clearly had control of his mind. Anyone in that moment would be severely tested emotionally, and the viewer is able to empathize with Tony's emotional struggle. But everyone also knows he would have acted differently if he'd learned his friend Rhodey had been brainwashed and used in similar fashion. Giving in to rage, he attacks Steve's lifelong friend and seeks to murder him in cold blood; vengeance consumes him, making Cap step between them, and Zemo, although captured, truly wins. It's a Shakespearean superhero tragedy.

The ending of the movie shows T'Challa helping Steve and Bucky. Natasha has defected to their side. Vision is upset and conflicted (and we'll find out later he starts sneaking out to meet Wanda). A crippled Rhodey says *"it hasn't changed my mind... I think."* And we already know Tony's broken the Accords, and later puts Ross on hold and doesn't respond as Cap frees the Avengers incarcerated on The Raft. Upon close examination, it seems clear which side the narrative is seeking to validate. Tony has pretty much abandoned the Accords at this point as well, and we don't see him waiting for U.N. approval before action in subsequent films. Steve's message to his friend says, *"I know you're doing what you believe in,"* but honestly... Tony doesn't. Bottom line?

Tony: *I'm trying to keep you from tearing the Avengers apart!*

Steve: *YOU did that when you signed.*

TEAM CAP motivations

Rights (and responsibility) of the individual - Sam Wilson wonders aloud how long it will be until the government wants to "LoJack" them and start tracking their actions. Where will government control stop once they sign away some of their rights? It's evident that people with powers are being viewed as less than human, much like mutants in the X-Men stories where the government sought to create a special "registration." Secretary of State Ross even refers to Banner and Thor simply as 30 megaton warheads. They're weapons to him, not people. When Steve argues that they should be able to retain self-governance, Tony disagrees, speaking from the personal history that has caused him a lot of guilt. But Steve points out the flaw in his logic.

Tony: *...when I realized what my weapons were capable of in the wrong hands, I shut it down. I stopped manufacturing.*

Steve: **Tony, you CHOSE to do that. If we sign this, we surrender our right to choose.**

Cap explains further that he'd rather take responsibility for his own actions than sign a document that just shifts the blame. He doesn't want the Avengers to be able to hide behind the "I was just following orders" defense. This concept comes into focus later when a bunch of government operatives are given the go-ahead to shoot Bucky Barnes on sight for the bombing of the Wakanda Embassy (which he didn't do). If they'd killed him—only to find out later it was Zemo—who would have been held responsible? They were just "following orders."

Innocent until proven guilty - Some viewers came out of the film seeing Steve as the one who was emotionally compromised by his childhood friend Bucky. It's true he's emotional, and Steve even acknowledges the tension, but Rogers has previously evidenced the kind of noble character that would give the same benefit of the doubt to a complete stranger, so this accusation falls flat. His defense of Bucky is coming from a place of principle as much and more than it is personal. Some also critique that he leaves team and country behind and risks it all for this one lost friend, but who does that remind us of?

"What man of you, having a hundred sheep, if he has lost one of them, does not leave the ninety-nine in the open country, and go after the one that is lost, until he finds it? And when he comes home, he calls together his friends and his neighbors, saying to them, 'Rejoice with me, for I have found my sheep that was lost.'
- Luke 15:4-6

Steve's belief that there was more going on, that Bucky was not responsible, is proven correct. He spends a goodly portion of the film protecting a broken-but-innocent man and ferreting out the true plot against the Avengers. Sadly, Team Tony's interference slows this down, and Zemo's complex chess game subverts everyone's efforts.

Changing agendas vs. unchanging principles - As stated, Captain Rogers is a man of principle. When asked why he doesn't like the Accords' handing over control to the U.N. he says, *"It's run by people with agendas, and agendas change."* No matter what we think of the United Nations, Tony's instant response is *"that's good!"* And here we see the primary difference in worldview, from Cap's assumed, objective foundation of principles and morality to Iron Man's more "progressive" view of moral relativism and subjective ethics. These ideologies are like oil and water (and inevitably clash). The former also more clearly resonates with the "objective truth" view found in scripture, whereas the latter doesn't.

Friendship - It's clear—from his devotion to Bucky to his final voicemail left for Tony at film's end—that Steve doesn't place his trust in systems, institutions or governments, but rather in trusted relationships with individuals, or perhaps a "made family" of like-minded comrades on mission. Compromise to systems outside that family has only caused heartache and suffering—or corrupted the mission—so he and several of the Avengers go their own way. To be fair, friendship as motivation plays a part for Team Iron Man as well, and I'll circle back to that at the end. But first, let's compare…

Civil Wars, Great Schisms, and the Church Today

"Peace if possible. Truth at all Costs." - Martin Luther

Not unlike the Avengers, the church has had its own share of civil wars over the years. Frankly, from major movements to historical denominations to splits and fights in individual churches, there have been more than we might count. Below are but a few, and there are some not-surprising parallels with the motivations we see in our superhero schism above:

• **Team Catholic or Team Eastern Orthodox** (1054 AD)

• **Team Luther or Team Leo** (1517)

• **Team PCA or Team PCUSA** (1973)

• **Team RCA or Team ARC** (2021)

At many junctures in the history of Jesus' church, people have sought to compromise its integrity, and sadly many from within have been compromised in terms of doctrine, morals, or principles. The church knows and expects the world—its institutions and systems—to attempt to bend, amend, change or sway our assemblies to their ways of thinking. The church strives to be on guard against that, to plant our tree and say *"No, YOU move."* Despite our best efforts, however, some on our own team are lured into compromise for many of the same reasons we see Team Iron Man fall prey. Let's look again at:

Guilt - The church historically has made mistakes—individual and institutional—and still does today, so people inside and outside her congregations will play on that guilt to demand *more* than just consistency with that we believe. They go further and say we must compromise what God's Word says to appease them. They'll cite a lack of love, then bend that concept to suggest Christians must "be nice" while also changing definitions of what is or isn't sin. They trick the church into overcorrection, bending on orthodoxy and practice, rather than living out the truth of our scriptures.

"Peace is not to be purchased by the sacrifice of truth."
   - John Calvin

Legalism - Whether it's something massive and doctrinal like adding a theology of works on top of grace, something secondary like outlawing drinking or dancing, or something trivial like fighting over pews versus chairs in the sanctuary, legalism has divided many a church. Recent divides have been over worldly trends in social justice, as congregants demand others sign onto their bandwagon.

Pragmatism - *We're in danger! People just aren't attending like they used to! We're losing families with kids! We need to pay the mortgage!* Sometimes churches water down doctrine or compromise worship music integrity, using gimmicks and distractions and caving to cultural trends over godly worship. I'm not against contemporary, contextualized services but when we dilute teaching and start ear-tickling, we've signed worldly accords. This can be insidious: perhaps a church's denomination just went liberal, and they face a choice: stop teaching the truth or lose their building. It's sad to see professing Christians surface who want continuity of trappings over truth. This may happen by way of *majority* or *authority*, with congregants falling in line because it seems the majority or authority of the church says it's the right way to go.

Emotionalism - Churches will say they follow God's Word and sound doctrine until it gets personal. A pastor's son or daughter will embrace an unbiblical lifestyle… and suddenly the pastor changes their view. They teach their congregation and subvert them, then seek to get their denomination on the same page. This has been the recent trend in progressive American churches, splitting many denominations. Emotionalism and anecdotes win over biblical truth and enduring principles. It's just like when Tony Stark was swayed by the boy's death in Sokovia, and then the home-hitting reality of his parent's death. Tony even knows he's not being reasonable; he tells Steve *"I don't care. He killed my mom."*

(It's worth noting here that Rogers is NOT without fault: he made an error in judgment that poured gasoline on Tony Stark's emotional fire. Some undefined time in the past—between the events of *The Winter Soldier* and *Civil War*—Captain America uncovered the fact that his brainwashed friend was the assassin who pulled the trigger on Stark's parents, and Steve opted to avoid the awkward the conversation of revealing and explaining this to Tony. Despite my critique of Stark's emotionalism, I fully believe that in a calm situation—well before the events of *Civil War*—Steve could have unpacked that history and Bucky's condition in a way Tony may have digested and come to terms with rationally. Instead, Tony has his mom and dad's murder and their killer's identity thrown in his face all at once in a fraught situation. If that heart-to-heart had happened between them earlier, Zemo's plan would have fallen like a house of cards. Steve's path of principle is the right one, but he is ALSO culpable for the falling out.)

While my point is that biblical parallels make it obvious Team Cap is the proper place to plant one's tree, I'll make a brief case for the alternate view: one could argue that Team Cap embodies the idea of the independent church, beholden to NO denomination or outside accountability. Some reading this book might wholeheartedly agree with that model, but I think the Vision's logic (being the best case for Team Iron Man) is worthy of consideration here. I agree with him: *oversight is not an idea that should be dismissed out of hand*.

Here's where it gets personal for me: my first decade in ministry was with a functionally independent church that imploded in 2014 because of—you guessed it—lack of healthy oversight. After that, I joined one of the oldest denominations in the United States for my second decade in ministry, and found great joy in the continuity and shared unity of that accountability structure. We had our own "Accords" in the form of Reformed Creeds, Confessions, and Catechisms that we literally signed our agreement with. Were the checks and balances perfect? No, and in fact The Reformed Church in America had its own "Civil War" and churches have split (in our own version of "Team Cap") because the other side caved to progressive politics and sexual ethics, compromising God's Word for the approval of the world's counsel. Still, the churches who left didn't do so individually; we left together, and created/signed all new documents so we would again be in one "accord."

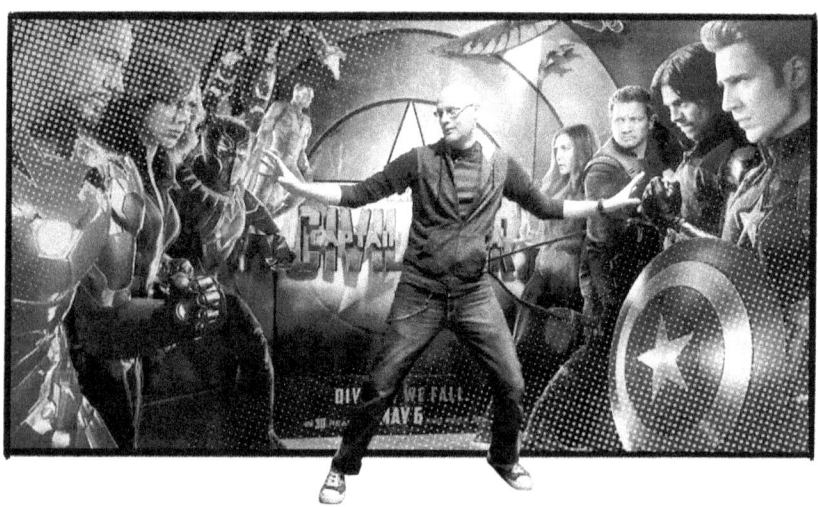

Okay, I think we ALL need a time out...

While it may never be perfect, I agree with Vision: **oversight is right.** But the reason I'm not Team Iron Man is the same reason our church left the Reformed Church in America. The arguments to stay, sign, and be accountable were not sourced in *principle*. We see Team

Cap wasn't wholly *against* oversight; they simply saw that the system as it stood was not healthy. The appeals to sign were emotional and anecdotal so as to obscure principle (much like most of modern politics today). It was hard to leave the denomination because the argument was emotional, much like Team Iron Man's. Their appeal was to unity and… wait for it…

Friendship - That's right, I said it was only fair to mention that this wasn't only a motivation on Cap's side of the schism. Team Iron Man's motivation was also friendship. One of the most heart-wrenching moments is near the end between Steve and Tony:

Steve: *He's my friend.*

Tony: *So was I.*

Both men were trying to keep their friends together. However, Tony was determined to do anything, which included abandoning the basic principles with which he once aligned (Stark long eschewed government oversight through the entire Iron Man trilogy, knowing how problematic that would be, yet acknowledging the need for peer accountability in other ways). In *Civil War*, he fought to keep the Avengers together *practically* at any cost, whereas Cap sought to keep them unified *principally*. We see the latter ideal lived out in the way Jesus defined family, as referenced earlier:

"While he was outside speaking to the people, behold, his mothers and brothers stood outside, asking to speak to him. But he replied to the man who told him, 'Who is my mother, and who are my brothers?' And stretching out his hand toward his disciples, he said, 'Here are my mother and my brothers! For whoever does the will of my Father in heaven is my brother and sister and mother.'" - Matthew 12:46-50

Therein lies the true philosophical divide here. Team Tony's motivation isn't really unity, except in location and token affiliation. Team Cap represents *true unity* in terms of foundation and focus. This is the same in the modern church, as progressives jettison orthodoxy but try to hold their denominations together *practically*, while those leaving to form new teams know they aren't unified *principally*. And if we aren't unified principally, Jesus explains divide is inevitable; from accords to the gospel, there will be civil war…

> *"And a person's enemies will be those of his own household."*
>   - Matthew 10:36

Somehow, amid all this heady and heavy material, the directors *also* brought in the hilarious antics of Ant-Man, and even arachnid comic relief with the MCU debut of Spider-man. There's a lot going on in this film, and I hope it isn't distracting from what is probably the meatiest of all the films leading up to *Infinity War*. It's worth getting past which characters you *like* better (siding with them for personal affinity reasons) and truly pondering the headier themes and principles as they apply to how and where we stand in our own lives. Otherwise, things might get… strange.

DOCTOR STRANGE: Time and Tony 2.0

> *"Your intellect has taken you far in life, but it will take you no farther. Surrender, Stephen."* - The Ancient One

Arrogance. Accident. Injury. New identity. I've said many times that all stories share similarities, and from Benedict Cumberbatch's facial hair to his character's prideful attitude—even a powerful glowy thing on his chest—this film wears those similarities on its sleeve. Swap science with the mystic arts and you have Iron Man's origin reimagined: just add magic, rinse, repeat.

Sure, there are little differences, from the actor's swagger to little personality quirks. One might say Tony worshipped his wealth whereas Stephen Strange worships his work, but both men equally evidence great pride in their intellectual prowess and power, their ability to be kings of their respective world, narcissistic and emotionally closed to others. Tony's incident was more ironic and inspired, gravely wounded by his own technology, whereas Strange seems to serve as a public service announcement about using your smartphone or screen while driving. Tony takes a blow to his heart, whereas Stephen's damage is his hands; while the second isn't fatal, it's fatal to his career, and thus all Strange holds dear.

Both men are subsequently helped and equipped by wise and older mentors—the Ancient One taking the role of Yinsen—and those characters lay down their lives. Tony and Stephen then take active roles in their newfound reclamation, learning to care about others and fighting similar foes; one a former colleague with similar armor, the other a former student with similar powers. Ultimately, they learn a lesson straight out of Rick Warren's book *The Purpose Driven Life*, which the Ancient One quotes verbatim after explaining that arrogance has kept Stephen from learning life's simplest and most important lesson, and the first of three lessons in this film:

1. "It's not about you."

We should be able to relate to this kind of self-centeredness, and this also indicts why many people who don't love God still seemingly help others. The former Tony Stark sold weapons and lived like a hedonist; he didn't have a comeback as compelling as Stephen might to accusations of selfishness. As a doctor, he argues that he helps others—heals others—but the Ancient One calls this bluff as well.

Steven: *I became a doctor to SAVE lives, not take them.*

Ancient One: *You became a doctor to save one life above all others: your own.*

Again, we don't have to be world-class surgeons to relate here. People argue that non-Christians still "do good things." But we must also question inner motives that, many times, only God knows for sure. The Ancient One might be speaking to any one of us:

"You may have helped thousands of people, but it was all for your own glory…"

The humbling of Stephen Strange comes from a pair of voices, the other being his ex-girlfriend Christine. When Stephen argues that she used to love coming to his speaking engagements, she replies *"no, YOU had fun. They weren't about us; they were about you."* He answers defensively *"not ONLY about me,"* but she levels the same verdict as the Ancient One:

"Stephen, everything is about you."

Intent matters. Heart matters as much as actions. One can save the world—or a single person—and then flash a smile and say, *"I AM Iron Man"* and bask in the glory, receive self-worship. We see this is true of Strange as he turns down patients because it's boring or won't bring him challenge or glory (blink and you'll miss that he turned down Rhodey's crippling injury from *Avengers: Civil War*).

Of course, an MCU film won't finish the thought here that leads to God and the gospel… that the purpose of our lives is far greater than our own personal fulfillment, peace of mind, or even happiness. It's far greater than our family, our career, or even our wildest dreams and ambitions. If we want to know why we were placed on this planet, we must begin with God. Still, planting the seed that *"it's not about you"* is a great and valuable lesson.

2. A Changed Worldview

"I do not believe in fairy tales… or the power of belief. There is no such thing as spirit! We are made of matter, and nothing more. We're just another tiny, momentary speck within an indifferent universe." - Stephen Strange

There are things to reject in this movie, just as when we watch Harry Potter or even Lord of the Rings: sorcery is not something to be toyed with in our real world, and things like chakras or energy and other pagan practices aren't to be emulated. However, the movie breaks the stubborn Stephen of his materialist worldview, and that's another step on the path to knowing God and embracing true faith. Unless there is from a mind and order above and over the universe, purpose is whatever we want it to be. Real, consistent atheists agree:

"Unless you assume a God, the question of 'life's purpose' is meaningless" - Bertrand Russell

This ties into the core exploration in my first book about the reality that there are only two stories: *life under the sun* or *life transcendent*. Stephen is certain that life under the sun is all there is, and he lives his life accordingly. Selfishly. Without greater purpose. He assumes transcendent stories (fiction and religion) exist to distract us from Bertrand Russell's sad reality that we're momentary. That is, until the Ancient One literally knocks Stephen's spirit from his body and makes him face the reality of things that transcend this meaningless life under the sun. Strange also learns from another source, who offers humbling advice congruent with scripture:

"I once stood in your place. And I, too, was… disrespectful. So might I offer you some advice? Forget everything you think you know." - Mordo

"Woe to those who are wise in their own eyes and clever in their own sight." - Isaiah 5:21

"For the wisdom of this world is folly with God."
- 1 Corinthians 3:19

Strange has all his pride and prowess stripped away piece by piece. He realizes he's been looking at the world through a keyhole and is unable to widen it by his own means. He was knocked down and determined to find his "own way" back. However, he must submit to the wisdom, teaching, and radically different worldview of others.

A narrative element *Ant-Man* and *Doctor Strange* share is a facet many former films in the MCU didn't focus on. Tony Stark didn't share much screen time with Yinsen. Bruce Banner mostly suffered alone. Steve Rogers was battle-tested on the battlefront. Odin ran Thor through a discipline-by-trial rather than hands-on training. Until Ant-Man, most of our characters were **trained by trial,** which certainly DOES parallel with aspects of the Christian life. But it's nice to see an equal value emerge in the MCU where characters are **trained by tutors**, receiving valuable teaching from their forebears. We see this in scripture with Paul and Timothy, Apollos with Priscilla and Aquila, and more. Trials will come and test what we've learned, but there is a richness and humility in sitting under the teaching of others. This humbling and equipping ultimately leads Stephen to a…

3. Unique, Sacrificial Death

Stephen Strange: *This is how things are now!*
You and me. Trapped in this moment. Endlessly.

Dormammu: *Then you will spend eternity dying!*

Strange: *Yes, but everyone else on earth will live.*

Dormammu: *But you will suffer!*

Strange: *I can lose. Again. And again. And again. Forever. That makes YOU my prisoner.*

Someone pointed out to me that this is the first Marvel movie where the bad guy isn't beaten with fisticuffs, missiles, shields, etc. It's unique… a true defeat of the mind instead of shooting and hitting things, which shows that Strange's greatest gift—formerly used for his own glory—has been redeemed and pointed to good purpose. Also somewhat unique is that victory is achieved by dying —over and over and over again—for the world. Or IS it that unique?

Evil being driven out by a sacrificial death surfaces in a lot of stories… and religions. The "repeating element" makes sense here, as Strange's mystical connections are more Eastern than Western. According to Hinduism, the god Vishnu incarnates on earth from time to time to eradicate evil and restore balance, often achieved through his death. In the Bhagavad Gita, it says Vishnu does this *"to reestablish the principles of righteousness"* and that *"I manifest myself, millennium after millennium after millennium."* Some Hindu traditions even point to Jesus as connected to this process in various ways.

Strange's ordeal shares a parallel as he suffers again and again and again for the world, until at some point Dormammu is done away with forever. Some clarity is needed here, because some Christ followers even fall into an errant belief like this, depending on one's understanding of the Eucharist or communion. According to some Catholic tradition, the communion mass *"perpetuates his one sacrifice that stands outside of time."* In a "strange" way then, each communion is the sacrifice occurring repeatedly in our time while outside time in terms of God. They even purport that it repeatedly becomes the actual body and blood of Christ. While dovetailing with our movie in a fascinating fashion, it contradicts scripture:

"We know that Christ, being raised from the dead, will never die again; death no longer has dominion over him. For the death he died once for sin, once for all, but the life he lives he lives to God." - Romans 6:9-10

Even more powerful than false religion or a Marvel movie, Jesus' one death gave us a singularity that was powerful enough to overcome death and defeat the real Dormammu, Satan, without any bargains (and let's not forget also atoning for sin). We can't let a desire for parallels and connections make us distort scripture. At the same time, those pagan "incarnations" and repeated superheroes sacrificing life and overcoming death reveal that we're longing for something higher, longing for salvation and victory from God above and relationship with him. Unless we come face to face with…

GUARDIANS OF THE GALAXY VOLUME 2: God's Ego

"See I rob banks, I pull pranks, sometimes I eat franks…
Stick 'em up punk, it's the fun-lovin' criminal…"
- Fun Lovin' Criminals

When last we left our alleged Guardians, they were committed to guarding others, with a caveat for being bad; a **"bit o' both"**, as Peter exclaims. In the opening scene, that commitment is fully realized; they're hired to *guard* batteries, but Rocket *steals* some. Most of us laugh, but then ought to ask: should we? No matter how pompous their golden employers were, it doesn't justify theft. Right out of the gate, a Christian should question our attraction to the fun-loving criminal; we like to laugh at lawbreakers and justify it by saying it's just fantasy (never mind Jesus says fantasizing in our hearts makes us just as guilty as if we'd done it ourselves). But I won't belabor this point.

This dysfunctional team's shared faults aren't Rocket's kleptomania, however, but rather shared arrogance. As they evade their newly minted enemies, an ensuing argument between Peter and Rocket causes a spectacular and nearly fatal crash. Gamora points out that they almost died because of Peter's arrogance in particular. Pride goeth before a fall, and they fall spectacularly (though Drax takes the brunt of it). Even Drax boldly claims *"I too am extraordinarily humble."* It's fitting, then, that when the mysterious stranger who aided their escape introduces himself as Peter's father, his name is literally Ego. Sometimes a metaphor in a movie is so obvious, so in-our-face, that we miss it, but the not-so-subtle message in Guardians Vol. 2 is…

1. Confronting our (own) EGOS

See, it's not just Peter who confronts his ego, but the whole cast… and not the character played by Kurt Russell, but rather their own sense of self-importance and overinflated self-esteem. They're broken, at their lowest, at odds with each other because of their egos…and when the namesake villain shows up, where does the film immediately take us? The scene switches to a brothel where we find the disgraced Yondu, Peter's surrogate father, and a glimpse of where ego eventually takes us all. It's a great moment of contrast and foreshadowing, building to the climactic moment in the film when the washed-up Ravager confronts the equally ego-ruled Rocket and declares *"I know who you are, boy… because you're ME!"*

"What is your goal here? To get everybody to hate you? Because it's workin'…" - Peter Quill

Characters like Rocket (and most of the Guardians) may be funny on the surface, but not worthy of emulation. We wouldn't actually want Rocket for a friend. He's a funny "movie friend" but we'd hate him in real life. The movie makes it clear: without change, he will become Yondu: full of regret, surrounded by idiots and no real friends, filled with despair. Now, one might argue that Yondu has an amazing, redemptive and reconciliatory moment at the end. Okay… but is that really what we should hope for in this life? Screwing everything up but going out in a blaze of glory? A horrible life with some eleventh-hour redemption? And what are the odds we get that *"I'm Mary Poppins, y'all"* moment? More likely we'll find ourselves humiliated and cast out, like Yondu was exiled by Stakkar from the true Ravagers.

"…at the end of your life you groan, when your flesh and body are consumed, and you say "how I hated discipline, and my heart despised reproof. I did not listen to the voice of my teachers or incline my ear to my instructors. I am at the brink of utter ruin in the assembled congregation. - Proverbs 5:11-14

The Guardians movies need careful viewing, lest we miss the point. There's a dangerous fantasy here we must reject, some kind of self-serving life that has some kind of final inning win that gains us all our respect back and a ticker-tape parade. We should be seeking honor in life, not just in our death. We may see flaws and quirks and all sorts of things in these characters we relate to, so long as we don't take away the message *relate and emulate*. A movie like this is not just about relating and laughing and going about our badly behaving business. It's about relating and *changing*.

But change to what? And whom do we learn from? That makes us turn to another major theme of the film:

2. Looking to FATHER for identity

Sadly, many boys today—like Peter Quill—grow up today with absent fathers. Yondu didn't have a father because his dad sold him into slavery. Peter didn't have a father and looks to male celebrities from his past (Kevin Bacon, David Hasselhoff) as role models. Even Gamora and Nebula had a terrible "father" in Thanos that gave them all the wrong lessons. Now, Peter finds his father and after some initial hope and wonder, it becomes another nightmare.

Boys and young men naturally look to fathers for purpose and direction, to help comprehend their origins and provide a launching point for where they're going. Even Ego himself says *"I desired meaning… purpose."* And sometimes we look to a father—or father figure—trying to sort that out. The alternative (which the evil Ego has done) is self-determination, fabricating one's own foundation, and Ego wants Peter to join him in what turns out to be a very selfish path.

> *"He may have been your father, boy, but he wasn't your daddy. I'm sorry that I didn't do none of it right. I'm… lucky you're my boy."* - Yondu

For better *and* worse, Peter comes to terms with the reality that much of his shaping came from Yondu (and realizes this only as the former Ravager gives his life for his surrogate son, in one of the most emotional scenes in the MCU saga). The "tough exterior" and bravado that made Yondu never admit his true motivation for keeping Peter is the similar face that "Star-Lord" wears. While not a good man, Yondu kept Peter because he realized Ego had killed all the other "offspring" he delivered and couldn't conscience handing him over. Quill's "good but bad" duality comes from the disgraced Ravager: Yondu, also, was a *"bit o' both."*

Whether intentional or not, we often emulate aspects of our fathers. At a fundamental level, this isn't a bad thing but something intrinsic to our nature, physically and spiritually. Christians understand that we often emulate our *earthly* fathers in temporal ways, in keeping with our original design in terms of imitating our *heavenly* Father in a godly way. We were not simply made in the "image and likeness" of our Father God in heaven; we were created in such a way so as to **magnify His image,** which may be the strongest—and most controversial—theme in this movie.

3. Magnification of IMAGE

The first Avengers film questioned man's existence and our "natural state" as kneeling before a god. One can redeem that idea by pointing out Loki is a false (and puny) god, but it's reasonable to assume the idea came up in part to question aspects of organized religion, including Christianity. It's even harder to dismiss what James Gunn is aiming at here in terms of the celestial Ego and his godlike plan. Again, there's no subtlety: it's about as on-the-nose as you can get in terms of distorting a biblical idea.

Ego has planted aspects of himself in many planets, including earth, and what is his ultimate plan? A radical magnification and "expansion" of image. He calls his son—his child—to join him in that expansion.

> *"Over thousands of years I implanted thousands of extensions of myself on thousands of worlds... to grow and spread, covering all that exists..."* - Ego

> *"So God created man in his own image, in the image of God he created him; male and female he created them... and God said to them, 'Be fruitful and multiply and fill the earth and subdue it..."* - Genesis 1:27-28

It's difficult to imagine this isn't a sly, rebellious attack on a biblical worldview. Opponents of Christianity typically hate the idea of an externally determined purpose, a godly template that we're meant to image and magnify. That like Peter, we are "God's children" and intended to help him subdue worlds and imitate his godly image. In other words, they'd say God has an "ego" in a bad way. Now, there's a wealth of theological resources dealing with why a perfect being (who created all things) can and should glorify himself; I won't go down that rabbit trail here. Suffice to say, this doesn't make me reject the movie's narrative but rather redeem it, no matter the authorial intention. The reality is, Ego isn't God. He's a finite creature who is not omniscient, omnipresent, or omnipotent (proven by the fact that the Guardians defeat him). He couldn't even stop a goofy blue Ravager from hiding Peter from him for years!

Like Loki, Ego is just another false god, and many false "gods" have sought to have their image magnified throughout history. The entire concept of faces on coins came from ancient cultures and their rulers; Roman emperors put their faces on coins so that their image would be with every person: in their hands, the face of their wealth, their currency, their power, it would all be an "expansion of their image". In the 21st century, with everything from YouTube to TikTok, we all can aspire to this godlike magnification of image for our own glory. "Ego" simply represents the godlike egos of those who are gods in their own minds. He represents the temptation that is within all of us: to magnify our *own* flawed image and ego instead of the one who *actually* created us to image Him.

Perhaps our error is in imaging our earthly fathers, when we should be magnifying our heavenly Father. In the end, Guardians Volume 2 at least rejects the former.

SPIDER-MAN, HOMECOMING: Getting Schooled

Peter Parker: *I just wanted to be like you.*
Tony Stark: *And I wanted you to be better.*

Welcome to the MCU, Peter Parker… hope you survive the experience! After his literal crash-course introduction in *Captain*

America, Civil War, the amazing Spider-man swings into his first solo film… or more accurately his "third first" solo film, following former forays in wall-crawling with actors Tobey Maguire and Andrew Garfield. Tom Holland brings a fresh take to the web slinger in his formative high school years, and director Jon Watts splits the difference between Marvel action and high school comedy as a young superhero tries to prove his worth.

This Peter Parker has grown up in a world of mighty Avengers that he and his classmates idolize. After Iron Man whet Parker's appetite for super heroics in *Civil War*, Peter's hungry for more. Tony Stark, on the other hand, regrets rushing him to the big leagues and encourages the teenager to slow his roll, much like Midtown High School's public service announcement encourages him:

> ***"Hi, I'm Captain America. Here to talk to you about one of the most valuable traits a student or soldier can have. Patience."***

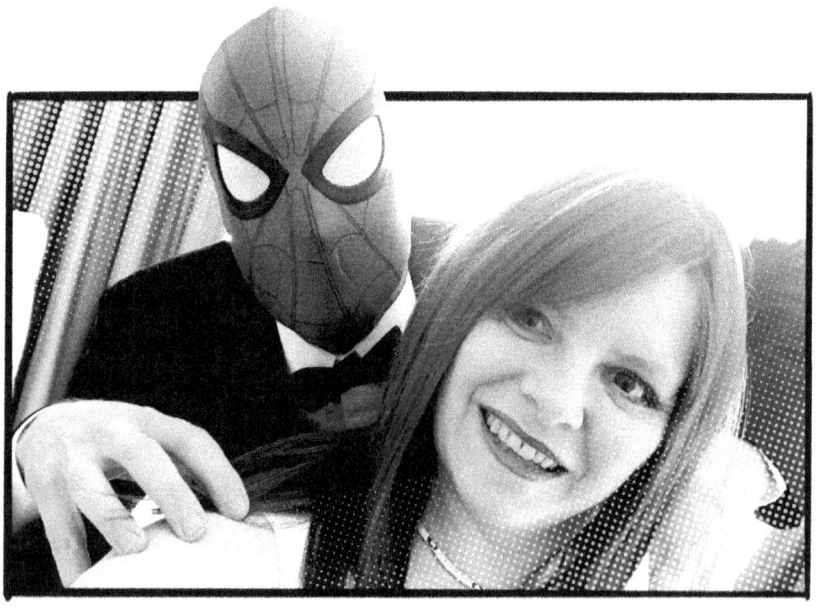

But I've been crawling the walls waiting for this!

Meanwhile, we're introduced to a hardworking blue collar family man named Adrian Toomes, who also feels held back by Tony when his salvage company loses a lucrative contract to a Stark subsidiary. Both feel unfairly held back, and thus we see Peter repeatedly disobey his mentor while Toomes and his coworkers turn to crime. If one verse existed to sum up both men, it's Hebrews 13:5…

"Keep your life free from love of money, and be content with what you have…"

Peter isn't content, and like most teenagers—and many adults—he tests (in this case breaks) just about every boundary given. Like his mentor Tony's perennial sin, he *"thinks of himself more highly than he ought,"* and almost dies for it in his first tangle with the Vulture. Next, he nearly gets others killed during the ferry fight. His desire to help isn't sinful, but his impetuousness most certainly is.

"So I just, um, feel like I could be doing more. You know? Just curious when the next mission is gonna be. So yeah, call me back. It's Peter. Parker."

It's common to desire a larger or more important role than we've been given, especially when we're young. We want to take on the world, but we aren't ready… or maybe that's not our calling. It's easy for Christians to all want to be the apostle Paul, forgetting that for every Paul there's a Timothy. Many Christians, especially young men, want to go out and metaphorically slay Goliath. Sometimes we need a reality check.

"You're not David!!!" - Pastor Matt Chandler

Now to be fair to Peter in this story, he's young, naive, and makes poor decisions… *but* he is also underestimated. Instead of a narrative one-trick pony, the film holds two realities in tension. When Peter complains to Ned that Mr. Stark treats him like a kid, Ned replies *"but you ARE a kid!"* At the same time, Happy Hogan certainly looks down on him, and Tony—God bless him—is not the greatest teacher. He's hands-off and offers Peter soundbites, and when Peter makes his grave mistake Tony says he's taking his opportunity away *"forever."* Stark admits he was wrong at the end, and in this we see a counterbalance to Peter's deserved admonition. In Paul's first letter to Timothy, the apostle encourages him not to let anyone look down on him simply because he is young. Similarly, while Peter thought too highly of himself, others thought too little.

As Spider-man spars with Adrian Toomes, we're also treated to one of the MCU's more nuanced and interesting villains. The character (and Michael Keaton's performance) evokes a *Breaking Bad* vibe, the tragic and beset middle-aged man who feels compelled to crime for the way society—and life in general—have dealt him a bad hand. It's also great that—like the character of Walter White—we can *empathize*, but the narrative never makes us feel he is *justified*. He's not a victim, and so we see compassion in Peter's handling of the situation without condoning Toomes' behavior or letting him play the victim card. Peter learns a lot from his experiences.

"For everything there is a season, and a time for every matter under heaven." - Ecclesiastes 3:1

In the end, Peter's growing maturity shines in the way he declines Stark's offer to join the Avengers. He realizes that Tony was right the first time, and that he does need time and lower stakes situations in which to be tempered. It's much like the reason church leaders (elders, deacons) are not supposed to be "new converts." He needs more training and superhero field work before going off on the big missions… if that even IS his destiny or calling.

"Can't you just be your friendly neighborhood Spider-man?"
-Tony Stark

Paralleled with the Christian experience, some of us want to be Paul, not Timothy: the biblical equivalent of Batman, not Robin. Most of us may not even be Timothy. Most people aren't called to be far-flung missionaries; for every Paul, there were whole congregations living life in their neighborhoods, doing local mission and financially supporting the "Pauls" on their journeys.

"But we encourage you, brothers and sisters… seek to lead a quiet life, mind your own business… work with your hands as we commanded you, so that you may behave properly in the presence of outsiders…" - 1 Thessalonians 4:10-12

May we have the humility, maturity and discernment to know when we're called to be our friendly neighborhood missionaries.

THOR, RAGNAROK: Laughing at the Apocalypse

"I know what you're thinking... how did this happen?" - Thor

Tonally, *Ragnarok* bothered me from the start, a jarring left turn for the Thor franchise into comedy more light and cheeky than *Guardians of the Galaxy*. While *Guardians* director James Gunn managed to juxtapose silliness with serious moments, the destruction of Asgard—the titular Ragnarok—occurs only to be instantly undercut by a joke voiced by the director himself. If some enjoyed it and didn't feel director Taika Waititi overplayed his hand, most feel he did with his follow-up, *Thor: Love and Thunder.* This felt more like watching an extended SNL comedy sketch of the MCU, but I digress. Despite being filled with improv and many mindless moments, the movie offers a few bon mots worth considering.

Thor has, without explanation, been regressed to the arrogant, prideful self we meet at the beginning of the first *Thor* film, joking sarcastically and full of himself as he fights the fire demon Surtur and believing he's successfully stopped Asgard's apocalypse. And so, we have a second helping of humbling for Thor, similar but sillier than his earthbound testing two movies back. He uncovers Loki's ruse, but then loses his father Odin. The discovery of an older, more powerful sister brings him low, hammer destroyed and exiled once again, this time to Sakaar. He's humiliated by the Grandmaster, but reunited with the Hulk, and together with Loki, Valkyrie, Korg and others manage to break out and return to Asgard. However, defeating Hela can only be achieved by one course of action, and Thor is forced to face a hard truth:

"This was never about stopping Ragnarok... it was about causing Ragnarok."

Ragnarok was a prophesy and meant to happen. Strangely enough, Thor and his crew play a part in it. What Thor previously feared, and tried to stop, was ultimately something that worked out for good as they defeat Hela and save the remaining Asgardians. There's a parallel here with the biblical apocalypse; it's strange to me, but sometimes I meet Christians who seem overly concerned about judgment day, even talking about trying to stop it. They conflate opposing the biblical Antichrist with thwarting what the

Bible says will happen, and so on. Certainly, Christians in the end times should oppose anti-Christ agendas, but the apocalypse is something prophesied; something our Lord has said *will happen*. No man—or Marvel hero—will thwart it. (This reality also happens to be one reason I'm the minority fan that likes *Terminator 3*…)

> *"Judgment Day is inevitable."* - the Terminator

> *"…the day of the Lord will come… the heavens will pass away with a roar, and the heavenly bodies will be burned up and dissolved, and the earth and the works that are done on it will be exposed."* - 2 Peter 3:10

> *"I should have realized it was never our destiny to stop Judgment Day, it was merely to survive it, together."*
> - John Connor, *Terminator 3: Rise of the Machines*

Indeed, some will survive Judgment Day, and here we see a little glimmer of gospel in the ending of *Thor: Ragnarok*. After all, Allfather Odin's firstborn son is the savior at story's end, redeeming a remnant of Asgardians and leading them out of the fires of judgment day toward the promise of a new home. Biblically, we hold to the promise that the one true God and Father will gather to himself a remnant, saved by the work of God the Son (Jesus Christ). Those people—Christians—are called his church, a term that is frequently misunderstood as the place where Christians meet, and this film taps into another idea that illustrates what it really means.

> *"Asgard is not a place. Never was. This could be Asgard. Asgard is where our people stand. Even now, right now… those people need your help."* - *Odin*

As with Asgard, the church is also not a place: it's a people. As I mentioned back in the first Avengers film, the word church means "assembly." It's not the building (or the planet) it's the people who populate it, who comprise it. And just like Asgard needed Thor, the church needs Jesus; in fact, even more so.

A final note on this film is the reality that shared experience—and tragedy—can sometimes mend a rift, or turn a heart, when words and actions seem to fail. Thor sought for multiple movies to reach his brother's heart to no avail… but between the death of their father and the destruction of their home, Loki begins to evidence signs of change and renewed brotherhood. Perhaps a bit of reverse psychology helps when Thor expresses that their paths have diverged: that he knows and accepts that it's too late. For those with estranged friends and family, it's an encouraging moment, and we know through prayer and the Holy Spirit, we may even "get help."

BLACK PANTHER: Longing for King and Kingdom

"I have seen gods fly. I have seen men build weapons that I couldn't even imagine. I have seen aliens drop from the sky. But I have never seen anything like this…" - Everett K. Ross

In contrast with a light-hearted and shallow ending for the exotic land of Asgard, our introduction to the world of Wakanda is replete with depth and wonder, visually and thematically. After teasing us with T'Challa and his foreign nation in *Civil War*, we finally cross the border into a story that is simultaneously bleak and hopeful. The opening flashback to 1992 gives us our first, tragic theme.

"And those of you who are left shall rot away in your enemies' lands because of their iniquity, and also because of the iniquities of their fathers they shall rot away like them." - Leviticus 26:39

Sins of the Father is a theme that stains the narrative of an otherwise wondrous-seeming Wakanda. The killing of King T'Chaka's brother N'Jobu leads to a cover up, as well as his son being left behind. N'Jobu's traitorous actions, and subsequent death, are scrubbed from the record, but editing the truth never goes well.

"We left him. We had to maintain the lie." - Zuri

"For nothing is hidden that will not be made manifest, nor is anything secret that will not be known and come to light.
    - Luke 8:17

The past comes back to haunt Wakanda when Erik Killmonger arrives, and T'Challa must come to terms with the reality of his imperfect father. After all, there is no perfect *earthly* king. In the Bible, King David sought to cover up his own sins and it went just as poorly. Later, his son Absalom would try to take over the kingdom and tear it in half. As the bard would say, *"heavy is the head that wears the crown."* T'Challa, and his father, would agree.

"You're a good man with a good heart. And it's hard for a good man to be king." - King T'Chaka

When T'Challa is defeated—seemingly killed—and Killmonger takes the throne, loyalties are tested; in fact, the very focus of that loyalty is debated. Warrior woman Okoye claims that she would kill for Wakanda *"without question."* And so emerges our second theme: **where is our loyalty to be directed?** The King? The country? Or what it stands for? Okoye and Nakia argue over where their allegiance and fidelity should lie:

Okoye: *My duty is to the throne.*

Nakia: *It is my duty to fight for who I... for the things I love.*

It begs questions that have tripped up Christians and churches over the centuries; should our loyalty be to the church? The pope? God's Word? Our duty is not necessarily to whomever sits on an earthly throne, a seat at the Vatican, or the pulpit of our church. Our duty is to the one true King of kings, not an earthly kingdom or self-proclaimed leader. Jesus himself was killed, in the name of the kingdom, by Pharisees—earthly leaders—and the people who rejected him. Do we stand by a leader, or stand by what we and that leader are *supposed* to stand for?

"Is this your king? Is this your king? Nah, I'm your king!"
- Erik Killmonger

The third theme we see in the actions of a crowned Killmonger is another lie, that of **justice-veiled vengeance.** Killmonger talks about justice... for him, for "his people"... but it's really revenge. Yes, he's faced oppression and hardship, but there's no true justice when the oppressed become the oppressors. Erik admits as much:

"I lived my entire life waiting for this moment. I trained, I lied, I killed just to get here. I killed in America, Afghanistan, Iraq... I took life from my own brothers and sisters right here on this continent! And all this death just so I could kill you."

It's a daring message the film's director Ryan Coogler brings to the table (and some people probably miss it). Erik isn't the "real hero" just because his grievance has validity. Sadly, that errant state of mind is reflected in the world we live in today. One can claim the cause of justice yet harbor ill motives. One can play the victim card as justification for heinous actions, as Erik does:

> *"The world took everything away from me! Everything I ever loved! But I'ma make sure we're even. I'ma track down anyone who would even think of being loyal to you! And I'ma put their a— in the dirt, right next to Zuri!"*

If we can set down our grievances or ways in which we (or our forefathers) have been sinned against in the past, and think clearly, Killmonger's words are not the language of liberation. It's the call for counter oppression, for reversing the prejudice, and worse: it's hatred that calls for slavery or genocide.

> *"So we're gonna use their own strategy against 'em... arm oppressed people all over the world... so they can finally rise up and kill those in power. And their children! And anyone else who takes their side... the world's gonna start over, and this time we're on top!"*

What makes things even more lamentable is that Erik's plan perverts his own father's vision. N'Jobu wanted all nations to be overthrown, yes... but didn't say anything about oppressed becoming oppressors or killing children. His dream was to have *one* nation under *one* king, which we'll talk about in a minute. But here's something curious that Erik says (whether he's truly thinking it through or not). He argues with T'Challa, who asserts that *"our weapons will not be used to wage war on the world. It is not our way to be judge, jury and executioner for people who aren't our own."* But Erik counters:

> *"Not your own? Didn't life start here on this continent? So ain't ALL people 'YOUR' people?"*

Never mind the awkward fact that in this statement Killmonger basically just said "all lives matter". Whether you're a Christian who believes all mankind sprang from the garden of Eden, or an atheist who believes humans evolved from a similar geographic position called the fertile crescent, Erik makes a valid point; all lives have one source and should preferably be one people under one rule. Christians totally agree, though that king isn't T'Challa or Killmonger, it's Jesus. And one day every knee will bow, and every tongue confess, that he is Lord: one King, one kingdom.

In the meantime, T'Challa knows he isn't *that* king, and Wakanda can't be *that* kingdom. But once he's ousted the mad king Erik and taken back the throne, he does realize that changes need to be made. He rebukes the errant ways of his father and other kings:

> *"You were wrong—all of you were wrong—to turn your backs on the rest of the world! We let the fear of discovery stop us from doing what is right. No more!"*

Like the kingdom of Wakanda, Christians aren't called to remove themselves from the world. We're not called to hide in monasteries like the kingdom of Wakanda hides, we're not meant to isolate like M'Baku and his clan. Jesus lays out the role for those who belong to his kingdom: we are to be *in* the world but not *of* it. Christ calls his kingdom people to be beacons, lights on a hill pointing the way to a better life and a better kingdom. T'Challa's declaration is not dissimilar:

> *"Wakanda will no longer watch from the shadows…We will work to be an example of how we, as brothers and sisters on this earth, should treat each other. Now, more than ever, the illusions of division threaten our very existence. We all know the truth: more connects us than separates us. But in times of crisis the wise build bridges, while the foolish build barriers. We must find a way to look after one another, as if we were one single tribe."*

> *"Therefore, we are ambassadors for Christ, God making his appeal through us. We implore you on behalf of Christ, be reconciled to God."* - 2 Corinthians 5:20

Paul's parallel of ambassadorial status likens the church to embassies in the countries we live in, pointing people to a better way, a better life, and a perfect kingdom: one rule under one king, the *perfect* king. By the same token, we see T'Challa setting up

Wakandan outposts in other nations at the end of the film. And this brings us to a final theme, a final longing.

> *"We rally around heroes like the Black Panther because we hope that they can lead us to Wakanda."* - Greg Morse, desiringgod.org

In Act 1, I explained the effect *Avatar's* Edenic Pandora had on viewers, giving them what felt like a return to paradise, or a vision of heaven. Wakanda's reveal and ideal gave many a similar taste. As Okoye pilots the Royal Talon Fighter carrying Okoye, Nakia and T'Challa into the rolling hills of their country, she expresses something the viewer feels on an emotional level: *"We're home."*

The triumphal entry into Wakanda treats us to a vision of something both ancient and futuristic; past, present and future all rolled together with a harmonious blend of nature and technology, creation and creativity, and as the story goes on we see that same relationship between science and the supernatural. Though the story drags the fictional kingdom through a nation-shaking conflict, the vision at the film's beginning—a veritable utopia—struck a chord with black communities across America (and the world) although the feeling was not exclusive to them. When Everett K. Ross is injured, he awakens much like we might expect it will be some day when we pass away and awaken in heaven.

People of every tribe and tongue were captivated by this vision of thriving culture, rich tradition, and a land of plenty… a promised land. The idea of a hidden kingdom, just out of sight but holding so much hope, evokes something in every human heart because it resonates with a transcendent reality that is realized in the gospel. Especially considering how my fellow Americans rejected a monarchy centuries ago, it's fascinating to see the tug on our heartstrings for this universal ideal: an undiscovered country that we've never known, yet know, ruled by a monarch who truly knows and cares for us.

The surpassing joy of the Christian is knowing that this king and kingdom truly exists, and—like Wakandan emissaries—it is our great honor and endeavor to make it visible to others. And like the famous Wakandan slogan, it is truly *"forever"*. As T'Challa says, arriving safely in the borders of his paradise… *"This never gets old."*

AVENGERS, INFINITY WAR: We All Fall Down

Gamora: *Did you do it?*

Thanos: *Yes.*

Gamora: *What did it cost?*

Thanos: *Everything.*

And so we're here… the above interchange applies to more than just the mad titan's actions in the film… in a meta way it speaks to the audacious endeavor that is the MCU, culminating here with a cinematic crossover on a level never before attempted by Hollywood. And while it may not have cost *everything*, the budget and machinations were as gargantuan a gamble as Thanos' universe-spanning scheme. Yet in front of, and behind, the camera this plan succeeds in a way no one will ever forget.

Naturally, a moving mountain of movies creates a wide range of topics and ideas to explore, as the cosmos-spanning events are of borderline biblical proportion. The film opens with the death and defeat of main characters, rapidly establishing the stakes. Loki's redemption arc comes to a close here with his sacrifice; he briefly flies his Judas flag, but it's only an act as he tries to kill Thanos and loses his life in the attempt. Death in fiction is important, and part of what gives this film its gravity is that, when the credits rolled, we didn't know whose deaths might be undone in *Avengers: Endgame*. Hindsight (and ongoing Disney+ shows) obviously remove some of this weight, but as *Infinity War* unfolded this uncertainty gave it a heft not unlike *The Lord of the Rings*. Like that "old movie" Peter Parker references in *Captain America: Civil War* with a cliffhanger ending (*The Empire Strikes Back*) this film ends with a victory for the enemy and no clear resolution in sight.

> *"I know what it's like to lose. To feel so desperately that you're right, yet to fail nonetheless. It's frightening, turns the legs to jelly… Destiny arrives all the same. And now it's here. Or should I say, I am."* - Thanos

Not all deaths will be glorious, and it's important as Christians to remember this. Despite confident hope in the hereafter, that doesn't remove the lament of difficult and sometimes seemingly unfair endings in this life. The once vainglorious "god of mischief" turns over a new leaf, only to die an inglorious death. It's a painful but potent reminder to the Christian that our hope is not in a happy ending here, or victory before the end of this life and flesh.

"All flesh is like grass, and all its beauty is like the flower of the field. The grass withers, the flower fades..." - Isaiah 40:6

With death's inevitability in mind, it's worth exploring Thanos' motivation before going any further. Like other immensely powerful and even godlike beings, we've seen recurring justification throughout the Infinity Saga, from Ultron's judgment on humanity to Ego's overwriting expansion of image. Thanos' power and plan stoked a wildfire of conversation and debate when the film came out in 2018, even including an endless array of memes, reddit threads, and earnest debate that **Thanos did nothing wrong.** Is he truly the *mad* Titan or a *logical* one? I'm not sure I've seen this much debate about a movie since *The Matrix*, actually. Thanos' followers in the film certainly see him not just as reasonable, but messianic. Ebony Maw's explanation almost sounds like a sermon:

"Hear me and rejoice. You have had the privilege of being saved by the great Thanos. You may think this is suffering, no. It is salvation. The universal scale tips toward balance because of your sacrifice. Smile. For even in death, you have become children of Thanos."

Everyone is likely to have some kind of reaction about this, and most naturally against it. But if we stop for a minute to truly consider why we disagree, we're forced to ask ourselves: **by what standard?** Thanos has a point: the universe, and its resources, are finite. Many animal species—left unchecked—will absolutely decimate an area's resources. It's why humans occasionally cull herds of animals in various regions; it's necessary to protect the ecosystem. Even forest fires, which damage and terrify, are sometimes good for the environment, clearing out decaying foliage and even disease from woodlands, spurring fresh growth and even improving wildlife habitats in the long run.

The atheist, or secular materialist, has a difficult time arguing against Thanos on ethical grounds without appealing to something greater or transcendent. If we are simply highly evolved animals, his principle is sound. Even now, many say our own planet has an overpopulation problem with no solution in sight. And Thanos is not Hitler: he debates with Doctor Strange that he's not discriminating against rich or poor, young or old. There's no targeted, specific people group, no genocide. He doesn't purport to be a "master race." The culling won't even be a painful or torturous event, as he explains...

> *"With all the six stones, I could simply snap my fingers, and they would all cease to exist. I call that... mercy."*

Thanos' solution to the population problem mirrors the motivation of other villains in comic book history: Batman's nemesis Ra's Al Ghul (in the comics) has tried to enact this on a global scale many times. Unlike Ra's, however, Thanos doesn't even intend to rule those who are left in the aftermath. Strange asks him what he'll do after he snuffs out fifty percent of the universe:

> *""I finally rest, and watch the sun rise on a grateful universe. The hardest choices require the strongest wills."*

True to his word, we see in *Endgame* that he's retired to a fertile planet, taken off his gleaming glove, and taken on the humble role of a farmer. No world-conquering, no ruling with an iron gauntlet. And while his own life isn't taken in the universal culling, it *does* require he sacrifice the person he cares for the most (more on that later). Unlike many hypocritical villains and would-be warlords, we at least have to acknowledge Thanos is consistent with his worldview.

So... what DID Thanos do Wrong?

This is a great question to ask a room of people with mixed beliefs, because most will have the autonomic reaction that of *course* he's wrong. Part of that is because the heroes we've come to love over seventeen movies oppose him. Another part is that we've been raised in a culture that just generally *assumes* this (without considering the underlying principles that support it). The bottom line is, unless we're appealing to some kind of transcendent standard, we can't say he's *wrong;* we can only say we have a different *opinion*. In a world of simply "evolved creatures" there can be no inherent or overruling moral standard; Thanos' position is simply another point of view (thanks, Obi-wan). And, in a cosmos governed only by Darwin's survival of the fittest, it may even be the most sensible.

What many will be uncomfortable to admit is that opposing Thanos on *principle* inevitably means recognizing some kind of moral standard within the fabric of our universe—inherent rights and wrongs in the framework of creation—and this necessitates not only transcendent moral laws, but the one (or ones) who established them. It doesn't get us all the way to the God of the Bible, but it does make the Moral Argument for God's Existence (which I discussed in Act 1 of *Cinemagogue: the Director's Cut*).

The Christian has an answer to the question, of course, and to articulate it I'll literally take a page from fellow Popcorn Theologian, Richard Foltz, via his podcast episode notes for the film:

> *Marvel has finally provided us with an incredibly deep and interesting (and powerful) villain. What do we think of his goal? What do we think of his philosophy that it would be better to kill half of the universe so that the other half do not live in situations of suffering due to lack of resources? On a smaller scale, isn't this nearly the same argument used by those on the 'pro-choice' side of the debate on abortion? How should a Christian consider the argument that abortion "makes sense" in cases where quality of life would be severely poor for the child?* (It's just a smaller scale form of culling.)

> *Ultimately, as believers, we have a standard to look to in order to answer this sort of question. This question is complicated and messy apart from an objective standard, but we have God's Word; and what does God's Word say about the value of life?*

> **"You shall not murder."** - Exodus 20:13

> *How would God feel about the mission of Thanos?*

> **"I will require a reckoning. Whoever sheds the blood of man, by man shall his blood be shed, for God made man in his own image."** - Genesis 9:5-6

Would He approve of the logic that it makes sense to sacrifice half of humanity so that the other half can live in a better way?

> **"Rescue those who are being taken away to death; hold back those who are stumbling to the slaughter."** - Proverbs 24:11

We see here that God is clearly on the side of the Avengers, and Christians who have opposed infanticide, genocide, abortion, euthanasia and other murderous abuses throughout the ages. Ultimately, the value of human life as beings made in the image of God is so very high that this sort of thinking is completely foreign to Scripture. Praise God we have an objective standard!

Amen. You can see how simply unpacking Thanos' mission opens doorways to all kinds of conversations and ethical application for our lives today regarding ethical concerns. Along the same lines, a complementary theme appears that wrestles with theological concerns…

Is Thanos a critique of the biblical God?

Loki. Ultron. Ego. We've already had some powerful figures that many moviegoers made much of in terms of parallels for religious faith, views of God, and more. It seems inevitable that when a cosmic powered villain takes the center stage with a world—or universe—spanning plan, someone is going to compare them to the God of the Bible. In this case, it's understandable but off the mark.

A few surface-level events help create this comparison, one being the "snap" event and disappearance of half the universe's population. This evokes a very modern Christian eschatological view of "the Rapture" that has already worked its way into entertainment via Tim LaHaye's *Left Behind* book series (which has been adapted into a few movies as well). Without getting into a rabbit trail debate on whether the Rapture is even biblical, the idea is that all the believers on earth will disappear *"in the blink of an eye"* (or snap of a finger) and be taken away to be with God. The rest will be left behind to go through the tribulation and ultimately face judgment day. It's easy to see how this is backward. Those snapped away by Thanos face a quick death so that everyone else can live;

those whisked away by God are the ones actually being saved. There's no parallel here save for the vaguest visual cue.

Even if you squint and try to imagine Thanos as representing God in terms of ushering in an apocalyptic event that brings an end to many, "separating the wheat from the chaff" as it were, the motives simply don't align; Thanos isn't separating the wheat from the chaff, the righteous from the wicked, or anything resembling a day of judgment. He goes out of his way to explain his culling is not a moral judgment day of any kind, but simply pragmatism. Even looking at the Old Testament flood, God's issue wasn't overpopulation but human depravity. No good comparison here.

The only story beat that rings closer to a biblical bell is the sacrifice of Gamora by Thanos. Giving up the life of the child you love is a deep and meaningful aspect of Christian faith; Abraham is asked by God to sacrifice his son Isaac as an act of faith and devotion. However, before Abraham sacrifices Isaac God stay this hand and provides a ram, a substitutionary sacrifice. Learned Christians also know this is a bit of Old Testament foreshadowing by God as the ultimate substitutionary atonement, fulfilled when He sends his only begotten son to die for the sins of the world.

"…God shows his love for us in that while we were still sinners, Christ died for us." - Romans 5:8

The difference is that Christ came and did this willingly; it was a cooperative and redemptive plan (not to mention he also rose from the dead three days later). Jesus gave his life to save many, not as a power-grab by which God might take the lives of many.

"He has appeared once for all at the culmination of the ages to do away with sin by the sacrifice of himself." - Hebrews 9:26

Speaking of self-sacrifice, it's fitting to shift our focus to the far more Christ-like figure in the narrative: the Vision. We addressed some of those allusions in *Age of Ultron*, but here we see a more-than-human figure who repeatedly expresses his willingness to lay down his life, as a sacrifice to spare the rest of the world (or worlds).

"We don't trade lives." - Captain America

There's been criticism of the Avengers' stance on this issue by pragmatic moviegoers; after all, if they'd just killed Vision and destroyed the stone, wouldn't Thanos have been thwarted? However, this cold logic doesn't hold up; once he has the time-stone Thanos dials back Wanda's killing of Vision (which she'd done at Viz's insistent—again, willing—request). There's no limit to how far Thanos could move back in time at that point, so he could have simply gone back before Vision was killed at *any* point. Once again, our heroes are heroic precisely because they eschew pragmatism when it clashes with principle. Thanos is the one who trades lives, (like Gamora's), trafficking in death for what he perceives to be the greater good. Vision, on the other hand, offers his willingly to save, which is a very Christ-like mindset.

> *"No one takes it from me, but I lay it down of my own accord..."* - John 10:18

If anything, Thanos is a flipped script, a mirror image, a hodgepodge of godly motivations twisted 180 degrees for cinematic effect. As Jesus came with a plan of life, Thanos came with a plan of death. In fact, his name comes from Thanatos, the personification of death in Greek mythology. He's seeking the power of God for purposes that are antichrist, so god-like parallels are better found elsewhere (like *Guardians of the Galaxy Volume 3*, but I'm getting ahead of myself). And speaking of the Guardians, let's talk about…

The Problem with Peter (you know the one)

> *"…what master do I serve? What am I supposed to say, Jesus?"*
> - Peter Quill, Star-Lord

For the most part, our assemblage of heroes from a cornucopia of comic book movies combines and performs quite admirably. Loki and Heimdall give their lives early for the cause. Peter Parker leaves his friendly neighborhood to brave a bigger stage and performs admirably to the end. Bruce Banner manages to help despite a reluctant Hulk. The earthbound Avengers team up with Black Panther and the Wakandans for a battle Royale while Strange, Stark, a reformed Nebula and the other Guardians face the mad Titan. Thor returns with Rocket and Groot at a critical juncture. We see

Bucky Barnes fighting alongside his friends, and almost all have a chance to exhibit the growth they've experienced from all the lessons we've covered thus far. Since the movie title is "Avengers" almost everyone brings their A-game… except for Peter Quill.

In scripture Peter denies Jesus three times, so we might give this Peter some slack that he only screws up twice. While some of his fellow Guardians still rank as the least mature of these heroes, his flaws allow Thanos to eliminate half of all life in the universe. May we learn these lessons vicariously through Mr. Quill and not repeat them as we face relationships and trials:

1. Don't make promises you can't keep

You know one of my biggest pet peeves in movies? When the protagonist is about to go off to a climactic battle with odds against them and an uncertain outcome, and they tell someone—often a child—that they "promise" they'll come back, or that everything will be okay. Now in most action movies the protagonist survives, but about a third of the time the person does something heroic like lay down their life, and all I can think is… you lousy liar! You made a promise you couldn't keep, and what did it accomplish? A moment of comfort and a lifetime of trust issues. What's amazing is when a good writer has the hero respond in a *mature* way, admitting they *can't* promise that, but encouraging the child or love interest, etc. with a meaningful and heartfelt exchange. And all those other action heroes who DO come back? Well, they still shouldn't have promised something they couldn't know for sure… and they ruin it for everyone else.

"If a man vows a vow to the Lord, or swears an oath to bind himself by a pledge, he shall not break his word. He shall do according to all that proceeds out of his mouth." - Numbers 30:2

Oh, yeah, and it's biblical too… not just James' pet peeve. There are a host of verses about the importance of keeping a vow (or promise). Jesus simplifies things and says let your yes be yes and your no be no. All that to say, Peter hesitates and loses his chance to keep his promise to Gamora. Sure, you could argue he did pull the trigger, and it's not his fault Thanos turned it into a bubble gun. But if he hadn't stammered and faltered and given Thanos a chance to understand their pre-planned action, he would have made good on his promise.

"Oh, daughter… you expect too much from him." - Thanos

Better yet, Peter should have been more honest about his hesitancy and uncertainty, and she might have seen the folly in being at the forefront of confrontation in the first place. Rash vows bring a world of hurt, and we should watch our words and be more honest about what we can and can't commit to. In this case, Peter is rash because he's ruled by emotion…

2. Don't be ruled by emotion

"The end of all things is at hand; therefore be self-controlled and sober-minded…" - 1 Peter 4:7

We've already seen and discussed how ungoverned emotionalism can lead to chaos, even *Civil War*. Tony Stark has been frequently guilty of falling prey to emotional sway, but here he looks like Mr. Spock in comparison with Peter Quill. When Thanos admits to killing Gamora in the film's penultimate battle, as the team has the mad Titan on the ropes, Quill's emotional reaction dislodges Mantis' hold on their enemy's mind just as they're about to remove the gauntlet. Even *one* more second of restraint and they would have stopped Thanos right there, saving years of pain and suffering across the universe. The overemotional Star-Lord sacrificed the universe due to a lack of self-control.

"A man without self-control is like a city broken into and left without walls." - Proverbs 25:28

Don't get me wrong, I'm not a Peter Quill hater like many MCU fans out there after Infinity War. Peter in the Bible denies Christ three times only to be met by his risen Savior with forgiveness, and a commission to go and be a pivotal participant in the preaching of the gospel and proliferation of the church. I love a great redemption story, and the MCU started with one in 2008 with Tony Stark. Peter isn't the only one who's had a bumpy road of regression and repeated mistakes, and sometimes people's growth is slower than others. Star-Lord may need a demotion (Star-Baron? Star-Butler?) but not condemnation. If anything, his foolish moment should remind us to fortify ourselves for a time of trial.

On the other side, people may argue that it's not his fault; after all, wouldn't we all struggle in the moment with such grievous news? That kind of empathy can be helpful, but this goes too far. Christians can't justify a lapse, in self-control or any sin, because God's Word reassures that we can remain steadfast in those testing moments, and we have help:

"No temptation has overtaken you that is not common to man. God is faithful, and he will not let you be tempted beyond your ability, but with the temptation he will also provide the way of escape, that you may be able to endure it." - 1 Corinthians 10:13

A final defense of Peter here might be that Doctor Strange oversaw this battle scenario, having used the time stone to look at over fourteen million possible outcomes, and knew that *this* path was the only scenario where they could win… which means the only way to beat Thanos *included* Peter making his rash decision. But that doesn't let Quill off the hook; just because a *wrong* action may play out in cause and effect for an ultimately *right* outcome doesn't absolve someone of the deed. (Also, it could be that Quill screwed it up in all fourteen million possibilities!)

But that leads us our final reflection on *Infinity War*…

God's Foreknowledge vs. Strange's Foreknowledge

Part of the reason comparisons to God come up in this film is because of the Infinity Gauntlet, or more precisely the six sparkly gems Thanos attaches to it. The Infinity Stones—in some ways— mirror aspects of Godlike capability. When we speak of God's lordship biblically, we usually list three attributes: *omnipotence*, (God is all-powerful) *omnipresence*, (God is everywhere, or all-present) and omniscience (God is all-knowing). While the six gems tweak and fall short, let's consider what they do and how they relate.

1. **The Power Stone:** this one's easy. God has unlimited and unparalleled power, so this relates to His omnipotence.

2. **The Mind Stone:** From the name, one naturally thinks this would align with God's omniscience in terms of knowing things. But this is the first stone we see in the MCU, as Loki uses it to control people's minds and make them do his bidding. This also relates to omnipotence, as biblically God has complete and total control of everything, including human will and action. We see this plainly in scripture as he hardens Pharoah's heart, directs kings to discipline Israel, etc. Romans 9 explains in detail how no one can resist God's will.

3. **The Reality Stone:** again, omnipotence. Bending the laws of physics and reality itself show up in scripture, as God parts the Red Sea and Jesus walks on water. Beyond that, reality itself is not independent of God; it literally holds together by his power according to Colossians 1:17.

4. **The Soul Stone:** very little is explained about this stone in the film, though the directors explain in an interview that it does give the wearer power over souls. In Matthew 10:28 Jesus explains that many things kill the body but only God has power over the soul, so once again this best aligns with omnipotence.

5. **The Space Stone:** finally! We move to another attribute of God. This stone allows Thanos to instantly be anywhere he wants and functions like teleportation. However, we see he can still only be in one place at any given time, rather than being *everywhere* at the *same* time, so it's a weak approximation of God's omnipresence (one wonders if some people have this misconception about God).

6. **The Time Stone:** with the last stone Thanos obtains, we see a mingling of omniscience and omnipotence. In *Doctor Strange*, we see Stephen aging and de-aging an apple and even turning back time to stop the destruction of Hong Kong. He makes a time loop to defeat Dormammu, so it's certainly a power flex. Thanos uses that power to get the Mind Stone. However, Strange also uses it for unique and prophetic knowledge, to look at all possible scenarios and outcomes in battling Thanos and divining the singular one that will bring them success. He gains foreknowledge of future events, or *possible* future events…

...and here we must be careful, lest we foolishly import a movie's imperfect *mimicry* of omniscience and let it distort our view of God.

There is a weak-sauce theology out there that improperly views God as "looking down a tunnel of time" (not unlike Strange's meditation exercise) and making choices in light of that knowledge to direct affairs to His determined ends. Well-intentioned Christians build this model to reconcile some admittedly mind-bending aspects of God's will, human choices, the origin of sin, and more. The problem is that it contradicts scripture.

> *"...for I am God, and there is no other. I am God, and there is none like me, declaring the end from the beginning, and from ancient times things not yet done... I have spoken, and I will bring it to pass..."* - Isaiah 46:10-11

God has **declared the end from the beginning**; He is not responding to a timeline operating outside His direct control, perceiving all possibilities and adjusting accordingly. He is not constantly seeing and reacting. Scripture is clear: He has ordained everything. Most specifically, in terms of salvation he didn't look at fourteen million possible outcomes and determine that Christ was the singular one where victory could be achieved. Don't let a "Strange" movie idea distort your understanding of God's foreknowledge.

> *"For truly in this city there were gathered together against your holy servant Jesus... both Herod and Pontius Pilate, along with the Gentiles and the peoples of Israel, to do whatever your hand and your plan had predestined to take place."* - Acts 4:27-28

God's plan was predestined, and Ephesians 1 tells us this occurred before the foundation of the world. There is no multiverse, no variants, no million other possibilities God is navigating to ensure we arrive at His best outcome. There is *one* story: one beginning, one middle, and one ending written by the Living Word. God "foreknows" because he's the director, the screenwriter, the producer, and the main character. Just as the Space Stone was a diluted form God's omnipresence, the Time Stone is a distorted form of his omniscience.

With that in mind, (or Mind Stone?) we can appreciate a diluted parallel in terms of Strange's use of the Time Stone that reminds us of God. Stephen asks Tony Stark and the rest to trust in his knowledge and the outcome, but subsequently leads them on a course of action that (as credits roll on this film) appears to end in abject failure... including the death of Strange, in whom they put their trust.

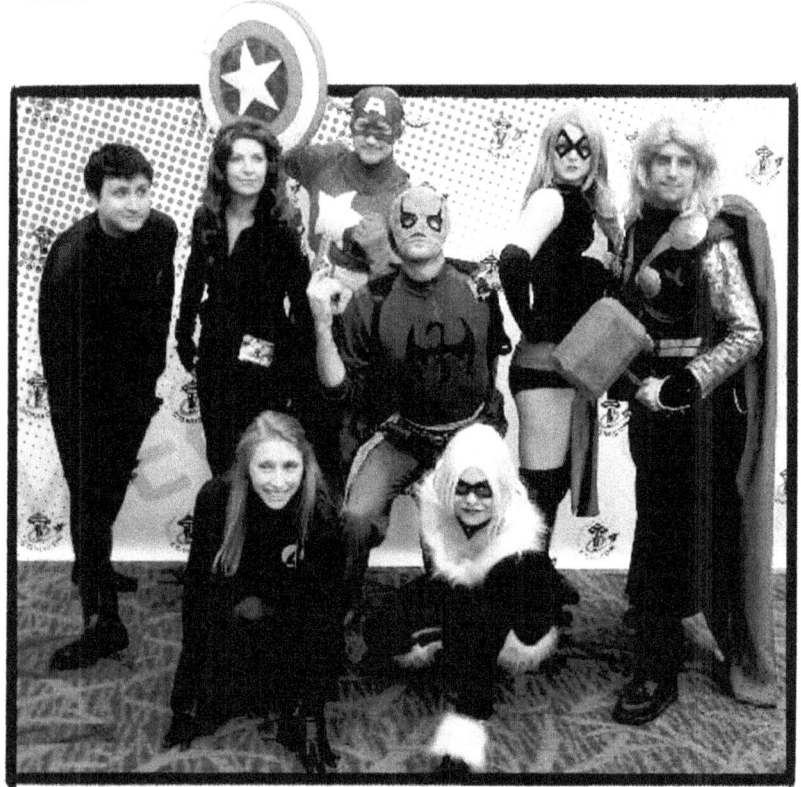

If Iron Fist and The Black Cat had been there, things might have gone differently...

Christians are called to trust in Him when things seem bleak, confusing, even hopeless. Believers must have faith that God knows better than we do, that His foreknowledge is not *strange*, but *supreme*. Consider the disciples when Christ was arrested, flogged, and crucified. Jesus even told them it would happen—*that it had to happen!*—for God's plan and victory to come to pass. But for three days, it looked and felt like utter failure... including the death of the one in whom they put their trust.

Avengers: Infinity War leaves its characters (and viewers) in the same emotional place as the disciples in those tenuous days between Christ's death and resurrection; despondent, questioning themselves and their mission, and wondering where it had all gone wrong. Thankfully Doctor Strange, and the Marvel Cinematic Universe (like Jesus) had an *Endgame*...

CAPTAIN MARVEL: Girl Power, Interrupted

"...you were the most powerful person I knew, way before you could shoot fire through your fists." - Maria Rambeau

Admittedly this film was more of a Captain Muddle for me, and one of several inaugural, cultural storytelling shifts that we'll talk about more extensively later in the book. Tonally, like *Thor: Ragnarok* the cheap laughs didn't work for me, (like how Nick Fury lost his eye) and the screenplay, direction, and other choices just fell flat. In similar fashion, we get a thematically mixed bag as well.

"...the god of this world has blinded the minds of the unbelievers, to keep them from seeing the light of the gospel..."
- 2 Corinthians 4:4

Jason Bourne, John Murdoch, Elly Conway, Neo, Leonard. The narratives of these characters (The *Bourne* movies, *Dark City*, *Argylle*, *The Matrix*, *Memento*) and many more provide us with a protagonist who doesn't truly know their past, or present: they've been fooled in some fashion for conspiratorial purposes. Nefarious powers are often manipulating them, and "Vers" (Carol Danvers) falls into this familiar and powerful story device. Characters like the Supreme Intelligence have blinded them from the truth, much like scripture describes Satan as pulling the wool over people's eyes in our real, shared story. That's why we need to be freed:

"For freedom Christ has set us free; stand firm therefore, and do not submit again to a yoke of slavery." - Galatians 5:1

A tale of truth discovery can always be a potent parallel for the gospel as we break free from the deception of the devil, or the false narratives of the world around us. Carol Danvers realizes how she's been fooled and decides she won't live in subjection to that delusion:

> *"I used to believe your lies, but the Skrulls are just fighting for a home... they won't submit to your rule. And neither will I."*

What's interesting about some of the other films above is that they deal honestly with the third deceiver we face: ourselves. Jason Bourne discovers that yes, he was subjected to experiments in the Treadstone program, but that he *volunteered* for it. In Memento, we see even more damnably that Leonard is *self*-deceived. This dovetails nicely with scripture; we aren't just deceived by the world and the devil, but by ourselves. As Romans 1 explains, we *"exchange the truth"* for a lie. Carol Danvers doesn't have that flaw... in fact, as Maria Rambeau and the movie tell us, she doesn't really have any. She was the best pilot. The best friend. The best... well, just the best. The only things holding her back are external forces, people and powers, symbolically and literally by the inhibitor on her neck.

> *"I've been fighting with one hand tied behind my back. What happens when I'm finally set free?* - Carol Danvers

Tony Stark was reprehensible. Bruce Banner has anger issues. Thor and Doctor Strange were full of pride. Black Widow has red in her ledger. Ant Man committed crimes. Almost all the great Marvel characters are introduced to us with significant flaws, and their growth and development is what makes them interesting. Captain Marvel's misstep is trying to convince us that the only problem with Carol is... everyone else. Even Captain America, who is introduced as a man of great character, is physically unfit and needs help from outside himself. That's the heart of Galatians 5 we just referenced; we needed help outside ourselves to gain the power to be free.

Unlike recent films *Doctor Strange* and *Ant Man*—who learn from teachers—Carol's teacher Yon-Rogg is presented as a man "holding her down". There's a misguided attempt in the film to make a statement about misogyny, or the patriarchy, neither of which hold up under scrutiny since the Supreme Intelligence isn't male (and in fact appears as female to Carol) and Yon-Rogg's chief lieutenant is the powerful, respected female warrior Minn-Erva. The story awkwardly tries to make an issue out of Jude Law's character telling

"Vers" she needs to control her emotions, seemingly to parallel men saying women are too emotional.

"Do not let your emotions override your judgment." - Yonn-Rog

Considering this movie comes on the heels of *Infinity War*—where half the galaxy is erased because Peter Quill **let emotions override his judgment!**—it's ridiculous to vilify Yonn-Rog's admonitions just to reinforce that Carol is perfect the way she is. The problem here is that the film is forcing a false, worldly narrative.

The Supreme Intelligence tells Carol that she's *"flawed. Helpless."* That she's *"only human."* This seems to galvanize Carol, who responds *"you're right. I'm only human,"* and then proceeds to wreck shop. Again, this is the world's narrative that would have us believe that we're perfect *just the way we are*, that *being human* is our focus: that we weren't *meant for more*, that we aren't *flawed*, and that we don't need anyone else to *empower, equip,* or *save us*. Sorry, but Captain Marvel's story of empowerment misses the mark.

To end on a positive parallel, however, we can redeem the image of the shattered inhibitor chip and Danvers' embrace of the full power she's been given. Hmm, wait a minute: this power isn't Carol's inherently, or from simply "being human". It's an alien power gained unintentionally (by either accident or providence, depending on your worldview). That matches more nicely with the Christian concept that we're given gifts and talents by God as we're set free from our yoke of slavery. As Carol proceeds to use those powers to help the refugee Skrulls and defeat the Kree, she casts off that inhibitor chip and soars to victory, evoking the exhortation by the author of Hebrews to go higher, further, faster:

"...let us also lay aside every weight, and sin which clings so closely, and let us run with endurance the race that is set before us, looking to Jesus..." - Hebrews 12:1

ANT MAN AND THE WASP: Loving Our Enemies

"I'm sorry for lying to you, for risking everything... I do some dumb things, and the people that I love the most pay the price."
   - Scott Lang

Janet Van Dyne sacrificed herself—assuming she was going to die and leave behind her husband and daughter—to save others. Scott Lang went to Germany and helped Captain America, but consequently screwed up relationships with Hank and Hope (and barely managed to keep contact with his daughter). Now, Scott finds himself in the deep end again when he's quantum-entangled with Janet, indicating she may still be alive. Scott finds himself struggling to find wisdom in facing these decisions.

"Plans are established by counsel; by wise guidance wage war."
   - Proverbs 20:18

The folly is easily exposed in Scott's decision to help Captain America. If he'd confided in Janet, he may have had more than counsel; she may have gone with him, adding another member to Team Cap. That may have even changed the outcome of the battle at the airport. Couple that with the fact that Hank Pym has no love for Stark, Scott may have gotten a few upgrades and tricks to bring to bear in the battle. He may have gotten *"wise guidance"* and *"waged* (civil) *war"* with better results. As it turns out, it takes the three of them—and Scott's X-Con partners—to resolve the crises in this film.

"Helping people isn't dumb... maybe you just need someone watching your back." - Cassie Lang

Counsel has turned up as a theme in many of these films, but the need for it here is particular; making similar choices in real life is difficult for first responders and others who put their lives on the line, and in another way it's tricky for Christians balancing ministry and family. Other jobs—surgeons, caregivers, even "normal" jobs with co-workers who still count on you—require juggling responsibility to the role with responsibility to family.

Bill Foster is also juggling responsibilities and difficult decisions of his own, as we find out he's partnered with the "Ghost" who turns up out of nowhere to steal Pym's technology. It's obvious he cares and feels responsible for the phase-shifting Ava Starr, and isn't convinced that Janet will be harmed by their plan to extract her quantum energy. Even Ava doesn't want to harm anyone unless it's absolutely necessary; she's a tragic figure acting rashly for survival. The only stereotypical "bad guys" in the film are Sonny Burch and his cronies.

Janet: *Your pain…*

Ava: *It hurts… it always hurts…*

Janet: *I'm sorry. I think I can help you…*

We've covered in several prior films that a sympathetic villain isn't justified in hurting others, so Ghost deserves to be held accountable for her wicked actions. And yet… we have a unique climax (or perhaps anti-climax) that sets Ant-Man and the Wasp apart from the typical Marvel film:

"But I say to you who hear, love your enemies, do good to those who hate you, bless those who curse you, pray for those who abuse you. To one who strikes you on the cheek, offer the other also, and from one who takes away your cloak do not withhold your tunic either. - Luke 6:27-29

Despite all she's done, Ava isn't repaid with an eye for an eye, a tooth for a tooth, or even incarceration. Sonny and his black-market compatriots get justice, but Ava receives a healing moment of grace, in keeping with how Jesus challenges us to love others despite what they've done to us. It's an inspiring and heartwarming ending. Well, at least until the after credits scene…

AVENGERS, ENDGAME: Loss and Redemption. Resurrection and Rest.

"Everybody wants a happy ending, right? But it doesn't always roll that way… part of the journey is the end." - Tony Stark

From one angle, it's one of the greatest achievements in cinematic history, bringing 22 films over a decade to a conclusion of universe-shaking proportion. The theatrical release dethroned the reigning box office *Titanic* and left an indelible mark on our culture. So, what deeper resonance might we find in its exploration of life, death and everything else in between? It's worth exploring the key characters we've followed.

"You know, I keep telling Some people they should move on. Grow. Some do. But not us." - Steve Rogers

What's fascinating about this film is that we see a well-balanced Tony ready to die at the movie's beginning, at peace with himself and his circumstance, naturally wishing things could be different but ready to accept his end… until an almost angelic sight swoops in and grants him an extension. It's a tribute to the growth Tony has experienced… but then again, sometimes facing death is easier than facing living in light of failure and loss. His initial return home, admittedly weak physically and mentally, sees him lash out. All the Avengers are ready to lash out in anger and resentment, and especially Thor, who lops off Thanos' head when they find him. Then this story really begins, as we see how our original Avengers faced the five years post-snap. At a glance, they reflect many different reactions and coping mechanisms we might relate to:

- **Captain America** is leading support groups and ministering to others, though it seems to have little healing effect for him.

- **Black Widow** has poured herself entirely into her job.

- **Thor** has let himself go, self-medicating and worse.

- **Hawkeye**, who previously appeared to be the balanced, well-adjusted family man, is lashing out in anger and bitterness.

- **Hulk**, typically the most dysfunctional, has surprisingly become well-balanced and seems the most adjusted, save for…

- **Iron Man.** Of all the characters we thought would be determined to find a solution to the problem, with sleepless nights and disheveled workstation, it would have been Tony Stark… or at least the Tony we've seen in many movies past. Instead, we see that instead of regressing (again) he's inculcated the many lessons he's experienced and moved forward. He's built a life, taken a wife, had a daughter, and is as settled and content as one may hope to be. We see from the picture of Peter Parker that yes, he has sorrows, but he also has true joy. When he's approached by the gang to help with the "time heist", he turns them down.

Steve: *Tony, I get it. And I'm happy for you, I really am. But this is a second chance.*

Tony: *I got my second chance right here, Cap.*

Set aside comic book and movie miracles like time travel devices for a minute and Tony is absolutely right here. Redemption doesn't rewind; second chances aren't do-overs. Even biblically, our reconciliation and restoration to God isn't a reversal of sin or a return to the garden of Eden: there will be a new heaven and a new earth, not a correction of the old. It's not a software patch, it's a whole new system. A new life, and what Tony has looks like it.

"Remember not the former things, nor consider the things of old. Behold, I am doing a new thing; now it springs forth, do you not perceive it?" - Isaiah 43:18-19

Now of course this IS comic book land, and so a time heist becomes a viable possibility. Then we see Tony wrestle with the self-same juggling act Scott faced in *Ant-Man and the Wasp*: where does his responsibility lie? Family? The greater call of mission? So this time, what does Tony do? What former lessons have taught him; he seeks the counsel of his helper suitable. And it's not a token gesture… he's really listening for her wisdom and insight and he's ready to go either way. Again, this is a testament to prior lessons learned. Pepper Potts lovingly talks her husband through the matter, and it's decided together.

Time hijinks ensue. Memorable moments are had between mothers and sons, fathers and sons. Thor's time jump takes him back to meet his mother Frigga, allowing for a similar scene of a man humbly receiving counsel. The motherly wisdom she gives her son addresses not just how we deal with loss, but also with failure.

"Idiot? No. A failure? Absolutely… do you know what that makes you? Just like everyone else. Everyone fails at who they're supposed to be…" - Frigga

This is a wonderful moment of humbling and level-setting, and recalls the biblical knowledge we need regarding our intended role as image-bearers of God, at which we have surely failed.

"…for all have sinned and fall short of the glory of God."
   - Romans 3:23

Like Thor, we've fallen short of who we were "supposed" to be, but that doesn't mean our story is over or that we can't move forward, living into the role God has for us, who we're *meant* to be. We may not be "worthy", but we find our worth in Him. And even in our brokenness, we can be of use. There's a poignant moment not long after, between the back-broken Rhodey and mutilated, robotic Nebula to that effect:

Nebula: *I wasn't always like this.*

Rhodes: *Me either. But we work with what we got, right?*

Flawed servants, committed to a path where they help others , is the recurring motif that brings us to what is, arguably, the most gut-wrenching and emotional core of the movie (there's only one other moment that carries comparable weight). Natasha Romanoff and Clint Barton (the latter with as much "red in his ledger" as the Black Widow, perhaps more) face a life-ending, sacrificial choice on Voromir, and both want to be the one who serves each other, and the universe…

"In order to take the stone, you must lose that which you love. An everlasting exchange. A soul for a soul." - The Red Skull

"Greater love has no one than this, that someone lay down his life for his friends." - John 15:13

There are so many verses, a depth of riches, that we could explore related to the scene where Clint and Natasha essentially try to out-Christ-like the other, talking about forgiveness and grace. A discerning Christian should be moved to tears:

Clint: *Natasha, you know that I've done. What I've become.*

Nat: *Oh, I don't judge people on their worst mistakes.*

Clint: *Maybe you should.*

Nat: *YOU didn't.*

Clint: *Tell my family I love 'em.*

Nat: *You tell 'em yourself.*

Nat and Clint literally fight to best the other, and there's obviously a clear "winner", as the Black Widow leaps to a sacrificial end. This scene perfectly captures the loving, servant-minded yet competitive nature of scripture:

"Love one another with brotherly affection. Outdo one another in showing honor." - Romans 12:10

Would we do this? Would we love family, friends, or just the world in general enough to not only accept this fate, but fight for the opportunity? Like Jesus, would we take up our cross and lay down our lives? There is a powerful inspiration to live out our faith in the mid-movie sacrifice of The Black Widow.

Clint: *It was supposed to be me…*

Hawkeye's tear-filled lament should also pierce our hearts and humble our spirits when we think of Christ, and how he laid down his life for our sins. It should have been us… and yet he substituted himself. He looks at us, like Nat looks at Clint, says *"It's okay,"* and instead of falling down he is lifted up (on the cross) so that we might have life eternal. May we ever have the tender and grateful heart of Clint Barton in response to what Jesus did for us. Because of him, we will stand one day with all assembled in love through Christ's victorious accomplishment in death… and resurrection.

Resurrection to Glory (Marvel style)

Before we get to the film's final sacrifice, let's pivot tonally to appreciate another significant image that packs a wallop of worshipful resonance. As the story slides inevitably toward a monumental confrontation, the recovery of the Infinity stones makes possible the return of the dead: all who had gone to ash (or dust). And while the reverie of the event is interrupted by a time-jumping Thanos and his army, this "Marvelous" resurrection is realized by a momentous gathering at the Avengers compound. Innumerable portals appear in the sky, and more comic book characters than we can count arrive from every corner of the globe, every tribe and tongue, from Wakanda to Kamar-Taj (and even outer space). Does it warm our hearts as purely fictional, or nearly biblical?

> *"After this I looked, and behold, a great multitude that no one could number, from every nation, from all tribes and peoples and languages..."* - Revelation 7:9

> *"On your left."* - Sam Wilson

For Christians at least—and maybe in the hearts of all who watch, though they know not why—there is a glimpse of our future reflected in part right here, as those resurrected rally around a hammer-wielding, weary-but-worthy Captain America.

> *"Then I saw heaven opened, and behold, a white horse! The one sitting on it is called Faithful and True, and in righteousness he judges and makes war. And the armies of heaven, arrayed in fine linen, white and pure, were following him on white horses.*
> - Revelation 19: 11,14

Avengers Assemble, indeed.

 Ready to follow their Captain into a noble and decisive conflict, an endgame that feels like the End of Days, characters from 21 prior movies each get to have their moment and participate in the glorious conflagration... but of course, one man is destined to strike the decisive blow.

Entering Our Rest

> *"Mr. Stark? Can you hear me? It's Peter. Hey, we won..."*

There's something in Tony Stark's eyes as he sits down, charred and scarred, looking up into the tearful eyes of his best friend, his surrogate son, and his loving wife. What is that look as they offer final words of reassurance? Is it resignation? Regret? To my eyes, it's a look of much needed relief.

> *"Comfort, comfort my people, says your God. Speak tenderly to Jerusalem, and cry to her that her warfare is ended, that her iniquity is pardoned..."* - Isaiah 40:3

There's a lot in that single, relieved look, for the character and the audience, maybe even for the actor. Robert Downey Jr. had spent more than a decade of his life, in nine films, pouring his heart, soul and acting skills into this character. Something tells me it wasn't hard to summon and channel a sense of relief into that moment. As for us? We'd seen him over the course of nine films (linked to a story spanning over twenty) and now an emotionally arduous three-hour conclusion. To have finally reached the climax brought a sense of relief, albeit tinged with sadness, looking into those eyes.

As for Tony Stark? He'd embarked on a long journey since his heart was forever changed in 2008, fraught with trials, obstacles, enemies, suffering… and his own stumbling, backsliding, regression and refinement. From Yinsen at the beginning of this journey, to Natasha who made it possible for him to snap stony fingers and win the day, he'd seen others make that ultimate sacrifice, and now… while Tony remains speechless, we might remember the exchange in *Iron Man* that he has with Yinsen, who shares the same look of relief:

Yinsen: ***This was always the plan, Stark…***
it's okay. I want this. I want this.

Tony: ***Thank you for saving me.***

Yinsen: ***Don't waste it. Don't waste your life.***

Everything comes full circle: it's Tony's turn not only to lay down his life, but to rest. We've seen since *The Avengers* that Tony was willing to give his life—to lose it—and in living that way he'd actually found it: blessed with love, home, and a family. Though not wanting to die, we see he was ready for the day when it came; he was at peace with it at the film's opening. His only concern seemed to be leaving his family behind, juggling the tension of responsibilities between mission and family that was explored with Scott in *Ant-Man and The Wasp*. That's the only reason we see Stark chafe at embarking on this final mission earlier in the film, but Pepper's encouragement gives him direction, even permission:

Tony: ***I can't help everybody.***

Pepper: ***Sorta seems like you can.***

Tony: *Something tells me that I should put it in a lockbox and drop it to the bottom of the lake... and go to bed.*

Pepper: *But would you be able to rest?*

As much as we may find ourselves blessed in this life, there is still a weight we carry. The world itself is under a curse, Romans 8 says the whole creation groans together. It also says Christians groan inwardly as we eagerly "wait for adoption" and the "redemption" of our bodies. We are waiting for a rest only found beyond this life:

"So then, there remains a Sabbath rest for the people of God, for whoever has entered God's rest has also rested from his works as God did from his. Let us therefore strive to enter that rest..."
   - Hebrews 4:9-11

To be clear, the Marvel Cinematic Universe doesn't give us any moment where Tony Stark looks to Christ for salvation or worships Jesus as Lord and Savior. Our "Iron Man" is missing a key (or more accurately, THE key) component to how we find this rest, not in our own works or transformation but in Christ alone. This is not mirroring a *literal* journey to that end, but a *symbolic* one; just as Tolkien's Middle Earth stories didn't include Christ in the equation, neither does our Marvel earth narrative. But keeping that in mind, we know this work of fiction has had a narrative hand at work, moving and in fact writing Tony's transformation. It is not by this fictional character's hand that he achieves this victory or is given this rest. Rather, by the grace of the storyteller he arrives at this moment, and the same can be said of OUR storyteller and our day of rest in Him.

"Come to me, all who labor and are heavy laden, and I will give you rest. Take my yoke upon you, and learn from me, for I am gentle and lowly in heart, and you will find rest for your souls."
   - Matthew 11:28-29

"You can rest now." - Pepper Potts

At Tony's funeral we see his "heart"—the arc reactor—floating on flowers, and it's hard to think of any other cinematic story that has been given the breadth and depth to so completely explore the "transformed heart" narrative. All that remains, as the film lingers a while longer, are a few final speeches and character beats to contemplate that add glimmers of hope to this dream of eternal rest.

"I'm hoping if you play this back, it's in celebration. I hope families are reunited, I hope we get it back, and something like a normal version of the planet has been restored. IF there ever WAS such a thing. God! What a world… universe now! If you told me ten years ago that we weren't alone, let alone to this extent? I mean… I wouldn't have been surprised, but who knew? The epic forces of light and dark that have come into play…"

Step back and consider Tony Stark's final message not with the moments of Marvel universe epilogue, but from our own hopes and dreams. What does he hope for in the end? Grand celebration, restoration… all the things the Christian waits for with confident expectation that we see in the verses from Revelation quoted a few pages back. It's amusing that Tony hopes the world will be restored to "normal" but also realizes that maybe it never *has* been. What a great parallel to the reality that we've never known a normal world, but a broken one under curse. The promise of the gospel is that someday we'll know what normal truly is, for the first time, as we celebrate in the kingdom to come.

We know Tony's comments about not being alone refer to aliens and other planets, but the exclamation rings with the same passion as the man or woman whose eyes are awakened to the spiritual reality of God… that there is so much more than this life, and to what extent? Who can possibly fathom? Even knowing what little we know, it is still mind blowing. And before anyone says I'm stretching here to make Tony's sentiments speak to more than the material world, fine… but consider the subsequent interchange between a grieving Hawkeye and Scarlet Witch.

Clint Barton: *You know, I wish there was a way that I could let her know... that we won, we did it.*

Wanda Maximoff: *She knows... they both do.*

I think of the various ways that different viewers can receive Wanda's words of comfort. For the atheist, do they *scoff* a little bit here? Do they assume they're the pat on the back equivalent of a fairy tale? Or the agnostic, do they find themselves *longing* in their heart that such a thing could be true, *but unable* to have any real hope? For the screenwriter in this scene, did they *intend* us to think that the Scarlet Witch—with her ambiguous powers—is speaking from actual knowledge here? Are they saying that (at least in the Marvel universe) there is an afterlife. Heaven?

Remember, in this world a "soul stone" exists, and we saw Thanos commune with the dead Gamora. Going all the way back to Yinsen—the first person to lay down his life in our MCU journey— even he shared this confident hope.

Tony: **Come on, you're gonna go see your family.**

Yinsen: **My family is dead. I'm going to see them now, Stark.**

From the MCU's beginning to its *Endgame* (and in a few subsequent films) it's clear they want to convey the hope of the afterlife, and perhaps even God. Certainly they see a path of righteousness as opposed to wickedness, the **"epic forces of light and dark"** and the need to oppose the one and strive to walk the other. In the end, the hope is not just rest, but reunion.

"For the believer there is hope beyond the grave, because Jesus Christ has opened the door to heaven for us by His death and resurrection." -Billy Graham

Reunion is where our movie rests, and the credits roll. Technically Steve Rogers doesn't die, but (unless some Marvel magic brings Chris Evans back) it is his character's "end". Like one generation passing the torch to the next, an aged Steve gives the shield to Sam. Note the order of sequence here. We see him old, having lived a full life, and then we see him reunited with the love of his life (who died in *Captain America: Civil War*). Sure, technically we *know* this scene isn't in the afterlife, as Steve achieves this by timey-wimey comic book means). But there's something ethereal, a dream-like quality to the camerawork, the echoing jazz music, as the long-suffering soldier dances with Peggy Carter, their image fading as this is literally the *movie's* end as well. We see a life well lived, a man satisfied and content, and then a reunion: a vision of dancing, a vision of love. A vision of heaven? It's not unintentional.

Avengers: Endgame gives us a glimpse of rest from a life well-lived and more: the hope of happily ever after.

> *"Blessed be the God and Father of our Lord Jesus Christ! According to his great mercy, he has caused us to be born again to a living hope through the resurrection of Jesus Christ from the dead, to an inheritance that is imperishable, undefiled, and unfading, kept in heaven for you... In this you rejoice, though now for a little while, if necessary, you have been grieved by various trials, so that the tested genuineness of your faith— more precious than gold that perishes though it is tested by fire —may be found to result in praise and glory and honor at the revelation of Jesus Christ."* - 1 Peter 1:3-4, 6-7

SPIDER-MAN, FAR FROM HOME: Timothy, Post-Paul

> *"He knew every mistake I ever made... The world NEEDS the next Iron Man and it's NOT gonna be me... it needs to be an adult, with experience, and that's good like Tony..."*
> - Peter Parker

The final words we have of the apostle Paul to his protege Timothy in the Bible are honestly kind of sad. In 2 Timothy chapter 4, he asks his disciple to come visit him soon because almost everyone else has flaked (except Luke). One man "deserted him" while two others left without explanation given, and he says a third "harmed" and "opposed" him. However, Paul remains confident and offers his apprentice some of the most rallying encouragements in scripture:

> *"As for you, always be sober-minded, endure suffering, do the work... fulfill your ministry. For I am already being poured out as a drink offering, and the time of my departure has come. I have fought the good fight, I have finished the race, I have kept the faith."* - 2 Timothy 4:5-7

We don't know for certain what happened to Timothy after Paul died for the faith, but standing in the shadow of this titan of the faith (not the Mad Titan, mind you) would have been intimidating for anyone. Who could be the next Paul? Peter's struggle in this film is not dissimilar. In fact, we see that the villains are actually an assemblage of disgruntled former Stark employees; just as Paul had associates that turned on him, Quentin Beck and his comrades oppose Tony's legacy and his successor, leaving it up to this web-slinging "Timothy" to stand in the gap.

The problem is, he's suffering from feelings of inadequacy and uncertainty about his future, and Beck—as "Mysterio"—preys on that inferiority complex.

"If you were good enough, maybe Tony would still be alive."
- Mysterio

Some might also fault Peter for flaking out, just wanting to be selfish and hang with his friends, but I think we can cut a 16-year-old some slack here: it's not wrong to want a break, particularly after the grueling *Endgame* experience and loss of his mentor. Beck plays on that too, telling Peter it's not wrong to want a normal life. And he's not wrong! That's what a good deceiver does, co-mingling truth with deception. A girlfriend, a summer trip, there's nothing sinful about these desires. Let's also not forget that there IS no real threat; Nick Fury (well, Skrull Fury) roping Peter into the mix is exactly what Beck wants. There's no real enemy except him and his plan to get the E.D.I.T.H. control glasses from Peter so he can access the orbital weapons (and more). If Parker hadn't been approached, Mysterio's scheme would have been derailed or at least seriously set back. *(As an aside, the REAL Nick Fury may have seen through this ruse, never involved Peter, and taken down Beck and associates, case closed. But that's another story. Maybe a "What If…")*

This narrative gives us a nice counterbalance of character, considering Tony's perennial problem with pride. Peter Parker often errs in the opposite direction, which can be an equal pitfall. Christians in particular may be so afraid of pride that they embrace a self-deprecating humility and never think themselves capable of anything… which is a detriment if God is calling us to fight the good fight of the faith. Will we chicken out because of what amounts to poor discernment of self? Or God's ability to equip us? We often think of Romans 12, which says we shouldn't think of ourselves more highly than we ought. But it goes on to say we should think of ourselves *"with sober judgment"*. God may have *given* us the skills and strength we need to face what's ahead, and we may indeed be up to the task.

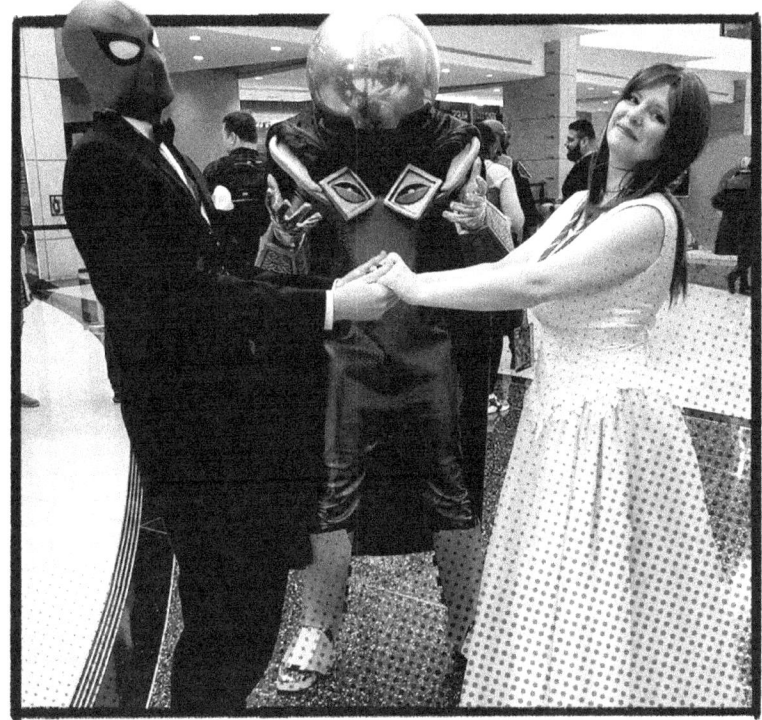

This guy came highly recommended and seems trustworthy, right?

On the other hand, I appreciate Parker's caution about his age, maturity level, and experience. E.D.I.T.H. represents great power, and Peter Parker knows that *with great power comes...* wait, we'll save that for later. In any case, he's trying to be sober in his judgment, and ultimately willing to listen to others, like Happy Hogan, who knew Tony Stark better than Peter.

> *"Nobody could live up to Tony, not even Tony. Tony was my best friend and he was a mess. He second-guessed everything he did. He was all over the place."* - Happy Hogan

Sometimes we put our mentors—parents, pastors, politicians, public figures or others we respect—on a pedestal; we start to overestimate them versus considering *them* with sober judgment. We know in the Bible that Peter still screwed up years after Pentecost, and the Old Testament is filled with fallible figures from Samson to David. They may have been men used by God, but they were also a mess. We can't elevate figures of faith or heroism in such a way as to stymie or stifle our participation in the same path.

> *"You got gifts, Parker… you've got to decide whether you're going to step up or not. Stark chose you. He made you an Avenger. I need that. The world needs that. Maybe Stark was wrong. The choice is yours."* - (Not) Nick Fury

The choice is ours. Will we step into the shoes of those who fought before us? Will Peter be the next Iron Man? Well, the first movie set after the Infinity Saga (and closing out Phase Three) ends with a news-shaking motif similar to the first Iron Man film: although Tony had the hubris to declare his secret identity to the world and tell the press that *"I am Iron Man,"* Peter's secret identity is shouted to the heavens by Mysterio (by way of Spider's long-time comic book nemesis, J. Jonah Jameson). This exposure is going to give him even more headaches than Tony had, but it still rings true with scripture that tells us *"what has been will be again, and there is nothing new under the sun."*

Scene 2: **Third Phase is a Charm**

And thus it ends, three phases over a "Marvel-Us" Decade-plus (mostly now on Disney+). After Phase One's cinematic gospel and Phase Two's cinematic growth, we reach an unparalleled climax with Phase Three's cinematic gallantry. There's more to examine beyond Marvel in this interesting era, but let's wrap up with a final summary of Phase Three's films:

13. **Standing true to principles brings division** (CA: *Civil War*)
14. **This life is not about us** (*Doctor Strange*)
15. **We're tempted to magnify our own image** (*Guardians Vol. 2*)
16. **We need sober judgment of self…** (*Spider-man: Homecoming*)
17. **…because a Day of Judgment IS coming** (*Thor: Ragnarok*)
18. **We long for a united kingdom & true King…** (*Black Panther*)
19. **…but in this life, we will know hardship** (*Av: Infinity War*)
20. **We can escape the slavery of this world…** (*Captain Marvel*)
21. **…and live differently, loving enemies** (*Ant-Man and Wasp*)
22. **One day there will be redemption and rest** (*Av: Endgame*)
23. **We thus persevere with confidence** (*SM: Far from Home*)

Okay, wow. That was a lot. But for better or worse, it's over…

…aw, who are we kidding?

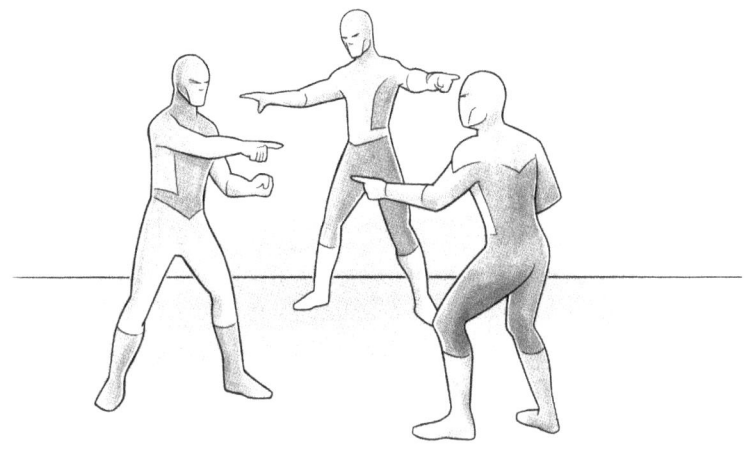

Act 5: **...and Beyond!**

or

"Acts, Apocrypha and the Old Testament"

Scene 1: **True, False, and Multiverse Choice**

They could have ended it right there. Called it good, or called the next one a reboot. But hey, Marvel's got a good thing going, right? Why cash out now? As of the writing of this book we're in the middle of Phase Five of the MCU, and... well, I think almost everyone can agree it's been a mixed bag. However, just as I (and a lot of other people) were about to check out, a burst of mutant-fueled healing factor has put posteriors in seats and money in the bank again. Two more Avengers movies are coming. And Robert Downey Jr. will return as Doctor Doom? What happens next is anyone's guess.

If we reframe the entire Infinity Saga (or the first three phases) as a 20+ Marvel movie "gospel"—with Tony Stark as its narrative center—what's happening now might be likened to the Book of Acts, or what happened after Acts; perhaps each movie is its own little post-Tony epistle. They're definitely different. Admittedly, some might even prefer that we render a few of these films or Disney+ series apocryphal, or not "canon" (or just forgotten altogether: I'm looking at you *Eternals, Marvels, Love and Thunder*). The "Multiverse Saga", as it's come to be known, has had some hits but many misses.

And speaking of canon, most people know there was a *decade* of movies before Iron Man birthed the MCU that bore the Marvel moniker, but certainly weren't "canon" in terms of continuity. What may be the best part of the mixed bag multiverse movies has been the ingenuity to recognize and lovingly embrace a host of "pre-MCU" Marvel films, folding them in and recognizing them as no longer apocryphal but perhaps akin to the Old Testament. Now, a whole new generation is going back and experiencing them for the first time as part of our "MARVEL-Us" era.

As a pastor, I've known many Christians who've read the gospels and some New Testament letters, but rarely dipped back into the Old Testament books of the Bible. They're not even sure if they're relevant, and some churches even downplay how foundational and essential they are to a full understanding of the New Testament, and what Jesus really came to do, all that he fulfilled and how all that prophecy plays into it. It's all important, and many NT passages reference the OT, folding them all into one framework.

Now, we're not comparing apples to apples here, but the reality is that we wouldn't have the quality or quantity of the Marvel Cinematic Universe if not for these founding father films: the original *Spider-man* and *X-Men* trilogy, just to name a few. And before them came *Blade*, who virtually saved Marvel from bankruptcy in the 90s and planted the first seed that has grown into a multiverse-branching and money-making Marvel tree.

So, we can use a few of the post-Infinity films as gateways into these OT (or O.G.) Marvel movies and see some of their value, the deeper discoveries and themes to be found within. And we'll also rocket back to check in on one remaining character from the Infinity saga who most desperately needed a narrative resolution.

Speaking of swinging, we'll pick up with the character who had just swung his way into a web of trouble…

SPIDER-MAN, NO WAY HOME:
History Three-Petes Itself

"Tragedy. What else can I call it? What more need be said? The damage, the destruction, you saw it with your own eyes. When will people wake up and realize that everywhere Spider-Man goes, chaos and calamity ensue? Everything Spider-Man touches comes to ruin." - J. Jonah Jameson

If we're being honest, we DO see what Jameson's saying with our own eyes. The central chaos and calamity in this film are the direct result of a rash decision made by Spider-man, though it's aided by Doctor Strange. The damage to his life, and his friends, from the reveal of his identity obviously hurts, but his cockamamie idea to erase the world's collective memory (and then babble incessantly so as to mess up Doctor Strange's mystical cocktail) causes all the resultant damage and destruction. Fortunately, not everything he touches comes to ruin, and an omelet IS made out of all the broken eggs.

Peter Parker (Maguire): *My Uncle Ben was killed… my fault.*

Peter Parker (Garfield): *I lost... I lost Gwen… I couldn't save her.*

Peter Parker (Holland): *I can still hear her voice in my head. Even after she was hurt, she said to me that we did the right thing. She told me that with great power…*

Peter Parker (Maguire): *…comes great responsibility.*

Great Power, Great Responsibility.

Spider-man is the most popular comic book character on the planet, and you'd be hard-pressed at this point to find someone who doesn't know his primary tagline. It's almost become a joke at this point (and that's a shame). This lesson, in every Spider-man story, is learned at great cost. In *Spider-man* (2002) Tobey Maguire's Peter gives us the most classic version of the tale, as his prideful negligence allows a crook to escape who later murders his uncle. In *The Amazing Spider-man* (2012) Andrew Garfield's Peter repeats that same sin of omission, then compounds it by promising his girlfriend Gwen's dying father that he'll stay away from her. His continued dalliance (not keeping one's promise, a sin we talked about earlier) indirectly leads to her death. And now, Tom Holland's Spider-man incites a chain of events that undeniably links to his Aunt May's tragic fate. If not for the crazy spell and scheme, there would never have been a Green Goblin to kill May. It seems that in every universe, the wall-crawler is destined to learn this lesson about power only at great and terrible cost: it's his original sin.

However, a failing we see in all three Spider-men (and the comics they come from) is that Peter Parker tends to take all the burden upon himself. While on one hand we discussed how Pete doesn't share Tony Stark's *obvious* form of pride (*see SM: Far From Home*) we see a more insidious forms, as he conceives his plan and seeks out Doctor Strange without ever discussing it with MJ, Ned, or May, the people he's doing it for! It's just another manifestation of pride comingled with guilt. The other versions of Peter at least have the excuse that no one else knows their secret identity, so outside counsel can be tricky. Peter has no excuse here, when in fact MJ herself reassures him that *"I wouldn't change a thing."* He decides to fix everything *for* them instead of fixing it *with* them, ignoring another important moral command that includes humility.

> *"Bear one another's burdens, and so fulfill the law of Christ."*
>   - Galatians 6:2

Spider-man's villains rarely share his sense of morality and will even mock him for it. Norman Osborne's split personality unleashed a violent, hedonist narcissist that plagued Tobey Maguire's Spidey.

> *"Your weakness, Peter, is morality! It's choking you! Can you feel it? I've watched you… struggling to have everything you want while the world tries to make you choose. Gods don't have to choose. We take."* - The Green Goblin

Norman represents someone who gives in to the lust of their own flesh. Otto Octavius was overwhelmed emotionally and gave into the lying voices of his robotic arms, seduced to do evil by an AI approximation we might liken to listening to the devil, the tempting and justifying whispers of our spiritual enemies. Pride in an overestimated intellect is the reptilian Curt Connors' downfall, whereas the sandy Flint Marko was originally tempted by easy money, and the electric Max Dillon plays the victim card to justify his abuses; in this cornucopia of characters we see the wide variety of temptations that can lead us astray from responsibly using the powers we've been given.

What's wonderful about this movie's multiverse magic is that it provides us a Peter Parker trifecta; the more experienced Peters can caution, protect, and even intercede where the newest Peter lacks wisdom. Part of this is sharing longer term sins that young Peter may be able to avoid. Maguire's Spidey confesses that he sought out his uncle's killer to exact vengeance. Garfield's Spidey confesses how a root of bitterness led to violence. James 5:16 exhorts us to *"confess your sins to each other"* while Galatians 6:1 warns us *"keep watch on yourself, lest you too be tempted."* While it's obviously odd that these are different versions of Peter confessing and cautioning himself, it's a reminder of the cathartic and communal way the church is called to be vulnerable with one another, so we needn't each make the same mistakes.

Initially, Peter rejects the idea of helping the villains; he simply wants to send them home so someone else can deal with them (until he realizes most of them will die, of course; that's a line too far for him). But it was May's expressed wisdom at the homeless shelter that puts Peter on the path, and here we come to the main theme:

Peter: *May, their chance of getting help is way better back where they came from. Sending them home, that's the best thing we can do for them.*

May: *For them? Or for yourself?*
Look around you. This is what we do. We help people.

(REALLY) Loving Your Enemies

Sure, *Ant Man and the Wasp* was the first obvious MCU example of **"love your enemies"** up to this point, but *No Way Home* truly brings it home as Peter (okay, Peters) literally find the cures for their legacy roster of villains. They confront them not to fight, but to heal. One by one, enemies are turned into allies. Otto even turns and helps them as they struggle to cure the others. Holland's Peter emotionally loses control against the Goblin and lashes out to kill him in vengeance, but Maguire's Spidey stays his hand (even takes a grievous backstabbing wound from Osborne) as an example that allows Holland/Peter's better nature to assert itself; together, they cure Norman Osborne of his insanity. As May encouraged Peter to her dying breath: they help people.

> *"You have heard that it was said, 'You shall love your neighbor and hate your enemy.' But I say to you, Love your enemies and pray for those who persecute you, so that you may be sons of your Father who is in heaven."* - Matthew 5:43-45

Then comes one of the most unique sacrifices yet for the MCU. Like Tony and Natasha did before him, Peter Parker chooses to lay down his life… only unlike them, he's going to have to live with it.

> Doctor Strange: *…you gotta understand… everyone who knows and loves you, we… we'd have no memory of you. It would be as though you never existed.*

> Peter Parker: *I know. Do it.*

Bear in mind that yes, he's concocting a plan and not getting much counsel again… but this is a world-ending, no time, snap-decision situation and quantifiably different. Also, he's taking responsibility for the grievous mistake he made and accepting the consequences. There's a nobility to it that almost surpasses the noble death of Stark and others, surprisingly connected to instruction Jesus gives about how we give to others:

> *"Beware of practicing your righteousness before other people in order to be seen by them… do not let your left hand know what your right hand is doing, so that your giving may be in secret."*
> - Matthew 6:1-3

No one will ever know what Peter did in terms of being Spider-man, from helping in the Infinity War or the Endgame or all his other actions. No reformed villain will remember that this Peter

Parker cured them. Ned and MJ won't remember how he loved them, and no one will know what he sacrificed to put the multiverse back together. Tony Stark got a funeral, tears were shed for Nat, but Peter Parker gives it all up and gets... nothing. It's the epitome of selfless sacrifice, unless perhaps there's someone loving watching from above. In fact, the viewer in a small way acts as the "omniscient" stand-in for God as we leave the theater, bearing testimony to what Peter Parker has done in secret. It's the comfort of the Christian that—as we find less far out, comic book ways to model this selflessness in our own lives—Jesus reassures us that our *"Father who sees what is done in secret will reward you."* - Matt. 6:4

In the end all the accolades have been removed, his relationships have been erased, and this Peter finds himself in the same boat that the previous Peters frequently suffered: no one to confide in. But the lessons he's learned from May and his more experienced Peter-peers has propped him up against depression or giving up. Instead, he's suiting up and swinging back to basics, ready to serve as your friendly neighborhood Spider-man. Personally, this is the way I like him, and I hope we'll see more New York, street-level stories (perhaps with Matt Murdock, whose cameo in this film gives me an entry point to talk about *Daredevil* later). I know some people like multiverse Spidey, and there is a whole "Spider-verse" for those who love that cross-universe craziness. But someone *else* will be getting tangled in the multiverse next...

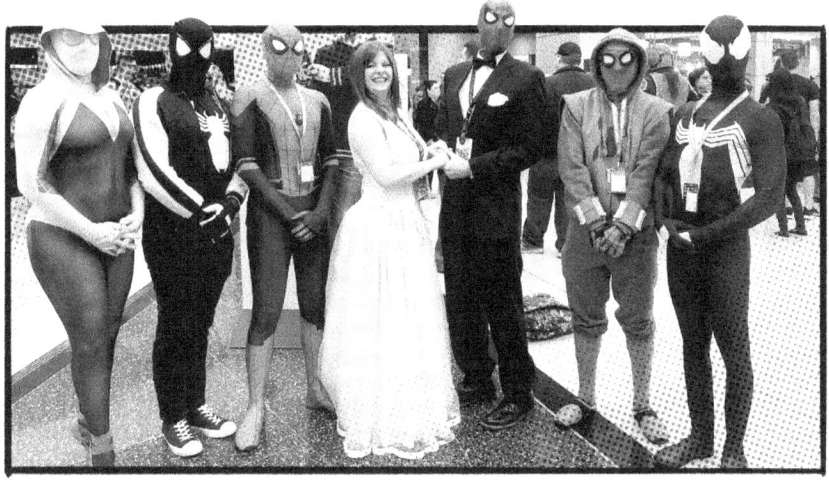

Just to be clear: you're going home with the one in the tux, honey.

DOCTOR STRANGE IN THE MULTIVERSE OF MADNESS: Vomit, Knives, and Happiness

"You break the rules and you become the hero. I do it and I become the enemy. That doesn't seem fair." - Wanda Maximoff

I enjoyed *WandaVision…* and I enjoyed this movie. The Doctor's second solo outing made big box office but garnered mixed reception with critics, some of whom were irritated at how they handled the Scarlet Witch. After getting to know her, and her resurrected paramour, in the first MCU Disney+ series, fans not only grew fonder of the character, but argued she had already learned a valuable lesson about tampering with people and reality in that series. She tried to force a normal life, husband and kids, by unnatural means… didn't she already learn and grow? Yet here she is, doing it again in an even more desperate and deranged fashion.

Our Metaphorical Vomit

Well, we've already covered this idea with Tony Stark in terms of regression, but—perhaps ironically—it bears repeating. There's a huge difference between learning a lesson and truly heeding its wisdom, between knowledge and application. And when it comes to not just Wanda's nature, but all human nature, our covetousness can easily drag us back into former sins. If comic book characters learn in a "one-and-done" story scenario, it may satisfy viewers but it honestly isn't very realistic. Even scripture returns to this topic.

"Like a dog that returns to his vomit is a fool who repeats his folly." - Proverbs 26:11

"What the true proverb says has happened to them: 'The dog returns to its own vomit, and the sow, after washing herself, returns to wallow in the mire.'" - 2 Peter 2:22

The film also features witchcraft and spirits by way of the evil influence of the Darkhold, the book which was a carryover from the end of *Wandavision* (and—in my opinion—clear foreshadowing). When our hearts are tempted, it doesn't help to have evil spirits egging us on, even influencing or entering non-Christians, pouring gasoline on smoldering, sinful desire. In fact, Jesus gives a grim warning about demonic influence:

"…they enter and dwell there, and the last state of that person is worse than the first." - Matthew 12:43

We may not like this narrative, but is it a truer narrative than we want to admit? How often do WE return to sins we "repent" of or learn from? The alcoholic, the addict, lust, etc. As for someone who "repents" but is apart from Christ? They are even more subject to spirits as much as Wanda is to the Darkhold. This might not be the narrative Marvel fans wanted for Wanda, but we can't say it's "bad writing" when it's an all-too-accurate depiction of human sin.

"Just because someone stumbles and loses their way doesn't mean they're lost forever." - Professor Charles Xavier

And just like that, this series embraced BOTH formative franchises in two films, back-to-back. *Spider-man: No Way Home* opened a portal to director Sam Raimi's original Spider-man film in 2002, and now *Doctor Strange in the Multiverse of Madness* (directed by Raimi, no less) pays homage to the 2000 *X-Men* movie (with music from the 90s cartoon), acknowledging the seeds and roots of the MCU's success. It also gives us a portal into the X-films which I'll discuss later in the chapter. Xavier's words ring true for Wanda as she does come to her senses in a way not unlike Samson in the Bible; her repentance turns out to be a death-bed conversion (not unlike Doctor Octopus in *Spider-man 2*) as she brings the building down around her to destroy the Darkhold forever.

Passing the Scalpel

"Because Stephen… you have to be the one holding the knife. And I always respected you for it, but I couldn't love you for it."
  - Dr. Christine Palmer

Doctor Stephen Strange was an undeniably skilled surgeon and usually at the center of every surgery he attended. Not long after, he rose quickly to be Master of the Mystic Arts… basically the center again, in another field. Then he had the unenviable task of knowing and directing critical affairs in the Infinity Saga, including the very clinical decisions to allow the "snap" and then years later send Tony Stark to his death. The critical moves and decision-making have been in his hands, and when one wields that control—and often does it well—it can be difficult to let go and trust in someone else. Here, we see the mantle of Master has gone to Wong—pricking Stephen's pride—and other variants of Strange have taken on more and more power to their detriment (and others). Yet, when the time comes to take America Chavez's power and be the one behind the wheel, he instead encourages and equips her to use it and ultimately save the day.

> "...and what you have heard from me in the presence of many witnesses entrust to faithful men, who will be able to teach others also." - 2 Timothy 2:2

In the Old Testament we see Moses struggle with "holding the knife" and overseeing all affairs of the people, until his father-in-law Jethro persuades him to delegate and distribute authority. The apostle Paul not only entrusts young Timothy with authority but also teaches him to pass it on as well. So, while a Christian might take issue with the modern Disney mantra of "trust yourself" (as Strange encourages young America Chavez) or "trust your heart", it's a redeemable message if what we *actually* trust in is what God has entrusted us *with*: a new heart and His Word. Just as America has been given her amazing powers, Christians are given a new heart—and accompanying gifts—by God. Sometimes we need that Strange—or Pauline—encouragement to live into those gifts and face our obstacles and spiritual enemies.

Wrong Question, Wrong Answer

Stephen Strange: *Are you happy?*

Wong: *That's an... interesting question... Sometimes I do wonder about my other lives. Yet I remain grateful in this one. Even with its tribulations.*

We find the question "are you happy?" Popping up at least three times in this movie, and both Strange and Wanda are wrestling with regret and what "might have been" in "another life". It's not an unusual human musing, though unlike the magic users in this movie we can't seek "multiversal" solutions. Wong dodges Stephen's direct query about happiness and instead speaks of contentment:

"But godliness with contentment is great gain, for we brought nothing into the world, and we cannot take anything out of the world. But if we have food and clothing, with these we will be content. But those who desire to be rich fall into temptation, into a snare, into many senseless and harmful desires that plunge people into ruin and destruction." - 1 Timothy 6:6-10

As the verse describes, Wanda has fallen into a snare; the "riches" she desires are the children she doesn't have. Similarly, Strange's desire to be "rich" would be to have Christine, and both are tested as they focus on where they are unhappy. The attitude Wong calls his friend to consider is far godlier, while even recognizing this life will contain tribulation.

"Count it all joy, my brothers, when you meet trials of various kinds, for you know that the testing of your faith produces steadfastness. And let steadfastness have its full effect, that you may be perfect and complete, lacking in nothing." - James 1:2-4

Wong is the steadfast soul we see in this film, and Stephen Strange is strengthened by that, even to the point of bowing respectfully to his friend in the end. Of course, there's a major plot point to be rejected wherein Strange uses the power of the Darkhold (evil) to combat evil… but the ending of the film indicates that it's probably an error that will have consequences in the future. And our MCU protagonists do tend to make poor decisions, especially…

GUARDIANS OF THE GALAXY, VOLUME 3: Perfected

"I don't learn. One of my issues." - Peter Quill

Earlier in the book I compared Tony Stark and Captain America with two pivotal biblical figures: the irrevocably altered Iron Man with the transformed Paul, and Steve Rogers with a *post-resurrection* Peter. I realized, while watching the end of the Guardians trilogy, that Peter Quill is also a lot like his namesake in the Bible, only in Quill's case he's the *pre-resurrection* Peter. Prior to Jesus Christ's pivotal weekend Peter is shown in scripture to be impetuous, speaking without thinking, stumbling and sinking and faltering on his road of faith. He's an example of "failing upward" and this is just as applicable to our stumbling Star-Lord. At the beginning of the film Peter's at another low point, and only Rocket's imminent death shakes him back into hero mode. At the end of the film, he knows this life course isn't sustainable, that he needs to slow down and learn what it truly means to live and be whole.

And yet, almost every character has been changed by their interaction and relationship with Peter Quill. Drax, Rocket, Nebula, Mantis, Groot 2.0 and even Gamora have grown in some fashion. It's a ray of hope in terms of how many of us—even in the midst of our brokenness—can be used by God as an example to others, sometimes even despite ourselves. As this movie opens, we see that the "new" Gamora and Quill have effectively swapped places; she's the Ravager out for herself, much like Peter was in Volume 1 (she belittled him outside the Broker's office when they first met, as she was already on a more virtuous quest to defy Thanos). While she isn't transformed back into her old self by the film's end, seeds have been planted and the warrior woman has been encouraged to be something more. The Guardian films seem to point out the reality that our hope is a slow, often laborious road toward perfection, one that is achieved by the influence of someone special in our lives.

"For by a single offering he has perfected for all time those who are being sanctified." - Hebrews 10:14

Peter is used as an archetype, pointing toward that sanctifying and saving path for many characters in the Guardians' narrative. This Star-Lord is far from the perfect "single offering", but he reminds us of another archetype that pointed toward the one who truly would be. Joseph in the Old Testament was sold into slavery, worked in the house of Potiphar, got imprisoned, but ultimately rose to become legendary with a high position, saving Egypt and Israel from a famine. Quill is likewise abducted into slavery, raised in the house of the Ravagers, imprisoned, but rises to be the legendary Star-Lord and save the galaxy. As a new testament parallel, he's akin to a Christian in community rather than a Christ-figure, so the growth is more mutual as they inspire one another. Groot was raised by this community, which leads to his saving of Adam Warlock, who is inspired by that loving act and in turn saves Quill's life in the climax. So, while he's not the "perfecter" referred to in Hebrews,

Peter Quill points to the need for sanctification and a savior… someone truly worthy of imitation.

Perhaps the one most changed by Peter through relationship over the course of these movies is Rocket… though we find out that it's not so much *changed* as *restored*.

> *"Someday I'm gonna make great machines that fly. And me and my friends are gonna go flying together, into the forever and beautiful sky."* - Rocket (Raccoon)

There's something sweet and innocent about the young Rocket we're introduced to in flashback, alongside animal friends that paint a portrait of love and family. But we also find out they've all been plucked from happier origins and placed in a cursed world presided over by a false god seeking his own vision of perfection.

> High Evolutionary: *All I wanted to do… was to make things… perfect!*

> Rocket: *You didn't want to make things perfect. You just hated things the way they are.*

This problem turns up in all sorts of demagogues and worldly systems that try to step into the role of curing our admittedly cursed world—and sin nature—a curse that only God and the gospel can address. Things aren't great the way they are, but a flawed creator almost always winds up making a Frankenstein's monster in their quest for perfection. The High Evolutionary's stated intent is to create a "perfect" society, but he's inherently flawed: jealous, spiteful, even self-loathing. How can he possibly create a perfect anything? When Rocket solves a problem that he couldn't, the "high" one can't rejoice that the answer is found; he's simply filled with rage that he didn't do it. The perfection he's seeking isn't for the world or anything lofty, but merely for himself.

From cancel-culture to Christian culture, men and women often step into the role of perfecting this world instead of trusting in the perfect one (Jesus) who has overcome the world. The perfection sought here is more like the Aryans trying to create their *Übermensch* or the Khmer rouge killing anyone with "imperfections". This is man playing God by way of social engineering.

152

"There is no God! That's why I stepped in!!!"
 - The High Evolutionary

Thanos, Ego, and now the High Evolutionary… a recurring theme in these movies is created beings with god complexes. From Joseph Stalin to Pol Pot (and the fictional Red Skull) secular leaders and their systems of government often devolve into fascist regimes that commit heinous acts in the names of a "better world" just like the High Evolutionary. Even Christians can go astray from their Great Commission (calling people out of this world with the hope of the kingdom to come) and instead believe they can force the kingdom now through legalism and legislation. Our modern, more secular Americana reflects this mentality as well with identity politics. We start deciding who gets to have a voice in the "better world" we're arrogantly creating. We effectively start acting like gods. Worse, like the caged animals we see experimented on and mutilated in the name of this better world, we keep making promises of utopia that the people we're promising them to are never going to see. The only way we might achieve such a thing is if we could actually pass the litmus test Jesus set before us:

"*You therefore must be perfect, as your heavenly Father is perfect."* - Matthew 5:48

As the High Evolutionary's Counter Earth demonstrates, we may find ways to restrain evil, but we can never neutralize the sin nature. Only God can fix that forever, and *Guardians* once again reminds us that no creature can step into the role of god or declare themselves Creator.

And the possibility of that real Creator is explored by Rocket's death experience; the flatlined guardian doesn't come face-to-face with God, but (like Thanos talking with the departed Gamora via the Soul Stone in *Infinity War*) our often-ornery raccoon gets a glimpse of the afterlife. Lamenting that he has no purpose, that he was *"made for nothing"* and is just something *"to be thrown away"* he is encouraged to consider a different view by his deceased friend:

"There are the hands that made us, and then there are the hands that guide their hands." - Lylla

This acknowledgement of a Creator, working behind the machinations of men and monsters with a purpose and intent that perhaps Rocket—and we—*can* put our trust in is a powerful message of hope. The message here is not to believe in ourselves, or put any faith in perfecting ourselves individually or corporately, but to trust that hands beyond our sight are working all things for a higher purpose.

> *"And we know that for those who love God all things work together for good, for those who are called according to his purpose."* - Romans 8:28

Although the *Guardians of the Galaxy* series might be a story where we consider the characters are growing and being perfected by happy accidents, shaped simply by bouncing off of each other and their shared circumstances, *Volume 3* intimates that there is providence at play… that there is a divine direction sculpting these characters into the roles they've been called to embody, even despite the intentions of their earthly fathers or masters. For Rocket, this leads to his becoming leader of a new team, the baton-passing (or knife-passing) notion we just glimpsed in the Doctor Strange sequel now manifest in the next generation of Guardians, discipled by imperfect peers and moving forward with the hope that they're being perfected and directed by higher, guiding hands.

> *"No one has ever seen God; if we love one another, God abides in us and his love is perfected in us. By this we know that we abide in him and he in us, because he has given us of his Spirit."*
>   - 1 John 4:12-13

If someone as reckless and mean-spirited as Rocket can find a comic book style sanctification, then maybe there's even hope for…

DEADPOOL AND WOLVERINE: The Anchor Being

> *"We need you to hope again…"*
>   - Professor Charles Xavier, *X-Men: Days of Future Past*

Was the MARVEL-Us era over? As many were fearing that the MCU had passed its prime in 2024, or perhaps faded into irrelevance with poorly produced (and poorly received) entries like *The Eternals, Thor: Love and Thunder, The Marvels* (and some Disney+ shows best forgotten) a couple veteran superhero actors suited up to breathe life back into the box office and perhaps show us that the injured Marvel brand had a healing factor after all. In doing this, fans also got a love letter surpassing *Spider-man: No Way Home* and *Doctor Strange in the Multiverse of Madness* in terms of recognizing, embracing, and celebrating all things Marvel at the movies.

The MCU might have sprouted in 2008 and blossomed through 2019, but Ryan Reynolds decided to expose its roots, stretching back into the previous century. Much like a memory-addled Wolverine, Marvel's film history stretches back further than many recall, and the current era owes its present success to key "anchor beings" in its past.

Blade saved Marvel from bankruptcy in 1998, looking a lot like *The Matrix* in terms of style and effects though actually preceding it by a year. The vampire, of course, is a powerful metaphor for the sin nature (I covered this in the first *Cinemagogue* book and won't repeat it here). However, the character of Blade—a "Daywalker"—as some kind of unexpected "incarnation" strikes a fascinating figure. Part man and part vampire, yet with none of the latter's weaknesses, he's an evil-opposing hero who can literally "walk in the light"… another pale but provocative image of savior that the Christian can clearly see. And without his trilogy, we might not have the MCU.

Similarly, *Spider-man* topped the box office at the turn of the century and helped spawn more Marvels like *The Fantastic Four, Daredevil, Elektra* and others. But a few years before *Spider-man*, the world was introduced to Hugh Jackman and his family of mutants courtesy of 20th Century Fox (ushering in the 21st century with its release in 2000). If *Blade* was Marvel's conception, *X-Men* was the real birth. Or perhaps *Blade* is grandfather and *Spider-man* and *X-Men* are effectively mother and father to these MARVEL-Us offspring. Without these movies, and Wolverine in particular, the MCU wouldn't exist as we know it today… which is fitting, then, that two of these legacy characters now enter the MCU and seek to save its existence in a very meta fashion.

"What IS this place?" - Wolverine, *X-Men*

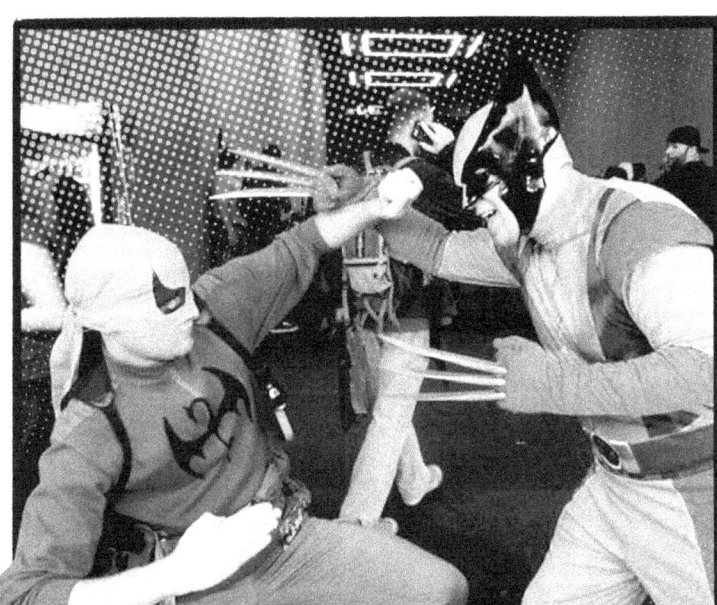

Deadpool's right, he'll be doing it 'til he's 90…

A Brief History of [Logan's] Time

I could devote *almost* as many pages to the X-Men saga as the Infinity Saga (and perhaps I did, in some alternate timeline) but instead, let's take a flashback look through Logan's lenses at the groundbreaking superhero series that got us—and him—here today. It's fitting, as I've often referred to the original three X-Men films as not truly being X-Men movies at all, but rather comprising the "Wolverine/Rogue" trilogy. The viewer follows a male and female protagonist as they encounter two mutant titans—Professor X and Magneto—and their philosophies, with the respective X-Men and Brotherhood of Mutants as mostly supporting characters.

Much has been made of Professor X and Magneto evolving into a parallel for the civil rights movement in the 60s, juxtaposing the peaceful, non-violent methods of Martin Luther King and the more aggressive, violent methods of Malcolm X. One is for teaching and modeling equality, believing co-existence is possible, while the other is for supremacy, segregation and using force to achieve goals. It's a fair comparison, and many writers used the comic to speak indirectly to ethnic prejudice. This would be a primary theme until the franchise was co-opted by the LGBTQ+ community in the 1990s.

The character of Marie (Rogue) best represents the original idea of the X-Men comic, in terms of troubled teenagers taken in by a caring school. Mutant powers triggering in one's teens always made it a metaphor for puberty, when many feel confused with growth spurts, body changes and more, often isolated and even bullied while trying to navigate the transition. They seek people and peers who understand what they're going through. Rogue goes from being shunned and outcast from her family and the world she knew to a new family with special gifts… from people who shrink from her to people who care for her. It's much like the early church, or places where being outed as a Christian means excommunication (or worse). The X-Mansion is a great metaphor for the church, as this new family even features unique "gifts" to help each other and the stranger. In terms of fit, the church may be the best metaphor.

Rogue is brought into this world, chooses to follow Xavier's dream, and invests in this made family of X-Men. Wolverine's story is quite different, and ultimately the prime focus: in each film we see a distinct area of growth for the character of Logan. It's a trilogy of transformation:

- **X-MEN: From Selfish to Sacrificial**
  Logan is a lost creature we meet—like an animal—in a literal cage. He's just existing, getting money and booze and cigars, without a past and no thought of future… barely more than a beast (and no, not THAT Beast). In act one he's indifferent to Rogue and begrudgingly helps her. He's also a mocker of Xavier—*"what do they call you, wheels?"*—and the X-Men, but develops a genuine respect for them (save for Scott) and encourages Marie to stay with them. By the final act, he's willing to risk everything, even his life, to save her.

"…count others more significant than yourselves. Let each of you look not only to his own interests, but also to the interests of others." - Philippians 2:3

- **X2, X-MEN UNITED: From Solo to Sibling**

  Logan met the X-family in the first film, but still drove away at the end. He appreciates them, but is still a loner. This second story forces him to take on the mantle of an older brother or uncle as he protects the X-students, especially Bobby, Rogue and John. He uncovers some of his lost memories and former identity, forced to confront not only who he was, but who he will become. Encouraged and inspired by this mutant family, we see him near the climax holding a child, leaving his past (i.e. William Stryker) and choosing Charles Xavier's ensemble.

"Therefore, since we are surrounded by so great a cloud of witnesses, let us also lay aside every weight, and sin which clings so closely, and let us run with endurance the race that is set before us..." - Hebrews 12:1

- **X-MEN, THE LAST STAND: From Training to Teaching**

  We meet Logan in the danger room training students, and it's a great progression parallel of the Christian life: one goes from seeing the image of Christ in the gospel, then going from lost to found and having Christian family, and finally growing from just being a disciple to discipling others. When Logan's leading both the X-Men and the army men for the final fight, we see he's grown into the role Xavier encouraged him toward. And the final part of that is putting his old self to death... which is represented in his killing of the character Jean Grey, who has effectively become the feral creature he was at the beginning of the first film. On top of that, he doesn't kill her from a seat of rage, but a heart of love. Many people don't like the way they shortchanged the classic Phoenix storyline, but in terms of a *Wolverine* trilogy it's a fitting finale.

"Put to death, therefore, whatever belongs to your earthly nature... You used to walk in these ways, in the life you once lived. But now you must also rid yourselves of all such things as these: anger, rage, malice... put on the new self, which is being renewed in knowledge in the image of its Creator."
  - Colossians 3:5-10

That might have been the end of it. *The Last Stand* came out in 2006 and was met with mixed reviews, but we all know two years later *Iron Man* made superhero films cooler than ever, and Twentieth Century Fox saw more potential in mutant movies, so Hugh Jackman took up the mantle again in the poorly reviewed *X-Men Origins: Wolverine* in 2009. The lackluster film at least filled the non-comics crowd in on some facts they didn't know about Logan, like his real name (James) and lengthy lifespan (born in 1832). That's why he looks the same age when we see his cameo in *X-Men: First Class*, the soft reboot prequel trilogy that started in 2011. Adjacent to that, however, Logan would get another solo film.

THE WOLVERINE: Immortality, Blessing or Curse?

"Eternity can be a curse. It hasn't been easy for you, living without time. A man can run out of things to care for, lose his purpose." - Ichiro Yashida

2013's *The Wolverine* put director James Mangold at the helm and gave us the deeper character study we wanted of a character who is seemingly immortal. Grieving the loss of Jean Grey from *The Last Stand*, it seems Logan has reached a point of his life where he feels the weight of Solomon's lament in Ecclesiastes: all things bring weariness, life has shown its tiresome repetition, and there is nothing for him except cursed, repeating cycles of grief under the sun. In real life, this is part of why God sent man out of the garden when evil entered the world; immortality in a sinful world would eventually feel just slightly north of Hell. This is why the young man Logan met in World War II, now a dying billionaire tech mogul, offers to "help" the weary Wolverine by removing his immortality.

Sadly, Logan is being manipulated by Yashida, and violent hijinks ensue. Despite all his talk about the value of a normal life and a meaningful death, the old man simply craves Logan's power and hides his true view of immortality until the end, as he taunts:

"Your mistake was to believe that a life without end can have no meaning—it is the only life that CAN."

This profound statement from the mouth of the film's antagonist contains a LOT of truth. In the grand scheme of things, what is a "meaningful death" (or life, for that matter) in a world where we go to ground, and that's it? The dead won't remember or retain any satisfaction in it, and resonance felt by friends or those around them eventually fades. In our hearts, we sense the importance of the eternal.

> *"I have seen the business that God has given to the children of man to be busy with. He has made everything beautiful in its time. Also, he has put eternity into man's heart…"*
>   - Ecclesiastes 3:10-11

The hole in Yoshida's logic is that a life without end—in our sin —amounts to nothing more than condemnation, now and forever. We need redemption first, then immortality.

> *"So we do not lose heart. Though our outer self is wasting away, our inner self is being renewed day by day. For this light momentary affliction is preparing for us an eternal weight of glory beyond all comparison, as we look not to the things that are seen but to the things that are unseen. For the things that are seen are transient, but the things that are unseen are eternal."*
>   - 2 Corinthians 4:16-18

Logan doesn't find Christ, of course, but instead of his nemesis' selfish immortality, or his own wallowing in guilt, the Wolverine ultimately decides to return to the meaning and purpose he knew before, the "gospel" of Charles Xavier, and just in time for…

X-MEN, DAYS OF FUTURE PAST: Perfection

As I mentioned earlier, I consider 2014 the zenith of the MARVEL-Us Era; this year not only gave us two of the best MCU films—*Captain America: The Winter Soldier* and the *Guardians of the Galaxy*—it also offered us *Big Hero 6,* one of Disney's best (underrated) animated films also based on a Marvel superhero comic. Even the Academy Award for Best Picture (and director, screenplay, and cinematography) went to *Birdman*, starring Michael

Keaton playing a washed-up superhero actor. The year would also yield three other marvelous franchises, but I'll get to those later.

On top of all this, the banner year gifted us with the crowning achievement of the *X-Men* franchise. The prequel series would focus more on how Charles Xavier and Erik "Magneto" Lehnsherr slowly became the old men we know… and yet their second film would stand out among the rest because of our claw-wielding fan favorite, as well as using time travel to bring the casts of the original and prequel series together.

"Just because someone stumbles and loses their way, doesn't mean they are lost forever." - Professor Charles Xavier

Imagine what it would be like to travel back in time with the task of motivating a down-and-out apostle Paul to get back to his job of missional evangelism… and now imagine you've been among the greatest doubters of that mission in your very rough-and-tumble Christian walk. This shares similarities with Logan's task in the film, motivating his former (or future) mentor to stay the course and hold on to the very dream Xavier would one day instill in him.

What's fascinating about this film is that it explores the flaws in both Professor X and Magneto's philosophies. While I paralleled Charles' school with the church earlier, the reality is it falls short; this is also why I put his "gospel" in quotes. The fact is that Erik rightly sees the irredeemable depravity in man; his assessment is truly biblical. Where the master of magnetism errs is in his response, taking vengeance into his own hands and acting out of hatred without mercy or love. Our wheelchair-bound Professor promotes (and acts in) a more Christ-like manner, but his faith in human nature is often his own undoing. Something *more* is needed, and the character Mystique in this film rejects both men to walk a middle path… one that more closely reflects the gospel and the church.

The blue, conflicted mutant played by Jennifer Lawrence sees through Charles' optimism but also rejects Erik's pragmatism. On their best days you could say Charles reflects mercy while Erik brings justice, but Mystique sees the need for both. She doesn't believe in Charles' dream of full integration but also rejects segregation. It's the tightrope walk that communities of Christians must walk: to be in the world but not of it, offering love and mercy to enemies and leaving vengeance to the Lord. Believers look to days of future blessing rather than expectations in this life, because someone incarnated in our world and planted the seeds for peace.

On our podcast episode for this movie, my Popcorn Theology co-host Miles Wallace said that at the end of this film—when Wolverine awakens in a time-transformed future—it's almost a vision of heaven. Those once dead have been raised to new life and the world has been healed of the curse that afflicted it, their enemies defeated. There is a relief in this film that rivals *Avengers: Endgame* and makes it one of the greatest superhero films of all time. There is a new X-Mansion and a changed earth, a comic book style foreshadowing of the new heaven and earth believers will see on that day we pass from this life to new life, with a holy city or "mansion" with many rooms: one for all who are in Jesus' school. The long struggle will be ended, and faith will be rewarded.

Happily ever after, right Wolverine? Well, at least until…

LOGAN: Seeking the Illusory Sun

"Where we're going, 'Eden…' It doesn't exist." - Logan

If *X-Men: Days of Future Past* is a shining example of a "Life Transcendent" story, the third solo Wolverine movie, *Logan*, arrived in 2017 and gave us an Oscar-worthy entry in "Life Under the Sun". Both films stand out as some of the best superhero entries in the genre, while embracing the North and South Poles of storytelling.

Despite all the optimism of previous entries, we find a former Wolverine broken again, a shell of the man he once was, now in the role of caregiver for a dementia-suffering Charles Xavier. The X-Men are dead, and mutants have seemingly been hunted or bio-engineered out of existence. Logan himself is finally succumbing to age and adamantium poisoning, carrying a bullet made of the same metal coating his claws, and contemplating suicide. Once again, he's lost hope. One might consider that all these ups and downs are due to different writers jerking the character in disparate directions, but

I've lived long enough to see people of faith go through as many or more shifts in life.

> Logan: *I always thought we were part of God's plan. Maybe... Maybe we were God's mistake.*

> Charles Xavier: *What a disappointment you are... When I found you, you were pursuing a career as a cage fighter. You were an animal... but we took you in. I gave you a family.*

Once again, we're forced to realize that the hope and faith Logan (and all these characters) have are in earthly things that don't last; naturally the "heaven" at the end of the last film faded. People age, they die, tragedies happen: there is no Eden to be had on this earth. And like a metallic cancer in his veins, Logan keeps sinking back into the darker parts of his own nature. His only motivation comes when confronted with the young, savage Laura who is effectively his daughter. While it's impressive to see Logan step up and run one final gauntlet, to give her and a few surviving mutants a chance for a better life, it isn't much more than the survival instincts of an animal, a Wolverine, fighting for its life and that of its offspring, the perpetuation of one's genes or species. Laura's eulogy—quoting the movie *Shane*—is a tearful reflection on life and human nature:

> *"A man has to be what he is, Joey. Can't break the mold. There's no living with the killing. There's no going back. Right or wrong, it's a brand. A brand that sticks."* - X-23

This might have been the final word in the Wolverine saga, a bleak finale that mirrors a secular worldview. It's also true, in terms of man's ability to ultimately change or fix himself, but of course the good news of Jesus Christ is that the mold *can* be broken—we can be more than we are—thanks to an intercessor and intermediary. The "brand" of our sin can be removed, thanks to the Son of God who came into our world. And while I cringe to make the comparison, Wolverine gets another chance thanks to someone who miraculously enters the world of the MCU.

DEADPOOL: Marvel Jesus?

Let me be crystal clear: Deadpool is not Jesus. The fact that he makes a reference like this in *Deadpool and Wolverine* upset some Christian friends of mine. It's also worth noting that every fourth sentence out of Deadpool's mouth is wholly inappropriate... yet I don't consider what he said to be actually blasphemous in this case. DP makes no claim to be Jesus in the film, only to be *Marvel's* messiah. Adjectives matter, and if Aslan can be a messiah in C.S. Lewis' *Chronicles of Narnia*, then in a fictional story set in another reality Deadpool could be that universe's savior. In some ways, he is... at least from a box office perspective as mentioned earlier. Part of Deadpool's humor is making meta-commentary, and the MCU was flatlining before he and Hugh gave it a shot of adrenaline. They also brought back a simple narrative approach and may yet save this cinematic universe from the sin of preaching identity politics in lieu of good storytelling (more on that in chapter 8).

The first *Deadpool* film debuted at the end of Twentieth Century Fox's X-Franchise, which officially became an ex-franchise in 2020, lasting two decades with thirteen films and two television series. Wade Wilson, the mocking mutant mercenary, made quite an impression, breaking the fourth wall and making fun of comic book movies while at the same time loving and reveling in them. *Deadpool 2* brought more of the same, while thankfully walking back some unnecessary sex and nudity. They even released a more family friendly version, *Once Upon a Deadpool*, because his snarky wit appeals to all ages. There are verses against mocking that give some Christians pause, but contextually those warnings are against mocking God, or the things of God. Personally, when I read Elijah mocking the prophets of Baal in 1 Kings 18, I hear Ryan Reynold's voice. And when Jesus says the Pharisees ***"strain out a gnat and swallow a camel"*** the hyperbolic language sounds familiar.

Mockery has its place, and in *Deadpool and Wolverine* (oh look, we're finally back to the actual film this section is about!) we see a form of mockery that points out faults and flaws from a place of love. It's clear that the hands behind the movie (actors, screenwriters, director) treasure the *X-Men*, *The Avengers*, *Spider-man*, *Blade*, while at the same time mocking all things Marvel *because* they love it and are willing to have fun with it. They know that Twentieth Century Fox made mistakes, Disney has made mistakes, Marvel comics makes mistakes, not to mention other mistakes. (*Green Lantern*, Ryan?) The two title characters are flawed and make numerous errors. It reminds me of some Christian wisdom I received years ago, that we should take God seriously and ourselves less so. When we take ourselves and our man-made endeavors too seriously, we tend to (alternately) take God lightly.

So, on the one hand *Deadpool and Wolverine* doesn't take itself seriously… yet surprisingly, beneath the snarky veneer there is some multi-layered meta-commentary that's worth considering. Deadpool is a fool, and the "worst Wolverine" we're introduced to in the film carries guilt and shame; they embody the same traits the Guardians of the Galaxy did and follow that same narrative parallel with God (or the screenwriter) using foolish things to shame the wise. We should understand that trope by now. More interesting is the concept they come up with about what holds universes together.

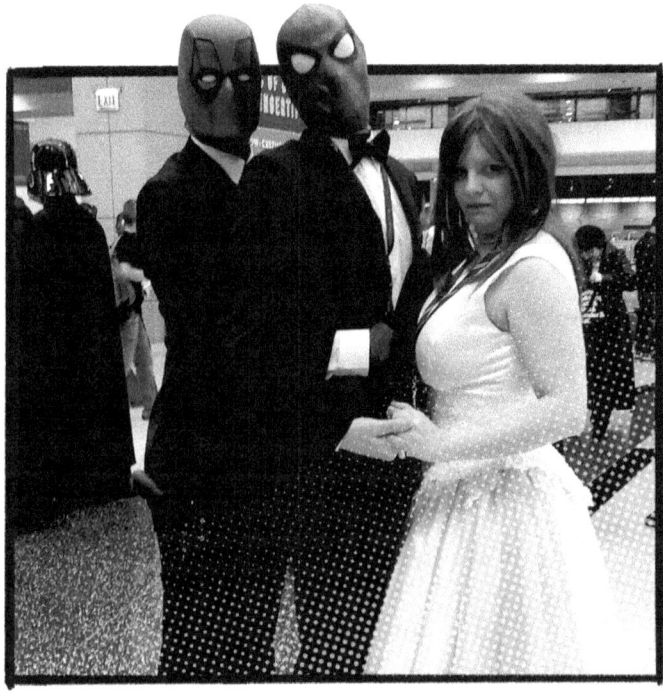

Umm, Wade? This isn't what I meant about holding things together.

"This is your universe, Mr. Wilson. That is what happens when a universe loses its anchor being. See how it decays from the inside? This is how a reality dies... an anchor being is an entity of such vital importance that when they die, their whole world slowly withers out of existence." - Mr. Paradox

The movie, of course, is playing with some meta-commentary here. The X-Men franchise withered after the movie *Logan* (where he died). Likewise, the MCU has been struggling since its formative character—Tony Stark—died in *Avengers: Endgame*. It's also true of any fictional "universe" formed around a central character. You can't have a lasting "Spider-verse" without Spider-man. Many franchises have flailed and failed after the fan favorite character is killed (or the central, popular actor leaves the show). They were the "anchor beings" without which the story can no longer be sustained. The question is, does this point to something deeper here?

"Long ago, at many times and in many ways, God spoke to our fathers by the prophets, but in these last days he has spoken to us by his Son, whom he appointed the heir of all things, through whom also he created the world. He is the radiance of the glory of God and the exact imprint of his nature, and he upholds the universe by the word of his power." - Hebrews 1:1-3

This is your universe, Mr. Christian. Jesus is the anchor being that not only spoke our universe into existence, but according to scripture it is upheld—its very fabric sustained—continually by his power. Without him, reality dies. Fortunately, his incarnation and death didn't lead to our withering out of existence, because he rose again three days later. In fact, his death was necessary to keep us from withering and decaying in our sin. He's the creator, director, show runner, lead actor and main character.

The problem is, some of us are like the arrogant Wade Wilson, and the proper response is Mr. Paradox's laughter and correction:

"Can you imagine if you were the anchor being? Haha. Ah. No."

Wade faces the humbling reality that he's not the anchor being of the story, yet he has a part to play. This is the lesson every Christian faces in the light of truth. We're not the anchor being in the universe or even in "our story" but (like Deadpool) we can be used to accomplish things, hand-in-hand, with brothers and sisters in Christ.

Logan believes he's done something for which he can never atone. He believes himself beyond redemption, and it takes someone breaking through into his universe to pick him up in his brokenness and put him on a path of redemption. Uh-oh, here's where Wade Wilson gets another Jesus-parallel (don't let it go to your head, DP). Logan turns back to the comic book "gospel" of Charles Xavier, and literally accomplishes things hand-in-hand with his new brother in arms, Wade.

And here we have a simple restorative journey that highlights both sides of the gospel coin and its effect: the proud get humbled, and the broken get lifted out of the mire, both put on that narrow road down the middle, trusting that there is an anchor being holding us, and everything, together.

Scene 2: **A Few Final Lessons**

Without bullet-pointing Wolverine's X-filled films individually, we can close out this MARVEL-Us journey with some final lessons:

- **We need confession and community…** *(SM: No Way Home)*
- **…as we seek to have grateful hearts.** *(Doctor Strange: MOM)*
- **In our sufferings together, we can have hope.** *(GoTG Vol. 3)*
- **We may struggle mightily to hold on to it.** *(X-Men to Logan)*
- **That hope requires an intercessory being.** *(DP & Wolverine)*

Where will the MCU go from here? It's hard to say, and difficult to know if *Deadpool and Wolverine* truly revived the universe or simply gave it one last ride. I predict the MARVEL-Us Era will officially end in the 2020s; there will surely be comic book movies, as ever, but the primary Hollywood focus will move on. The main thing I'm looking forward to after this book publishes is the revival of my favorite entry in the MCU that I simply can't do justice here…

DAREDEVIL: (soon to be) Born Again

"I'm not a religious man, but I've read bits and pieces over the years. Curiosity more than faith. But this one story... There was a man, he was traveling from Jerusalem..." - Wilson Fisk, *Daredevil Season One*

Comic books have always been, by nature, episodic: monthly installments with ongoing story arcs that many times aren't the best fit for feature films. Consider an entire season of Captain America in World War II, or Tony Stark's decline in *Iron Man 2* playing out across 13 episodes. The MCU did an amazing job weaving together the Infinity Saga, but there are character moments and story beats that would have benefited from a slower burn. This is exactly what we got in the first three seasons of *Daredevil*, and in my opinion it's the best the MCU has to offer, cinematically and spiritually.

Relying more on practical effects and amazing fight choreography, set in a dark and gritty New York City, it's stylistically closer to Christopher Nolan's work on *The Dark Knight* trilogy than what we're used to seeing in the MCU. Bringing us not only the title character but also the best version of The Punisher, *Daredevil* additionally gives us the most fully realized MCU villain in the form of Wilson Fisk (the Kingpin) played by Vincent D'Onofrio. The series is so rich in spiritual and moral themes, a whole book could be published examining the storylines and character quotes episode by episode. Hmm…

"I was pretty angry at God and bitter toward his world. How could a loving God blind me? Why? {Father Lantom} told me God's plan is like a beautiful tapestry, and the tragedy of being human is that we only get to see it from the back. All the ragged threads and muddy colors, we only get a hint at the true beauty that would be revealed if we could see the whole pattern on the other side, as God does." - Matt Murdock, *Daredevil Season Three*

"And we know that for those who love God all things work together for good, for those who are called according to his purpose." - Romans 8:28

Alternately, one could argue there's no need to do a commentary to sift metaphors and parallels in the series, since the conversations are so overt! When the first episode opens with actor Charlie Cox's blind (but alternately gifted) Matt Murdock confessing to a priest in a church, and the first season climaxes with the villain relating the story of the Good Samaritan and proclaiming himself to be the villain described in the parable, this show doesn't shy away from Christian themes but embraces them, wrestles with them, rejects them, and frequently returns to them. There are conversations about God, the devil, doubt, human nature, evil, justice, mercy and more, frequently between Daredevil and a man of the cloth. Matt Murdock is a doubting Catholic struggling with everything he once believed. Christianity isn't demonized or poorly stereotyped as it often is in Hollywood fare, though naturally it presents with Catholic trappings (because the clothes and cathedrals are the most visually dramatic, on both the comics page and the screen). The metaphysical musings feel natural and serve the story instead of forced moments for preaching. Christian filmmakers could learn a lot from this show; come to think of it, so could modern Hollywood.

Thankfully, Disney's original plans to reboot the character with new characters, recasting, a lighter tone and other terrible ideas got nixed as they saw how audiences were reacting to their post-Endgame direction. Things seem hopeful now that they've reversed course, though I'll be curious to see if the House of Mouse is daring enough to keep the "Devil of Hell's Kitchen's" musings about faith and God. If they disappoint fans yet again, it may signal that it's time for some of their comic book competitors to take center stage.

Speaking of that Distinguished Competition—with characters who make use of (bat-shaped) signals—perhaps it's time to shift gears and look at how Warner Brothers helped usher in, and then piggy-backed on, the MARVEL-US Era as well. While lacking in the same level of acclaim and success, the last decade of DC's offerings is rife with as much or more religious symbolism that's worth exploring.

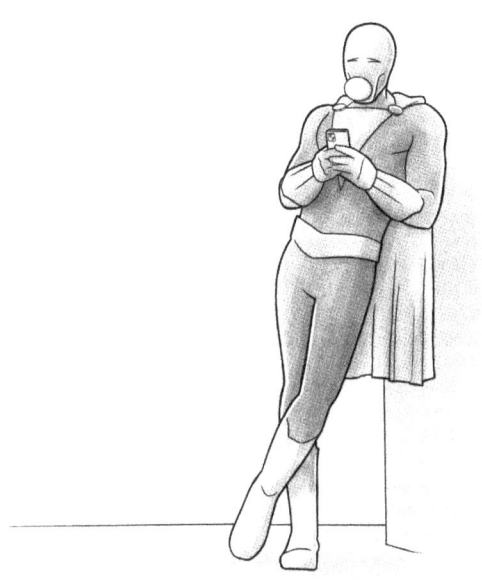

Act 6: **Justice Lag**

or

"Up, Down, and Sideways..."

Scene 1: **Credit Where Credit is Due**

"You really started something..." - Jim Gordon, *Batman Begins*

Before Iron Man's film began with ACDC's "Back in Black", Bruce Wayne had slipped back into black three years earlier; sure, it was *The Dark Knight* that would make the world take notice, but the full Nolan trilogy is at least equally responsible for the resultant superhero-dominated theaters of the decade that followed. And perhaps Bats owes a bit of his return to the black-leathered X-Men and Blade before him, much like we discussed how the MCU benefited last chapter. Still, if we go further back than *Blade* in 1998, we see the primary heroes of DC dominating the box office for twenty years. Superman essentially owned the 80s and Batman claimed the 90s (both started in 1979 and 1989 respectively, but then cashed in on sequels throughout the subsequent decade).

Beyond film, DC's animated shows garnered the most acclaim and viewership, from Batman and Superman to the Justice League and beyond (*Batman Beyond*, to be precise). Marvel had some great cartoons as well, but when it came to film most entries were forgettable, or downright embarrassing: anyone remember the 1990 *Captain America* film? Or *The Punisher* with Dolph Lundgren? *Nick Fury* played by David Hasselhoff? I know, you're trying hard not to. And to be fair, DC had a habit of running its franchises into the ground; both Superman and Batman burned out after four movies due to poor studio decisions that produced diminishing returns. I think I'd rather watch Dolph Lundgren's version of Frank Castle than suffer through George Clooney's Batman.

All that to say, the baton seems to have been passed back and forth between the "Big Two" (DC and Marvel) for decades. In 2012, when *The Dark Knight Rises* and *The Avengers* both broke into the billion-dollar club, it looked like there was room enough to share this time around. Sadly, Warner Brothers just didn't seem able to manifest the "lightning in the bottle" that their comic sparring partners produced; covetousness seems to have made them overeager, perhaps some producers overbearing. Directors were rushed, plot lines compressed, creative minds muddled.

Still, just as 20th Century Fox produced gems like *X-Men: Days of Future Past* parallel to the MCU's heyday, DC gave us several spiritually fascinating entries that would ALSO marvel us, if not technically "MARVEL"-ing us. So, let's test their mettle first with…

MAN OF STEEL: Two Fathers, True Conviction

"You will give the people an ideal to strive towards." - Jor-El

"You have to keep this side of yourself a secret." - Jonathan Kent

At first glance, it seems redundant to examine Superman considering how central he was to my explanation of Life Transcendent stories in the first Cinemagogue book. When this film premiered in 2013, however, it was mind-blowing to see mainstream media embrace the same conversation: examining, discussing, mixing and matching all the ways Clark and Christ compare. It's a great day when a conversation on how our modern mythology mimics Jesus moves from Cinemagogue to CNN. I even received an invite to attend a free screening for pastors, complete with notes on how to mix the movie in as sermon illustrations.

Since I've covered a lot of ways in which the Man of Steel measures up to the messiah previously, it felt more poignant to discuss the amplified ways in which the film is a love letter to dads, while also addressing two of the film's most controversial moments. The trailer featured dialogue from Superman's Kryptonian father (Jor-El) and his adopted Terran father, Jonathan. Based on the trailer alone, it seemed as though the advice from these men might be in tension or conflict.

Whereas Jor-El anticipates and hopes that his son will become "like a god" to the people of earth—someone for them to follow— Jonathan tells his son that the earth is not ready, and that his identity must remain hidden. In the context of the movie's narrative, however, we discover these ideas are NOT in conflict, and it all comes down to a question of timing. Jonathan Kent realizes that the son he loves has a destiny; while he is Clark's earthly father, the boy has a "true father" and needs to be patient so that his mission begins at the right time and place. As Pa Kent explains:

> *"I have to believe that you were... that you were sent here for a reason... and when that day comes, you're gonna have to make a choice... to decide what kind of a man you want to grow up to be, Clark; because ...whoever that man is, he's... he's gonna change the world."*

In numerous flashbacks, we see the maturing Clark Kent struggling to submit himself to the will, timing and counsel of his Kansas farmer father... and later, when that day finally arrives, Clark (or Kal-El) is assisted and led by his cosmic father's "spirit" (thanks to the wonders of Kryptonian technology). When Jonathan first reveals his son's extraterrestrial origins, the teenage someday-Superman is understandably overwhelmed. Adoptive father and son share this tearful exchange:

Clark: *Can't I just keep PRETENDING I'm your son?*

Jonathan Kent: *You ARE my son! But somewhere out there you have another father too, who gave you another name…*

This scene was so moving it made me choke up along with Jonathan; it serves as the emotional core of the story and makes me wonder if this is how Joseph felt raising Jesus. What was interesting to me is how the film focused on Superman's obedience to his father's will, and his willingness to act (or not act) according to the will of both earthly father and—dare we say?—"heavenly" father. When the adult Clark/Kal meets the recorded construct of Jor-El's consciousness (insert Holy Spirit parallel here) this father also asks his son to follow him, to submit to his will and the intended purpose for his Son.

The way this Jor-El instructs Kal is even more direct and specific than the scenes between Marlon Brando and Christopher Reeve in the classic *Superman: The Movie*; Russel Crowe's version literally tells his son to turn this way, turn that way, strike a wall, etc. and the young man trusts and obeys. Jor-El explains he sent his son out of love… to change the world. To save it. And similar to Christ, he does. Unlike the 1978 version, where the son ultimately defies his father's will and turns back time to save Lois Lane, here we have a portrait of the father and the saving son working in unity.

"Father, if you are willing, remove this cup from me. Nevertheless, not my will, but yours, be done." - *Luke 22:42*

"For I have come down from heaven, not to do my own will but the will of him who sent me. And this is the will of him who sent me, that I should lose nothing of all that he has given me, but raise it up on the last day." - *John 6:38-39*

Again, I've chronicled the myriad ways Clark mirrors Christ elsewhere, but *Man of Steel* managed to make some Superman fans furious. Between David Goyer's script and Zack Snyder's direction, the film had two major strikes against it (and enough for some people to decide it struck out). However, as a Christian I respected and appreciated both choices; let me explain…

"Strike" One: Jonathan Kent is a @$%&#!!!

Clark Kent at 13: *What was I supposed to do? Just let them die?*

Jonathan Kent: *Maybe; but there's more at stake here than our lives or the lives of those around us. When the world finds out what you can do, it's gonna change everything.*

This is a case where a trailer can sometimes be a curse; I remember they cut right after Jonathan said "maybe" and Superman fans exploded. Everybody freaked out that Superman's adoptive Dad told him to let a busload of children drown! How could he? What a horrible person! However, as any Bible-reading Christian knows, **context matters**. The rest of Mr. Kent's sentence matters. Jonathan is a man-in-progress, working through the ethics and morality of a lot of issues, including patience, timing, family, etc. Let's look at ten steps to understanding why Jonathan is right… or at least "maybe" right, from a superhero perspective:

1. *Every* time a Spider-man (or ANY hero) changes clothes in a closet after a villain starts wreaking havoc, every injury or death in that interim is equivalent to the hero prioritizing "keeping his secret" over those people's lives. It's not principally different.

2. *"But a clothing change is only a few minutes!"* That doesn't change the *principle* of the argument: 3 minutes or 30 years, the principle is the same. A hero chooses to let someone get hurt or die while they put their underwear on the outside and mask up.

3. The reason for not acting in their civvies is often the protection of loved ones. If bad guys find out Matt Murdock is Daredevil, they'll hurt Karen, etc. Likewise, Jonathan is thinking of the consequences of a boy carelessly exposing his household to harm.

4. This is also looking at *the long game*. Calculated use and timing allow them to help more people over time. It's a variation on the thought experiment called the Trolley Problem. Save a bus, get exposed and put in a cage by the government. Wait for the right timing: save billions…which, of course, turns out to be the case.

5. *"But he's SUPERMAN. The government can't hold him, he can fly around the world in minutes, he can save the bus AND the world."*

Awesome: are you enjoying that hindsight? Jonathan doesn't know this. He's a dad who knows he has a 13-year-old *child...* with indeterminate powers, of unknown origin. We seem unable to recognize the story of a parent in the midst of a *process*.

6. You could argue that every time Clark Kent has lunch with Lois Lane, his super-hearing *could* pick up crimes: theft, rape, murder, etc. Basically, ANY time he takes time for himself or those he cares about? He's "letting someone die." Do we expect the same of our other heroes? Of ourselves? Are people being hurt while you're wasting time reading this right now?

7. If we mix our messianic themes with Superman and say "Jesus wouldn't let a busload of kids die"... actually, Jesus was incarnate for 30 years without record of miracles, and also withdrew frequently during his 3 years for solitude. There were people he didn't heal, help or save in the imminent sense. He raised Lazarus from the dead: could he not have saved his friend John the Baptist from beheading, or miraculously reattached it?

8. Again, Jonathan isn't telling Clark "hide forever, bury your talents." Whether it's by God or aliens, Pa Kent assumes a time and reason will be revealed: he's advising *patience*.

9. These complex issues are something people in real-world, life-or-death situations face, especially in wartime. Sometimes a town has been sacrificed for the sake of keeping code-breaking abilities a secret; millions of other lives are saved as a result. These are hard, "greater good" decisions we don't like to weigh, but unlike us (with our armchair quarterbacking) Jonathan Kent has been given a rare and unprecedented situation to navigate them.

10. Finally, Jonathan is internally consistent: we hear his logic that is essentially "maybe there ARE times to let events take their course and not intercede" and we assume he's selfish, or a coward. But his logic is tested when he's metaphorically "on the bus": he's injured, tornado coming, his son wants to intercede... and he puts his mortality *money* where his philosophy *mouth* is.

"For everything there is a season, and a time for every matter under heaven: a time to plant, and a time to pluck up what is

planted; a time to kill, and a time to heal; a time to break down, and a time to build up... a time to tear, and a time to sew; a time to keep silence, and a time to speak; a time to love, and a time to hate; a time for war, and a time for peace."
  - *Solomon*, Ecclesiastes 3:1-8

All in all, Jonathan Kent in *Man of Steel* provides what I think is one of the more earnest, admittedly conflicted, but ultimately ethical versions of Jonathan Kent we've ever had. Instead of a one-dimensional morality PEZ dispenser we have a very moral, real human, thinking through implications we often take for granted for the sake of his son, his family, and the greater good. He's a man of conviction, another key area of focus in the film.

Man of Steel asks us: **what would we give up for our convictions?** What do we believe, and what would we sacrifice for it? What would we cast aside, willingly lay down? And where do we get the courage of these convictions? How do we hold to them in the face of trial and temptation? Would we compromise for something like career advancement? Lois Lane gets the scoop of the century... and decides to pass on it. Why? Because she believes in Superman: his convictions, his character, his goodness. Would we do this? For someone else, or the world in general?

Many would compromise these things for their own glory and pursuits, and that's how we find the state of Krypton at the beginning of the film. In *Man of Steel,* it's a world that's lost its way, and is going to be destroyed. The people of the planet have been slowly destroying themselves from within, engineering themselves away from the image it was meant to bear. We see a sober reflection of the brokenness of our own world, and thus we see Jor-El as a man of conviction, putting his family at risk. What if he'd been wrong? What if Krypton hadn't blown up? He would have sent his only son away and made his wife complicit in stealing the codex that they send with baby Kal. He's certain of his convictions and in this case, of the truth.

But Zod (played brilliantly by Michael Shannon) carries himself with equal conviction; he's not a one-note villain. When confessing that he killed Jor-El, Zod explains:

"I did. And not a day goes by that it does not haunt me. But if I had to do it again I would. I have a duty to my people… I exist only to protect Krypton. That is the sole purpose for which I was born. And every action I take, no matter how violent or how cruel, is for the greater good of my people."

Note the phrase *"the greater good"* (I heard you *Hot Fuzz* fans just repeat those words in monotone). We see Jor-El and Zod doing these things for "the greater good" and trying to make Clark/Kal see and submit to their vision. We witness Jonathan and his adopted son, struggling to see what that greater good truly is, because men (like Zod) can tread a path in the name of righteousness that isn't headed where they believe.

"There is a way that seems right to a man, but its end is the way to death." - Proverbs 14:12

"Strike" Two: Zod's Dead, Baby. Zod's dead.

Men of conviction must make hard choices, and men of conviction stand by them. That doesn't always make them right, of course. Comic writer Mark Waid famously stood up at the climax of *Man of Steel* and shouted, *"THAT'S IT, YOU LOST ME, I'M OUT!"* Other professing Superman fans went ballistic like he did, crying out with conviction that the character *"doesn't kill. Full stop."* They couldn't handle that he broke his enemy's neck. Director Zack Snyder, with equal-but-opposite conviction, has done multiple interviews suggesting that this comic book rule is archaic, juvenile and stupid, doubling down on his interpretation of Superman and Batman saying that if the characters can't kill, they're "irrelevant".

Personally, I find both passionate positions to be lacking, uninformed and irrational. First, Superman killed the three Kryptonian villains in the now classic 1980s Superman comics by John Byrne. Even Chris Reeve's Kal-El kicked the Kryptonian cronies—without their powers, mind you—screaming down into a black, icy chasm beneath the Fortress of Solitude in *Superman II*. They never show up again… hmm. He killed the villain Doomsday. He's also killed other aliens (sentient ones, not just animals) in cartoons like *Justice League* because it was wartime. It's just never his preferred choice: like a soldier, or a policeman pushed into a lethal force situation, there are rare times he has killed in comics and film. He's amazing enough to have many other options at his disposal, but he reserves the right to sanction when necessary.

Zack Snyder's responses seem a bit too bloodthirsty for my tastes as well, and I wish most Superman fans on either side of this would just simmer down. But my main concern is that Christians might let a comic book love of Clark Kent impair their vision of the real Superman: *Jesus*. When our image of these heroes—one fictional, one real—focuses on the *nice* to the exclusion of the *just*, we limit and remove aspects of either's character or capability. Superman will stop to help a kitten out of a tree, but he also has the power and position to take a villain out of play permanently.

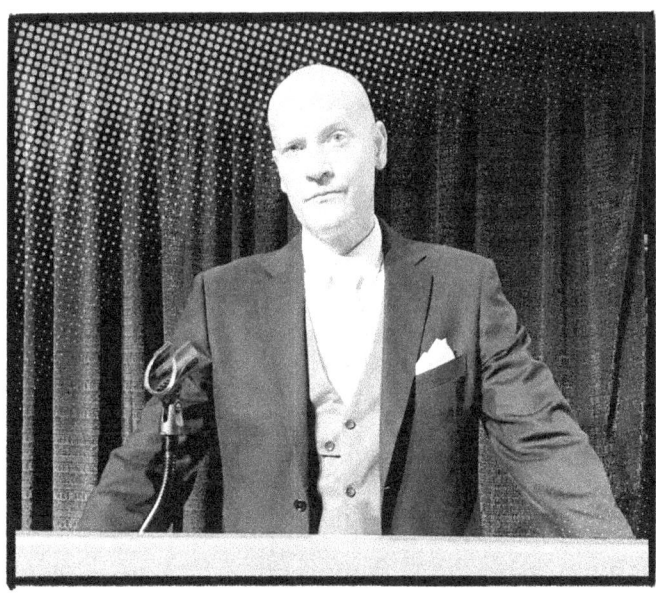

C'mon, I would have made a better Luthor than Eisenberg…

Similarly, Christ in his incarnation did not kill anyone (although when you read the gospels, he's not always nice… subject for another time). However, in John 5:27 Jesus proclaims that God *"has given him authority to execute judgment… for an hour is coming when all who are in the tombs will hear his voice and come out, those who have done good to the resurrection of life and those who have done evil to the resurrection of judgment."* Those outside of God's grace will be judged and die eternally. Revelation describes him with a sword, on a white horse, striking people down. The gospel is the grace he's given us, serving us like helpless kittens stuck in trees… but he also holds the power and position to take sinners out of play permanently.

Another thing some people apparently didn't pay attention to, after Zod's neck snapped like Gwen Stacy's, was Superman's emotional reaction. Henry Cavill's passionate performance shows us Superman falling to his knees, a primal scream from his lips and tears in his eyes. We see clearly that Kal's desire was not death for Zod… yet it was necessary, and just.

> *"This is good, and it is pleasing in the sight of God our Savior, who desires all people to be saved and to come to the knowledge of the truth."* - 1 Timothy 2:3-4

Oh, and I didn't just reference Gwen Stacy above for kicks; consider that we see the depths of Spider-man's pain when Gwen dies in comics and film. She's someone Peter loves who is both a romantic partner and *friend*. In *Man of Steel*, we see Kal-El express an equally powerful lament out of love for his *enemy*. Loving enemies is something counterintuitive that Jesus calls us to do. All in all, this version of Superman seems the most overtly Christ-like of all.

And behind every good Superman, there is a…

WONDER WOMAN: It's Not About "Deserve"

> *"What one does with the truth is more difficult than you think. I learnt this the hard way, a long, long time ago. And now, my life will never be the same…"* - Diana Prince

Two years before *Captain Marvel* appeared, with some people praising it as if there'd never been a strong female lead character in comic book movies (or cinema in general) DC gave us a wonderful entry and added to the annals of heroic women in film, done in a way that still overshadows Marvel's attempts. Having already led her own television series in the 70s, the amazing Amazon's story was deftly directed by Patty Jenkins and follows the classic "hero's journey" motif. Our protagonist must leave their ordinary world, answering a call to adventure, meeting and learning from a mentor, facing tests, making allies and finding others to be enemies. The classic structure serves this classic character well.

Of course, the "ordinary" world for Diana is her island of Amazon warriors, while the strange new world is ours (though set back in the lesser depicted World War I). The hero's journey often includes the central character embarking on a quest and—in the first act—they tend to have ignorant or misinformed views of the world. The second act challenges those, the third act corrects them, and they come into a new understanding. Gal Godot plays the part perfectly: that of a strong and capable woman who, nevertheless, still has lessons to learn. Just like the best male heroes, she has to glean knowledge and wisdom, and the film isn't afraid to have that come from a man (in the form of Steve Trevor, played by Chris Pine).

"There's so much… that you don't understand" - Hippolyta

The narrative doesn't fall into the trap of trying to "elevate women" by diminishing men, portraying Steve or his comrades as inept or unnecessary while Diana is always right. They even deal with it directly early on, when she dismisses men as not being necessary but then learns otherwise. Her education up until meeting Steve has been book-based versus experience-based, and what emerges is a complementary relationship; they have much to learn from each other and truths to discover together about war, human nature and love. As Diana narrates:

"I used to want to save the world. This beautiful place. But I knew so little then. It is a land of beauty and wonder, worth cherishing in every way. But the closer you get, the more you see the great darkness simmering within. And mankind? Mankind is another story altogether."

Diana has a distorted view of human nature and fallen man. For most of the film she blames the war solely on Ares, the "god of war" in Greek mythology, yet in this film he is portrayed more like the tempter, (like Satan) prowling around and leading man into their worst impulses. She's not wrong that Ares is involved, and Steve comes to realize that his dismissive assumptions are off the mark; this movie's devil IS real. However, Steve's later assertions about mankind's inner nature are tragically more correct than Diana wants to believe.

Steve: *You don't think I get it, after what I've seen out there? You don't think I wish I could tell you that it was one bad guy to blame? It's not! We're all to blame?*

Diana: *I'm not!*

Steve: *But maybe I am!*

This movie challenges the modern notion that humans are essentially good; it belies the ideas in *Captain Marvel* and modern ideologies, that our real issues are external and that inside we're perfect just the way we are. This story dares to dally and deal with a countercultural question about human nature. It leans toward a more biblical understanding:

"As it is written: 'None is righteous, no, not one; no one understands; no one seeks for God. All have turned aside; together they have become worthless; no one does good, not even one.'" - Romans 3:10-12

Steve Trevor is humble enough to admit he's part of the problem: that we all are. We even see this reflected when Steve's friends raise a glass together and say:

Charlie: *May we get what we want...*

Steve: *...and may we get what we need.*

Sameer: *But may we never get what we deserve.*

The word "deserve" turns up so often it becomes the obvious issue and question in the film. Diana's mother tells her to be careful in the world of men, and that they do not deserve Diana's help. Ares also tells her that mankind doesn't deserve her, hoping to sway her to his destructive side. He's simultaneously the tempter and accuser of humanity, again like Satan. Diana finally sees and acknowledges that indeed, humans are all corrupted... and in her resultant anger and confusion, Steve Trevor offers another view to consider.

Diana: *She was right, my mother was right... she said the world of men do not deserve you, they don't deserve our help...*

Steve: *It's... not about deserve! Maybe, maybe we don't. But it's not about that, it's about what you believe!*

Steve Trevor stumbles into a key component of Christianity and God's grace, in that He gives us what we don't deserve. Grace by definition is unmerited favor; we aren't worthy of it, we didn't earn it, and He's not obligated to it. He chooses to love us according to His mercy, He achieves it by His unparalleled power, and delivers it through the sacrificial death of Jesus. That's what Christians believe.

The film, of course, doesn't run this philosophical ball into the biblical end zone, but there are three pieces of story craft that might qualify as a field goal. Steve Trevor models what he believes by a sacrificial death. We see Diana strike down Ares with unparalleled power, and ultimately decide that while this human race doesn't deserve it, she will choose to love them efficaciously. Hmm... is this character truly a Greek creation, or a veiled vision of someone else?

"I glimpsed the darkness that lives within their light... Now I know. Only love can save this world. So I stay. I fight, and I give... This is my mission, now. Forever." - Wonder Woman

Christianizing Greek Mythology: the "god" killer

What shape, then, does this kind of world-changing love take? When does that love assume the form of fighting? The war of a sacrificial warrior? This film's fantasy draws on unbiblical views of gods and history, imagery of Zeus and ancient Greek beliefs. However, there's quite a deviation from the original myths here, and the reshaping of that mythological clay reveals a more Christian-shaped narrative. We've already talked about Ares' resemblance to Satan, but even more interesting is the nature of Zeus and the role of Diana as the revealed weapon to destroy the gods.

1. In Greek mythology, it's Prometheus who created mankind from clay (and Zeus wasn't happy about it). In the film, Hippolyta explains to Diana that Zeus (who is above all other gods) created

mankind *"in his image"*, a concept more akin to the God of the Bible. Her words paraphrase parts of Genesis.

2. She goes on to explain that Zeus' son Ares corrupted mankind, which also differs from Greek mythology. Again, while Satan wasn't God's "son" he was God's creation, and Ares more closely reflects the biblical tempter in the garden of Eden.

3. We discover in the film that Diana wasn't formed from clay, but is actually Zeus' offspring, and the only one who has the power to crush the head of Ares. In other words, Wonder Woman is the daughter of God, reshaping Greek mythology as a comic book parallel for the biblical Son of God. Consider, she is:

- …conceived and birthed by the God above all others.
- …to be savior to some and destroyer to others.
- …sent to vanquish evil: not a *god* killer but *devil* killer.
- …sent to dwell with us and show us the light.
- …sent to love us even though we don't deserve it.
- …sent to bring about peace.

This reimagined mythology is much closer to the story of Christianity than its Greek roots. Even the origin and function of the Amazons is bent to accommodate this too. Instead of a warrior race who was all about war in Greek mythology, here they serve a peaceful function.

Steve: *What is this place? Who are you people?*

Diana: *We are a bridge to a greater understanding.*

"You are the light of the world. A city on a hill cannot be hidden. Neither do people light a lamp and put it under a bowl. Instead they put it on its stand, and it gives light to everyone in the house. In the same way, let your light shine before men, that they may see your good deeds and praise your Father in heaven."
- Matthew 5:14-16

The movie portrays the Amazons as a people set apart, meant to bring light to the world… and through these chosen people the ultimate savior emerges. It's not far from God's working through a chosen people throughout the scriptures, from Israel to the church. On top of that, Hippolyta's isolationism adds another dimension to consider: a people "set apart" who have forgotten or forsaken their mission. She's forsaken the world, neglected the mission. This shines a light on Christians today: have we abdicated our outreach role? Are we distanced and cold toward those we were made to love?

> *"My father told me once, he said, 'If you see something wrong happening in the world, you can either do nothing, or you can do something'. And I already tried nothing ."* - Steve Trevor

This movie lassos and exposes three critical truths from a Christian perspective: a sober reminder of human nature and God's grace, a stylized reminder of the divine child he sent to save us, and our mission as Christians: to be set apart, but not removed, from the world and seeking to be a bridge to a right understanding of Christ.

Wonder Woman and Superman seek to give us stories of life transcendent, the hope of a redeeming savior, to contrast days when we feel all we have is this troubling life under the sun. We find a third such story not under the sun, but under the sea…

AQUAMAN: Monomyth, Mercy, and Dual Natures

> *"Jules Verne once wrote: 'Put two ships in the open sea, without wind or tide... they will come together.'"* - Arthur Curry

James Harleman once wrote: put three *stories* in the DC, and they will come together too… with storytelling symmetry. Clark Kent learns of his special heritage and goes on a journey; Diana leaves Themyscira to discover hidden truths about mankind and herself? And Aquaman? Here we are again, practically drowning in monomyth country, and this movie clings to the classic formula like coral to a rock. Watch this movie and then compare with the actual 12 stages of journey in Joseph Campbell's *Hero with a Thousand Faces*:

1. **The Ordinary World:** we see the hero in their everyday life.

2. **The Call to Adventure:** an inciting incident for the story.

3. **Refusal of the Call:** the hero hesitates and/or rejects the call.

4. **Meeting with the Mentor:** the hero gains the supplies, knowledge, and/or confidence to commence the adventure.

5. **Crossing the First Threshold:** the hero ultimately commits wholeheartedly to the epic journey.

6. **Tests, Allies, and Enemies:** the hero explores the special world, faces various trials, and makes friends and foes.

7. **Approach to the Innermost Cave:** the hero nears the center-point of the ordeal and may face a supreme danger.

8. **The Ordeal:** the hero faces their greatest challenge yet and experiences death and rebirth (real or metaphorical).

9. **Reward:** there are consequences and celebrations for the hero.

10. **The Road Back:** the hero returns to their ordinary world or continues to an ultimate destination.

11. **The Resurrection:** the hero has a final moment of death and rebirth, so they're pure when they reenter the ordinary world.

12. **Return with the Elixir:** the hero returns with something to improve the ordinary world.

I'll leave the reader (and viewer) to work out these parallels in *Aquaman* and only mention that mid-movie, director James Wan's story takes Arthur into a literal "innermost cave" and "special world". Later, Vulko literally declares *"the King is risen!"* I'm not complaining when I say the hero's journey beats are so on the nose; they make *Avatar* look subtle (I love both films). If you've read the first Cinemagogue book, and all the stories and parallels in this book thus far, and can't see how this movie maps onto the monomyth, well… either I've failed utterly in my call, or you're all wet.

"In this trident resides the power of Atlantis. In the hands of the true heir, it will unite all our kingdoms above and below."
  - King Atlan

Muddled, Merciful Messiah

Moving past Campbell's themes to the more biblical ones, we see clearly where *Aquaman*—and the monomyth—don't always map perfectly onto the gospel. They map more comprehensively with narrative threads throughout all of scripture; the "call to adventure" can be seen in the call of Abraham, for example. He's called by God out of his ordinary world, but Abram doesn't hesitate or refuse the call. Rejection can be seen in the story of Jonah, however, but he crosses the threshold after being swallowed by a whale.

Speaking of whales, Arthur Curry's aquatic epic gives us a narrative that includes an ocean of parallels: a fall, a divided kingdom, and an epic son whose dual nature is the key to reconciling them. There are some obvious cues even before he reaches adulthood that give him a messianic bent:

- A highly favored mother and a blue-collar father.
- A special birth, the boy raised in a small rural town.
- A legend (prophecy) of a king that will restore kingdom.
- An offspring who is an heir to the story's ultimate throne.
- The last one anyone expects would be that leader.
- A servant leader first, and king second.

"Legend has it that one day... a new king will come. Who will use the power of the trident to put Atlantis back together again." - Atlanna

Obviously, this falls short of biblical parallel: Jesus was not an illegitimate child, he was a virgin birth of the highly favored Mary and raised by his blue collar, carpenter stepfather Joseph. Jesus didn't drink his dad or disciples under the table; he was not so much the "everyman" as to join us in things we ought not do. Jesus never rejected the call; he didn't turn it down initially like Arthur does. Once again, we like to conflate our journey with the true savior's journey, and even some Christians reduce Jesus and depict him more like "one of the guys". We conflate the convert story with the Christ story; Jesus was set apart, more like Clark Kent than Arthur Curry.

Arthur does match up with some of the lesser archetypes, however: he's the learning, changing hero. Like Jonah (and Moses) he refuses the call. Like Daniel, he's tested; he faces a few variations of the lion's den. He also learns and grows in understanding and showing mercy. Early in the film he lets Manta's father die; he turns his back and leaves the man to his fate, letting him drown in front of his son. Maybe his fate was deserved, but Arthur does it with an act of smug, self-satisfaction and this comes back to bite him.

> *"It was up to me, and I let him die. I could've saved him, but I didn't. And now I've made an enemy. And he could have hurt you. And that would have been my fault."* - Arthur Curry

> *"Repay no one evil for evil, but give thought to do what is honorable in the sight of all. If possible, so far as it depends on you, live peaceably with all. Beloved, never avenge yourselves, but leave it to the wrath of God, for it is written, "Vengeance is mine, I will repay, says the Lord."* - Romans 12:17-19

Blessing the persecutor—Manta and his father—by saving their lives might have flipped the script, or at least—as scripture says—the act of mercy would have been like heaping burning coals upon their heads. Jesus turned enemies into friends and forgave sin. Those once opposed to him, like Paul, became his greatest advocates. Aquaman learns this lesson, as we see him at the film's climax extend mercy to Orm:

Orm: *Mercy is not our way!*

Arthur Curry: *Maybe you haven't noticed, brother… but I'm not one of you.*

One of these things is not like the other… Arthur's fitness for the throne turns out to be that he is unique. His singular makeup embodies and makes him a connecting point between two radically different kingdoms.

The Hydro-static Union

"You think you're unworthy to lead because you're of two different worlds? But that is exactly why you are worthy! I can see that now. The question is, can you" - Mera

Thematically, we might apply this quote to a lot of real-life issues: racial reconciliation, national conflicts. Arthur is essentially an ambassador because he bridges both. Biblically, this reminds us of the bridge that's needed between the Kingdom of God and the kingdom of man. In the movie, Arthur's two natures are that he's a creature of the land and of the sea, both united in one body; in the Bible, we see that Jesus is incarnate as both truly man, but also truly God (technically, we call this the hypostatic union). And why? Christ came to be a covering of mercy and forgiveness, to shield us from a deserved wrath. He serves as the only path of forgiveness and reconciliation.

Mid-movie, when the Atlanteans throw mountains of trash and human warships up onto coastlines around the world, the author and seeming crackpot Stephen Shin calls out the truth: that there IS a declaration of war against mankind, and that they're involved in a greater conflict than just the kingdom of man. He's told that he's insane, that there is no Atlantis and no declaration of war. He tells the reporters they need to open their eyes, because there is already a representative of that kingdom walking among them: Aquaman!

Like a comic book movie prophet, he's right of course… there is a declaration of war from another kingdom, angry at the way we've despoiled the planet we've been given. The narrative suggests, on one hand, that the accusation is legitimate… and yet the representative "walking among us" is seeking to create a bridge between kingdoms: not to bring us wrath but to bring us peace. Clearly this is reminiscent of the declaration of war against mankind in a spiritual sense, even more justly deserved in how we've maligned and marred the kingdom of God, not to mention poorly stewarding His creation. Sin itself is a declaration of war, and God's retaliation would be just.

Thankfully Arthur, like Jesus, pushes back against the one who would simply accuse us, devoid of mercy. Orm isn't a stand-in for God's righteous wrath in this story, but rather—like Ares in *Wonder Woman*—he's a stand-in for the devil, a self-proclaimed "master" of the kingdom but filled with selfish intent; he even initiates his conflict and builds his army by using deception. Arthur, the rightful heir, vanquishes and dethrones Orm, now poised to be a figure of reconciliation between the kingdoms. Like I said above, the metaphors are as muddied as the waters in the trench, but this story profited greatly from using them.

Ever wonder what made Arthur Curry's story go from a bad joke on Robot Chicken to a billion-dollar box office smash? Let's face it, to the world at large Aquaman has been the most mocked superhero, the "guy who talks to fish". Well, as *Wonder Woman* basically Christianized Greek mythology, this story borrowed heavily from the monomyth and biblical imagery to beef up a formerly floundering hero. One could argue that tapping into a Judeo-Christian worldview that is embedded in our western psyches might simply be a narrative cheat code, but obviously I believe it's deeper than that, much like the way men resonate with Aragorn and the "Return of the King". A prophesied monarch, a tested hero, and a servant leader that unites kingdoms and brings a perfect quotient of justice and mercy? A risen King? Told correctly, that story is always lightning in a bottle.

And speaking of lightning…

SHAZAM: Seduction of the Not-So Innocent

"You seek a pure soul, old man. But no one's worthy."
  - Dr. Sivana

Unlike the three previous DC heroes that cling closely to the messianic/monomyth form, Shazam mixes a different set of parallels and principles in a more comedic film. The ending credits of *Shazam* even mimic the ending of *Spider-man: Homecoming*, which is a clue that this story is riffing on the teen who learns that "with great power, comes great responsibility". Foster child Billy Watson seems even more troubled (and egotistical) than Peter Parker ever was, and even acknowledges he's not pure of heart. When the wizard explains the qualifications for possessing the power of Shazam, Billy's at least honest about himself:

"Look, man, maybe this is magic, and, I don't know, but the people you're looking for - good, pure people - I'm not one of them. I-I don't know if anyone is, really."

In a 21st century culture that often posits that people are basically good, this was a refreshing take on the character and a story worth consideration and conversation. As previously pointed out, the Bible does present the hard truth that no one is inherently good: mankind has a sin nature, we've all fallen far short. The fact that we're not worthy (and that we're folded into God's family solely by grace) is a horse pill a believer must swallow prior to the sweet elixir of salvation that washes it down. As Dr. Thaddeus Sivana explains to the wizard later, this is admittedly hard to hear…

> *"Do you know what it's like for a child to be told you'll never be good enough? No, you don't. What you said to me all those years ago made me realize who I really was. And you know something? I am NOT pure of heart."*

All the same, people can have totally different reactions when confronted with that reality: we can allow the truth of our condition to humble us or harden us. Realizing it's our present state doesn't mean it has to be our future. It's obvious which way Sivana chooses, as he embraces and takes on a life formed and fueled by sins in a very literal, comic book fashion.

The Magnificent Sevens?

The seven deadly sins appear as monstrous, demonic manifestations in this film, another very Christian-adjacent touch that dovetails nicely with an exploration of human depravity. These aren't the only sevens, however: we also learn there are seven wizards, and seven thrones in the cave-like "Rock of Eternity". When Billy Batson finds out where his birth mother lives, the apartment number is 707, and in the after credits scene, Mister Mind —the talking caterpillar—mentions the seven realms (or magic lands). While the film never truly addresses the odd obsession with this number, it has a scriptural parallel. The number seven is significant in the Bible, representing wholeness, perfection, and completion.

The creation of the world was in seven (literal or poetic, depending on your exegesis) days, and God set up the week as a complete cycle, ending on the seventh day with rest. Under the Sinai covenant with God, the Israelites were to observe seven holy feast days, as well as observing every seventh year as a year of Jubilee, resting and relying on God's provision. There are seven gifts of the Holy Spirit listed in Isaiah 11, and the root of the word seven in Hebrew is from a word that means "to be full".

Sevens turn up in Revelation even more than in Shazam: seven angels, seven churches, seven lamp stands, seven seals, seven plagues, etc. so it seems likely Shazam is playing with biblical ideas here. Why then, one may ask, are there only six people with the power of Shazam at film's end? Well, we can't forget the original "champion" the wizard speaks of, that will turn out to be none other than Black Adam (played by Duane "The Rock" Johnson in the subsequent DC film). Curious that the story begins with someone named Adam, who rebelled and did evil… followed by the need of someone with a "pure soul" to set things right. Adam fell; hence we need the messiah (the pure soul) to come… ah, I see what you did there, guys.

"Only the purest of hearts can resist their temptations. And you will never be worthy!" - The Wizard

Billy Batson is no messiah, however, and far from pure. Even without the need of manifest monster sins to drive him, his inherent defaults quickly become a "look at me" kind of pride, not to mention greed when we find him busking at the town center. He's been given the wisdom of Solomon, the strength of Hercules, the stamina of Atlas, the power of Zeus, the courage of Achilles, and the speed of Mercury (the first initial of each name spells SHAZAM, for the record) but—perhaps like Solomon did, despite his wisdom—he's wasting it trying to impress chicks. He tells his foster friend Freddie that he's ignorant about "superhero stuff" and it turns out that's not just a powers issue, but a character issue as well.

Shazam: *Could I, could I give you a little piece of advice? Don't be worried about everybody else. Always look out for number one. Gandhi said that.*

Mary: *I don't think he said that.*

Part of Billy's bad attitude is influenced by his abandonment issues, and perhaps subsequent treatment within the foster care system, but he bears responsibility for the bad attitude as well. We see the story judge him rightly as his reckless behavior almost costs the lives of kids on a bus, his relationship with Freddie, and the people who are seeking to love him like a son and a brother.

Focus on the Family

"All we can do is give him a place full of love. Whether he chooses to call it a home, that's up to him." - Victor Vasquez

That's right, it's another "made family" story, like the *Avengers* and the *Guardians* and *X-Men* over at Marvel. Instead of the biological family that failed him, he's brought into a mixed family of children from all over and encouraged to be a part of this blended family. It takes on a whole new dimension, of course, when he shares his powers with his siblings; none of them are truly the "pure soul" that the wizard was looking for, but united they can tackle Sivana and the sins, supporting one another with Billy at the center. This may be where we see that "wisdom of Solomon" have its moment; instead of being hardened like Sivana with the knowledge that he's imperfect, he's humbled enough by the truth to share his power with the others and accomplish the feat together.

"I open my heart to you, Billy Batson. And in so doing, choose you as champion." - The Wizard

What we get isn't a Christ-like parallel, but we might make an Old Testament nod to King David and his "mighty men" in scripture. David wasn't pure, but he was an archetype, a foreshadowing, and he achieved his victory alongside other trusted men of God. When the prophet Samuel anointed David, he didn't assume this kid would be perfect, or even the "capital M" messiah. He knew he'd be a king, but not the King of Kings.

A New Testament comparison for Billy and his family would, as we've touched on repeatedly in this book, be likening it to the church, a made family endowed with gifts to combat sin together. As for the "pure soul"? One might argue *Shazam's* narrative suggests that there isn't one, or perhaps one isn't needed. Maybe all we need are these made families pulling together? Alternatively, the gospel would say these archetypes (biblical, historical and fictional) point to a reality that is fulfilled in Christ.

Still, in the film the kids' foster father Victor calls the family to a time of prayer. They all put their hands in, but Billy abstains. Perhaps the film is slyly pointing us to what we need, but leaving some of the understanding up to the viewer. Will we put our hand in and call God's "made family" our home? As Victor reminds Rosa:

> *"...you said something that I'll never forget. You said, 'it's not a home till you call it a home. It's something you choose.'"*

Scene 2: **Flash in the Pan?**

All the DC films we've looked at so far had sequels that... well, let's just say they had mixed reviews. Others would say the follow-up films stunk, or sunk the franchise, although there are some ardent apologists, specifically for the polarizing *Batman v Superman*, which came too close on the heels of *Man of Steel* instead of giving Clark a proper sequel. Wonder Woman was followed by a pandemic-plagued *Wonder Woman '84*, and *Aquaman* got the waterlogged *Aquaman: The Lost Kingdom*. Lost in the middle was a much-maligned *Justice League* film, corrected as best as it could have been by Zack Snyder's extended Netflix version. But the damage had been done. Sprinkled in there were fun gems (like James Gunn's *The Suicide Squad*) and some rougher entries that didn't fare as well.

What went wrong? Plenty of speculation and opinions abound on this, and the reality is that it was a combination of bad decisions by many involved: producers pushing to duplicate the Marvel magic, some of director Zack Snyder's decisions in light of those pressures (not to mention the tragic loss of his daughter). By rushing things and admittedly failing with a few films, they upset fans who began to view everything preemptively through a negative lens, and then things spiraled. We've also entered a hyperbolic decade where nothing is middling; a movie is either "the best EVER" or "the WORST" with nothing in-between. True, I found many of the subsequent films lacking, but more average or mediocre than truly terrible. As mentioned at the start of this chapter, I believe covetousness got the better of the Warner Brothers powers-that-be, so they tried to move like the Flash instead of building momentum.

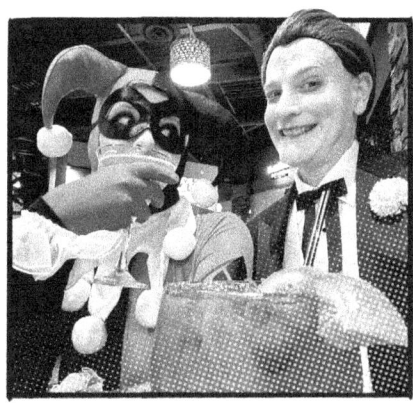

"Better luck NEXT time, puddin'..."

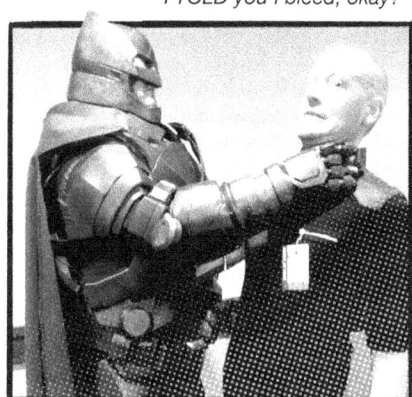

"I TOLD you I bleed, okay?"

Make no mistake: despite their questionable quality, there are plenty of themes that could be explored; Lex Luthor in *BvS* (although horribly miscast) makes some blatant correlations between Superman and God. But again, I talked about the character Lex Luthor in my first book. Perhaps in another decade I'll write a DC book, as James Gunn reboots that universe for what many hope is a more successful run.

However, before we leave Marvel's Distinguished Competition, it's worth looking at the final film in this series. If you, like many, didn't bother with it because the shine was off and the franchise was ending, I would recommend giving it a run-through.

THE FLASH: Knowing When to Let Go

Barry Allen: *We can't bring you back, can we?*

Batman: *You already did. You already did.*

Let's see... a comedy movie that involves time travel, the multiverse, and an attempt to fix an event that went horribly wrong in the past, featuring legacy characters from previous franchise

194

incarnations that forged the way for this current universe? That's right, *Deadpool and Wolverine* may have perfected this routine, but a year earlier, well... let's just say *The Flash* got there faster.

"Not every problem has a solution. Sometimes we just have to let go." - Barry Allen

Is there someone in your past you wish you could help? Something you wish you could change? Perhaps you feel you could have done more, or perhaps you contributed to the problem? Trauma is endemic to most superhero stories: Barry Allen's childhood scars make him similar to Bruce Wayne, and he feels responsible for rectifying it with the same haunted posture that weighs down Spider-man. When we consider our own past, most of us can think of something we'd be tempted to go back and "fix", which makes this narrative so compelling.

The main point of the film, however, is accepting the reality that we cannot fix everything, or save everyone. (One could also make this really meta: as the swan song for the struggling DC Extended Universe, this film is commentary that they can't fix it, or save it, and need to move forward.) It's about accepting limitations and being realistic, specifically about our past. It's an ode to the serenity prayer used in 12-step programs around the world:

"God grant me the serenity to accept the things I cannot change, courage to change the things I can, and wisdom to know the difference." - Reinhold Niebuhr

The original poem goes on: *"Living one day at a time; Enjoying one moment at a time; Accepting hardship as the pathway to peace."* It's true, many times these hardships are the things that made us what we are, shaped us into the godly people we've become, and the ripples extend far beyond us as well. This is what Bruce Wayne (or we might say Batfleck) tries to communicate to Barry at the beginning:

Barry Allen: *I could save her. I could save both of them. I... I could save your parents.*

Bruce Wayne: *Barry, those scars we have make us who we are. We're not meant to go back and fix them.*

Another wonderful plot point in *The Flash* is that we should listen to elder voices who temper or even counter our passions to "do good" with spiritual, experiential and practical wisdom. This is the exact opposite narrative that played out in *Spider-man: Across the Spider-verse* the same year. While that movie is beloved, and certainly has its own merits, it falls into the trope of the young people outsmarting the old, rejecting experience and wisdom to ***"do muh own thing."*** Spidey plans to risk a whole universe collapse to save his father, much like Barry ends up doing trying to save his mother. And I suspect the final Spider-verse film will turn out to be one of those stories where the experienced people are wrong, and the kid is right.

In *The Flash*, young Barry ultimately learn from his elders: he gets wisdom from not one, but two Bat-men, and ultimately a slightly older Barry must plead and appeal to the younger. The message is that strong desires need to be tempered with wisdom, and may actually cause more harm than good because we don't see or understand the big picture. From Tony Stark to General Zod to Barry Allen, this verse rises to haunt us again:

> *"There is a way that seems right to a man, but its end is the way to death."* - Proverbs 14:12

Barry Allen's rash decision reminds me of the apostle Peter in the garden of Gethsemane with Jesus, grabbing for his sword and cutting off ears when Jesus' arrest is a necessary event, a "canon event" if you will. We see the apostle Peter being rash even before that in Matthew 16:

> *"From that time Jesus began to show his disciples that he must go to Jerusalem and suffer many things from the elders and chief priests and scribes, and be killed, and on the third day be raised. And Peter took him aside and began to rebuke him, saying, 'Far be it from you, Lord! This shall never happen to you.'"*

> *"But he turned and said to Peter, 'Get behind me, Satan! You are a hindrance to me. For you are not setting your mind on the things of God, but on the things of man.'"* - Matthew 16:21-23

Peter's intentions for Jesus are caring, and yet his ignorance is met with a harsh rebuke from his master. Think about it: Peter desired to change the plan i.e. the atoning work of Jesus! Speaking of becoming Satan, this is basically what happens to Barry when we realize he, in his ignorance, becomes the Dark Flash. It's a great way of holding up a mirror and reminding all of us that we can become our own worst enemy. Thankfully, Barry sees how his zeal-without-wisdom is leading to destruction.

Flash reversing his decision, taking the tomato can out of the cart, is a physical act of repentance for Barry, admitting he's wrong and following up on that confession with action. It is also painful, tearful and powerful… and a rare narrative treat that we get a powerful story where the central protagonist is wrong and must face it. This is far more satisfying than the modern, predominant *"whole rest of the world needs to change and accept me for who I AM"* stories people are feeding on. It teaches humility and respect, realizing limitations, and living forward instead of backward.

> *"But one thing I do: forgetting what lies behind and straining forward to what lies ahead, I press on toward the goal for the prize of the upward call of God in Christ Jesus. Let those of us who are mature think this way…"* - Philippians 3:13-14

Some may have a few objections here: Barry still makes a minor tweak to get his dad off the hook, so he may not have fully learned his lesson. And with George Clooney showing up as the third Bruce Wayne in the film, it's clear there may be more mayhem for Barry to work through. But of course it ends this way, precisely because it isn't preaching: the movie is, first and foremost, a comedy.

A stronger objection may also be that the story's logic is more utilitarian than Christian: it reflects Spock's adage from *Star Trek* that *"the needs of the many outweigh the needs of the few… or the one."* Christians often point to the parable of the lost sheep (in Matthew 18 and Luke 15) to argue that Jesus would leave 99 to save one, but this is a misunderstanding of the parable: Jesus doesn't throw caution to the wind and risk losing 99 for the sake of the one. That's not the point. Jesus isn't giving special treatment to blood relatives or buddies in this parable over countless scores of other people. The parable of the lost sheep is about Jesus seeking the spiritually lost, which has applications in terms of evangelism, but not decisions on physical aid. Just ask a triage surgeon; getting stuck on saving one (perhaps because they know them) could cost the lives of a dozen others. You do what you can to save the most and accomplish the greatest good.

The Impulse to Help

Kara: *When you found me in that hole that they put me in, and I wasn't Kal-El, why did you help me?*

Flash: *Because you needed help.*

Barry's reflexive desire to help is a good one, a godly one, and there are always opportunities to come to the aid of others, including a stranger, as this story shows us with Kara/Supergirl. Here we even see Batman ready to walk past, but Barry insists, reminding us of another parable: that of the Good Samaritan. The film isn't afraid to show that we can grow cynical or callused with age, whereas Barry's youthful, earnest heart here is part of what revives that spark in the older Bruce Wayne. Just as the apostle Paul exhorted his young disciple Timothy, that no one should look down on him simply because he's young, Barry isn't all wrong. He's finding his footing in the vast DC universe and learning where and how to use what he's been given.

"Time has a pattern that it can't help reliving. Different people, different worlds, drawn to each other like magnets." - The Flash

This film brings us full circle to the events of *Man of Steel,* which is also why it's a fitting close to this cycle of DC films… and of course it reaches back much further, decades further than *Deadpool and Wolverine* did in terms of peering into the franchise's legacy; instead of a grizzled Logan, we get the amazing, grizzled return of Michael Keaton's Batman, and ultimately myriad incarnations of Supermen, Batmen, Flashes and more. It's a moment of reflection that in this MARVEL-Us era, even on DC's side of the fence, there's a recurring cycle of stories that have been told repeatedly (and will be told yet again, when Superman flies into theaters in 2025). It's a reminder that there's *nothing new under the sun…* but with a sense of wonder that suggests *there's nothing wrong with that*. It epitomizes what Cinemagogue has always been about; seeing beauty in the recurrences, then pondering and perceiving what they point us to.

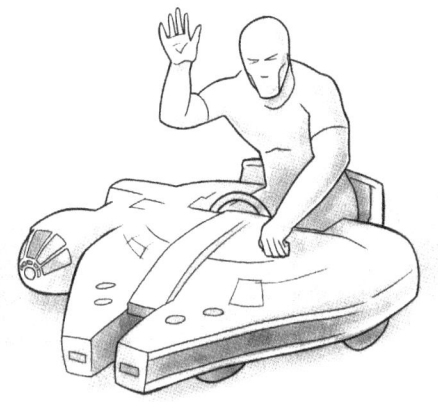

Act 7: **This is The Way**

or

"The Fast and the Franchise-Us"

Scene 1: **The Resurrection Business**

"There has been an awakening. Have you felt it?"
    - Supreme Leader Snoke, *Star Wars: The Force Awakens*

As I mentioned in Act One, Marvel's proof-of-concept made all the major studios double down on sifting their intellectual properties, seeing if there was a shared universe scenario they could create, or bring back to life. Sometimes the revivification just didn't take (looking at you and *The Mummy*, Tom Cruise) and the franchise plan was dead on arrival. Others have fared better, like the Monsterverse, and seem to be trending upward. The new *Jurassic* trilogy got mixed reviews, but the money for each piled high like dinosaur droppings. *The Fast and the Furious* franchise embraced superhero-level fantasy antics and put the pedal to the metal even if now—after a dozen films—it's running low on gas.

A few franchises have landed somewhere in-between, definitely resurrected and making varied amounts of money but—by fan standards and estimation—looking more like a Frankenstein's monster of the prior incarnation they loved. It's worth looking at some of the themes and takeaways from these other inhabitants that marveled us in this era where franchises (and Godzilla) were king.

Fans were split on J.J. Abrams *Star Trek* trilogy, though it did rejuvenate the hibernating franchise. Subsequent shows like *Star Trek: Discovery* have received an equally mixed reception. But a few months after the first *Avengers*, film, the world was rocked with the news that George Lucas had sold the Skywalker Saga to Disney, leading to the exciting prospect that the same year we'd meet the *Guardians of the Galaxy*, we'd also be returning to a galaxy far, far away. Star Wars would try to duplicate the Marvel formula with big sequel movies and spin-off solo films (and I don't mean *Solo* films, although they did that one for him so never mind). They even planned new theme park experiences to immerse fans in the Star Wars universe they loved. And we all lived happily ever after, right?

More than superhero fatigue, or franchise fatigue, or fan upset over choices made at Marvel or DC, perhaps nothing has been so vociferous as the verbal wars over Star Wars. When one thinks of the term "toxic fandom" different franchises may come to mind, but Star Wars probably beats them all in terms of the moniker being applied. Is the adjective deserved? Or have the creatives over at the House of Mouse bungled things so badly that all the criticism is deserved? Well, I think Peter Quill (Star Lord) put it best when he said, ***"bit o' both"*** and it's worth looking at some of the problems inhabiting both sides of the storytelling fence. If we're truly mindful, we might discover that some reasons we're upset have deeper meaning.

Scene 2: **A Wrong Time Ago…**

"That's NOT how the Force works!" - Han Solo, *Star Wars Ep VII*

Gwen Stacy was Dead.

I know what you're thinking: *wrong universe, buddy. Is this a misprint? Doesn't this belong in a Spider-man section?* But I'm not talking about a movie here, I'm talking about a comic book from 1973, an era where it was quite uncommon for a comic book character's supporting cast to be killed. Death was also more permanent in that decade; the lazy practice of routinely killing and bringing back characters wouldn't gain traction for several more decades. Because of this, the death of Gwen Stacy is considered one of the most important pivot points of the Spider-man story—core to his identity and the character—and had a major impact on the entire Marvel brand and comic books as a whole. All that being said…

… it would NEVER have happened today.

You know it's true. Marvel wouldn't dare to do it because of the instant backlash on social media; some fans would be mewling about Gwen being "fridged" while Pete and Gwen "shippers" would be screaming for the writer to be fired. They'd shriek that the previous book's writer would *never* have done this, while others would say the plot was ridiculous: Spider-man certainly would have caught her in time! Even if they dared to publish it, editors would freak out and make the writer find some way to undo it, retcon it, or reveal she wasn't *really* dead. Time travel, that'll do it! Or clones…

So, what changed? Honestly, fans in 1973 were upset too; angry letters were written, etc. However, the connection between creator and consumer wasn't as near-instantaneous as it is now. This allowed creators to be more daring, instead of getting instant feedback making them second-guess every choice due to what may be a vocal minority. And guess what? Over time readers realized that the gravity of the event, and its emotional impact on Peter and the rest of the cast, made for truly compelling storytelling. It subverted their expectations, went against what they *felt* they wanted… but in the long run it became one of the most beloved, albeit tragic, story beats of Spider-man lore.

"Stupid kid. You don't know what you want. None of you ever did." - Bruce Wayne, *Batman Beyond: Return of the Joker*

Bottom line? Fans only think we know what we want. Getting exactly what you expect can frankly become boring after a while. My wife almost always goes to Starbucks because she "knows what she'll be getting." It's reliable; it's also predictable. And thus, modern fans have turned their own franchises into the equivalent of McDonalds in terms of consumption. We want to be surprised, we love having our minds blown, but then we get upset when it goes outside the parameters of how we wanted things to play out. Instead of giving a story time, thought, and the long view, we throw fan tantrums like spoiled children.

Why belabor this point? Well, it has spiritual significance when applied to our own lives, in which God is a storyteller. Consider the screenplay of *your* life alongside your favorite fictions. Are there events in your life that don't play out the way you felt they ought to? Friends that don't do or say what you expect? People you thought you knew who suddenly made shocking choices? Relationships that fell apart? Things you never saw coming? God often subverts our expectations... and in the same vein we often rage about it, complaining about the latest chapter in our life or a "bad episode" we're experiencing.

Are some of the complaints about our favorite franchises projecting this kind of attitude? Do we respect the storyteller, or do we believe we "own" the narrative? *"I want them to surprise me, but not to do anything I don't want them to do with MY characters."* Wait... YOUR character? Who's in charge here?

"I've got a BAD feeling about this..." - Everyone, *Star Wars*

I'm not saying there aren't legitimate complaints to be had, especially within the Star Wars saga. But there's a difference between bad storycraft and one's preferences being betrayed. We can mindfully critique narrative weaknesses, but many toxic fans simply spew in disgust that the creator didn't take characters down the physical or emotional journey that *they* wanted. We even come up with terms like "head canon" to suggest we control what is actually truth about a character who—at the end of the day—we are not in charge of. It reminds me of people who like to pick and choose only parts of God's Word (and what Jesus said or did) like Thomas Jefferson did, cutting out the miraculous parts of the Bible he didn't agree with or believe.

That being said, I admittedly ignore the Star Wars *prequels* as if they didn't happen. See? I'm guilty too. And that's okay: Star Wars isn't even close to being as important as holy scripture. (If you get upset to the same level, truly pause and consider.) My concern is that the mindset begins to build a sense of entitlement and control in our hearts that may not be healthy in the long run. If we choose to ignore some parts we believe are poorly made (or simply don't fit our preferred mold) that's fine, but we may want to temper our vitriol. Our zeal should show when someone's distorting God's character. A make-believe character? Let's keep some perspective.

The latest version of Optimus Prime just came out in the animated film *Transformers: One*. Having been through five or six Optimus origins in my time, I saw the trailer for this one and rolled my eyes instead of rolling out as a young, would-be Prime traded Star-Lord style quips with his "blue-collar buddy" Megatron. I hear the animation is great, but the retooled background and characterization didn't interest me. Honesty time: did I feel irritation welling up within me? Sure. But do I need to go on an angry tirade about it on social media? No, I can go on with my life and rewatch the cartoons and movies I like. The end.

Now, about Star Wars… I enjoyed the sequels. Did I love them as much as the original trilogy? Not a chance. Do I have complaints? Yeah, but let's look at a few of those and see if some of them don't raise some biblical considerations:

STAR WARS: The Force ~~Awakens~~ Recycles?

"Chewie… we're home." - Han Solo, *Star Wars: The Force Awakens*

I remember our group being divided coming out of the first sequel, though everyone was generally pumped. It's easy for some to project backward from 2024 and feel disdain for all things Disney Star Wars, but most people I knew a decade ago either loved *The Force Awakens* or at least enjoyed it with qualifications. The main complaint in our small group at the theater was that it was just a rehash of *Star Wars: A New Hope*: The New Order, secret plans, a kid from a desert planet, a large planet-killer, etc. I get it. It does follow a fair number of story beats from the first film… but is that inherently a criticism? *Top Gun: Maverick* would do this even more blatantly in

2022 to both box office and critical acclaim. (Side note, the mission in *Top Gun: Maverick* is essentially the Death Star trench and target mission from *Star Wars* too.)

As any Cinemagogue reader knows by now, there are no "new" narratives, only repeating monomyths or life under the sun stories. What we think of as new is merely "fresh"… much like a freshly baked pastry. It's the same dough as yesterday, and maybe there's some modern contextual frosting or glaze put on it, but underneath the surface it's going to be similar. This Star Wars movie embraced that fact; whether it tasted fresh is a little more subjective.

"If you live long enough, you see the same eyes in different people." - Maz Kanata

Is it crazy to think history will repeat itself? I can see people complaining about The First Order being a retread of the Empire, but didn't that happen with World War II? Seriously, Germany again? The Imperial German Army is renamed the Third Reich? And only a generation later? We can't deny there's historical precedent. Even biblically, the book of Judges keeps repeating the same cycle: Israel behaves badly, another nation comes in to oppress them, and God raises up a judge like Shamgar or Samson to save them. Rinse, Rey, repeat. Everything old is new again.

As for Starkiller Base, or the "bigger Death Star"… isn't that what we do in real life too? We ended World War II with a nuclear bomb. What have we done since then? Made bigger nuclear bombs. Does this mean Star Wars writers are creatively bankrupt, or is this just art imitating life?

The other complaint centered around how immediate young Rey's aptitude for the Force manifests in the film. Admittedly, other movies of this decade with leading ladies would start falling into the cardboard cutout trope of the faultless, flawless female character, so this tripped some people's "Mary Sue" alarms. But come on… did we really want to have to wait through the slow Force growth this time around? Especially those of us exposed to some of the wild things Force users did in the animated Star Wars shows and video games, ripping all the rivets out of robots and yanking Tie Fighters out of the sky; weren't we all hoping they'd speed things up and get to the good stuff? Even in the prequel trilogy the Jedi seem FAR more power-laden than what we witnessed in the original trilogy. No one in-film suggests Rey was "better than Luke" or Anakin for that matter. She also is shown to have flaws throughout the trilogy, and a narrative explanation emerges later for why she and Kylo Ren are oddly, innately powerful.

Some of the hate for Rey seems more like bleed-over from portrayals of women in other films of this era. Well, and other women in the sequel, and the antics of the president of Lucasfilm… but we'll get to that shortly. All that to say, perhaps we should be mindful where we may be projecting (or blanket-condemning) characters when certain trends or tropes are frustrating us in other movies, like…

STAR WARS: The Last ~~Jedi~~ Straw?

"This is not going to go the way you think." - Luke Skywalker

I adore parts of this film; I loathe others. Rian Johnson gave us a mixed bag of ideas riddled with subversions of expectation that hit and miss. Sandwiched in the middle is some moralizing that felt out of place in Star Wars and out of sync with the previous film. Although still less overt than we see in other films of the era, there's an effort to make male characters act impetuous or inept while every female character is competent and superior. Poe and Finn appear to be "nerfed" to let Holdo and Rose take the stage… and not just a stage, but a metaphorical pulpit. The whole narrative excursus to the gambling planet feels like a waste of time that goes nowhere, save to stage a forced message about classism. It's all part of Hollywood's preachiness creep that I'll speak to in the next chapter.

Still, this isn't the main reason Star Wars fans hate this movie. We all know it's because…

"Luke would NEVER…!"

As I've said many times, I was a Han Solo guy. Not that I didn't love Luke, but I wasn't as beholden to him like my brother, who—as you might expect—hated *The Last Jedi*. I think we were all willing to believe a semi-retired Han Solo might slip back into a life of pirating, but some were wholly unwilling to believe that Luke Skywalker could err, or retreat, as we find out in this film. After all, we followed this character in the original Star Wars trilogy for *four whole years* of his young adult life; *surely* we know how perfect he would be for the rest of it! Destined for greatness, right? Right?

> *"I'm out of it for a little while, everybody gets delusions of grandeur."* - Han Solo, *Return of the Jedi*

Yes, I'm being sarcastic. We've rewatched Luke Skywalker's journey many times over four decades, but we only saw four years of his life. What I think is revealed here is that some people put Luke Skywalker on a messianic parallel, only to find out—and get furious —that he ended up more like King David. Consider the first four years we see young David in the Bible: stalwart, faithful, giant slaying. Destined to be king! Now we skip ahead several decades in our Bibles (much like jumping from Episode VI to Episode VIII) and we find an adulterer… a murderer. **Surely David would NEVER-!** Whoops. And let's not forget how David screws up raising his own sons, and the kingdom is divided (and later falls). Absalom basically pulls a Kylo Ren.

David was the man after God's own heart! How did this happen? This isn't the way the story was supposed to go! Let's get angry at the storyteller and—oh, shoot. *Sorry God.*

Now, to be fair, Rian Johnson isn't God… and from Marvel comics to Dark Horse comics to countless novels there are multiple fictional histories of Luke Skywalker's story after *Return of the Jedi*. It's fine to have our preferences, but refusing to believe a character might take such a radical turn reveals a blind spot in our own hearts and hopes. None of these characters are Christ, and all of them—like David—are thus narratively capable of doing things we don't want to accept. As I was writing this book, a pivotal high-profile pastor that has blessed millions fell into scandal when a 5-year affair was exposed. **But that man would NEVER-!** Oh, actually… he did. Closer to home, I've lived long enough to find out a mentor figure in my own life—a man vital to my discipleship and marriage counseling—stumbled into adultery, drug addiction, homelessness, and ultimately an overdose that took his life.

Now, the best pushback here is that many stories focus on being relatable or aspirational. Tony Stark and all his flaws are *relatable*; Clark Kent is so noble and set apart we find him *aspirational*. Luke apologists effectively reveal that they wanted Anakin's son to become exclusively aspirational. Notice I didn't say "remain" aspirational; let's be honest, Luke's pretty whiny in the first film, and flawed in the second film. He grows in ways that show him becoming aspirational, and this blossoms in *Return of the Jedi*. Angry fans can't believe other flaws might manifest later in life, whereas my experience with people over time is that there are peaks and valleys. *The Last Jedi* makes Luke a man instead of messiah.

> *"Pass on what you have learned; strength, mastery, but weakness, folly, failure also. Yes, failure most of all: the greatest teacher failure is."* - Yoda, *Star Wars: The Last Jedi*

> *"But he said to me, 'My grace is sufficient for you, for my power is made perfect in weakness.' Therefore I will boast all the more gladly of my weaknesses, so that the power of Christ may rest upon me."* - 2 Corinthians 12:9

Luke, however, becomes aspirational once again in *The Last Jedi*. Watch it again if you don't believe me; I think people tripped over how far he'd fallen and don't remember how spectacularly he picks himself back up. He schools a young and naive Rey, and also Kylo Ren, giving the latter a masterclass in humiliation. His power of Force projection is surprising and impressive (most impressive). Luke shares a heartfelt moment with his sister and goes out on top again, becoming one with the Force and vanishing much like former mentors Obi-wan and Yoda. If people wanted him to be "Star Wars Jesus" then I understand the disappointment. But it's still an ending of biblical proportion: he resembles Samson in the Old Testament, who (after falling from grace) got to stand and achieve victory with one last mighty exertion of power.

> *"Wisdom they held, but that library contained nothing that the girl Rey does not already possess…"* - Yoda

Some also took exception that Yoda seems to disparage the Jedi "sacred texts" in the film, suggesting Rey has everything she needs. The tree where the texts are kept bursts into flames, and here's where people who already didn't like Rey probably got angrier. Christians specifically took this as a secular dig at following written scriptures, advocating instead a more Disneyesque mantra of "trusting your heart". What they failed to realize was that the impish Yoda is being playful with Luke at that moment (hey, it's not the first time Luke's mentors fail to explain things plainly). Rey didn't just leave with her wits and heart, perfect as she is; she'd already taken and secured the sacred texts in the Millennium Falcon. And we see Rey reading and relying on those texts in the next film…

STAR WARS: ~~Rise~~ Rejection of Skywalker?

"Somehow, Palpatine Returned…" - Poe Dameron

Okay, this reveal was poorly planned and executed, and fans everywhere called it out, made it a meme and more. If they'd sprinkled a few hints into *The Last Jedi* that there was someone above Supreme Leader Snoke, it would have been enough. Unveiling it gradually in the first act of this film, instead of just dumping it in the opening scrawl, would have garnered less scorn. Still, a poor reveal doesn't mean it's not a great idea, both in terms of Palpatine being the enduring villain for all nine films and Rey's revealed parentage.

Like Sauron was to Middle Earth, Emperor Palpatine becomes the ever-watching eye and embodiment of what seems like undying evil itself. The Emperor had already shown up again—in comics and books before this movie that were beloved by many fans—and I for one was glad to see him. There was no way Snoke or any new face over just three films would match what had been cultivated over forty years and six films, so having Palpatine step out of the shadows (in a galaxy that had already introduced cloning and arcane powers, including resurrection) just makes sense. He then proceeds to comport himself like the Satan of Star Wars:

"I've been behind every voice you've ever heard." - Palpatine

We discover that Ben Solo's seduction and transformation into Kylo Ren was Palpatine-by-proxy, with a very devilish bent. He promises to give everything to Ben: it will all be his if he effectively bows down and worships the Emperor. Jesus was similarly tempted, but instead of saying "get thee behind me" Kylo bends… until he doesn't. Star Wars has always been a story of fall and redemption, and it takes Leia's spirit, calling her son back, to initiate that turn.

As for Rey's parentage, fans who kept up on interviews and comments outside of the narrative knew this was a retcon, but if you shut out that noise and enjoy the way it plays exclusively within the confines of the story… it works. Lest we forget: Darth Vader "murdered" Luke's father in *A New Hope*, then was retconned into being his father in *The Empire Strikes Back*. The myth of George Lucas having this all plotted out has long been dispelled. Personally, I like the way these three films play with our expectations. In the first film, we speculate Rey might be the offspring of a Jedi: perhaps Obi-Wan Kenobi? The second film throws us off, not because Kylo Ren knew Rey's parents were "nobodies" but because he'd plucked that idea and fear out of her own mind. Finally, the reveal isn't the horror that her parents are unimportant, but rather the worst thing imaginable:

Finn: *Rey, that doesn't sound like you. Rey, I know you-*

Rey: *People keep telling me they know me. I'm afraid no one does.*

Many fans were upset that Rey was being set up as a perfect woman warrior without flaws, and this movie shows that men like Finn believe she is. But *Rise of Skywalker* muddies the water with the dark truth of what's inside her, what's a part of her, where her power comes from: her lineage is that of Star Wars' darkest devil.

"You are of your father the devil, and your will is to do your father's desires. He was a murderer from the beginning, and does not stand in the truth, because there is no truth in him. When he lies, he speaks out of his own character, for he is a liar and the father of lies." - John 8:44

We live in a world that, like Finn, will tell us and reinforce that we're actually "good people", whereas Jesus in the gospels tells us that apart from reconciliation with a God we've rebelled against, our parentage is like Rey's: our dad is the devil. And Rey's journey is much like that of many Christian converts.

We often think—like she did living on Jakku—that we're part of something bigger. Then, as Kylo told Rey, the world says we aren't special: we come from nothing, there is no "big reveal" to be had in this material universe. Then the gospel comes along, telling us there's a big reveal, and the first part is the humbling fact that we're from a damned lineage. Fortunately, there's more to the story… and it turns out this can be redeemed; there's something even better than the Force by which we can have a new family. This is why I wasn't offended when Rey takes the Skywalker name at the end of the film; what a wonderful mirror for the good news in scripture that takes devil's daughters (and sons) and grafts them into God's family!

Not only that, but it takes the help and healing sacrifice of a biological Skywalker (Ben) to overcome the Sith's Satan and give Rey entrance to that new, adopted life.

Rise of… Complementarianism?

"The life-force of your bond… a dyad in the Force. A power like life itself." - Emperor Palpatine

The concept of the "dyad" crept into not just this movie, but the underrated *Matrix: Resurrections* in 2021. The term relates to chromosomes, chemistry and more, essentially a group of two things (or people) that form a pair in some special way, as by attraction or facilitation of a function or activity. In other words, two that "become or act as one" and are stronger for it. In the contemporary world we live in—which currently pits the sexes against each other, even telling women they don't need men—there's an interesting counter-cultural development that occurs in this film. Forget all that "Force is female" propaganda happening outside the narrative that has irritated and divided fans. In the actual film we hear Rey admit:

"I would have taken your hand. Ben's hand…"

In the first film, Rey barks at Finn to stop trying to take her hand, but in this story she recognizes the worth in this kind of joining.

Something has softened in the narrative, a recognition of the power of two, and specifically the portrait of one man, one woman.

"But from the beginning of creation, 'God made them male and female.' 'Therefore a man shall leave his father and mother and hold fast to his wife, and the two shall become one flesh.' So they are no longer two but one flesh. What therefore God has joined together, let not man separate." - Mark 10:6-9

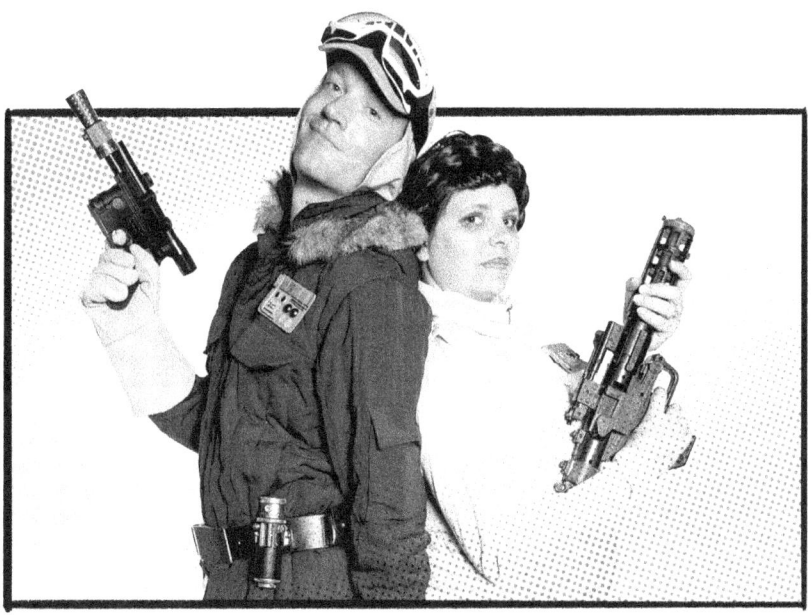
She loves me. I know.

The film upholds this amazing bond not just as something beautiful, but something powerful that enables them to overcome Palpatine and the power of the Sith. Rey couldn't have succeeded without Ben, without his sacrifice… which looks a lot like a husband's admonition in Ephesians 5:25.

"Husbands, love your wives, as Christ loved the church and gave himself up for her…"

Note that Rey even takes Ben's family name (on his mother's side). Not very progressive, mind you… and perhaps that's partly why critics were much harsher on this film, whereas they sang the praises of *The Last Jedi*. This trilogy takes us from the modern idolization of the autonomous individual to acknowledging that two becoming one is infinitely more powerful, and perhaps even designed and destined.

Say what you will about messaging in modern films (and the subsequent Star Wars shows on Disney+ that have truly tarnished the saga) but the sequel trilogy ends on a much more traditional note, filled with biblical imagery and ideas to play with just like the original films. For an old school Solo fan, seeing the former shoot-first skeptic confess full belief in *The Force Awakens* will always be a marvelous moment for me:

"I used to wonder about that myself. Thought it was a bunch of mumbo jumbo… the dark side and the light. Crazy thing is: it's true… all of it. It's all true." - Han Solo

Star Wars: The Force Awakens came out in 2014, a year I've mentioned was a mammoth moment in the MARVEL-Us Era, boasting some of the best comic book films that still stand as titans of the genre. (Side note: it also birthed an amazing franchise by the name of *John Wick*.) But on top of all this, another franchise resurfaced to remind us who the king of these titans truly was, with a fang-filled face I was familiar with from comics as well.

Scene 3: **The MONSTER-Us Era**

"Long live the king." - Dr. Russell, *Godzilla: King of the Monsters*

Marvel's Godzilla comics in the 1970s pitted the big lizard against The Fantastic Four, S.H.I.E.L.D. and even The Avengers (and those old stories were, pardon the pun, fire. I cut my baby teeth on the rubber-suited Toho features too. As of 2024, we not only have the Monsterverse movies but the accompanying Monarch series as well, topped off by Toho's own resurgence with animated movies and the live action *Godzilla Minus One*. It's a golden age for Godzilla fans.

(And Kong fans too, I suppose… I mean I like the big ape, but we all know who rules the roost, am I right?)

Some might point out that these movies are mostly fun while the plots—like the earth in the Monsterverse films—are fairly hollow.

But has this character lasted seven decades on such shallow premises, or like the ocean depths he calls home: is there something much deeper here? Rather than go film-by-film, let's stomp through the malleable mythos of this memorable monster.

The City of God(zilla)

The first Godzilla movie was a bomb.

Okay, it performed well critically and financially at the box office in both Japan and America. Perhaps it's better to say… it was *about* a bomb: a very particular bomb dropped on Japan by its foes in World War II, namely the United States. The reality is that "Gojira" (as the Japanese named him) represented the stomping they took from a mighty foreign power with nuclear capability. In other words, the monster was the U.S. and the destruction, and fallout, were emotionally coded callbacks for a recovering country. This is also why the movie was dramatically reedited for American audiences with a Hollywood actor inserted into the narrative as a reporter.

One might wonder then: how did such a focused, historically-fixed monster metaphor endure to become the longest continuously running film franchise recognized by the Guinness World Records? Mark Jacobson of New York magazine posited one theory:

"Very few constructs have so perfectly embodied the overriding fears of a particular era. He is the symbol of a world gone wrong… He rears up out of the sea as a creature of no particular belief system… a reptilian id that lives inside the deepest recesses of the collective unconscious that cannot be reasoned with, a merciless undertaker who broaches no deals."

Jacobson is hitting close to the atomic mark here, although I'd differ with him in terms of belief systems. While Godzilla's original designer cited no sources other than pursuing a "reptilian design" and adding the back plates for a unique aesthetic, a reading of the leviathan in Job 41 offers some uncanny similarities! It's worth pulling up images of Godzilla and reading the chapter in its entirety, but here are some select verses…

"Can you draw out Leviathan with a fishhook
or press down his tongue with a cord?
Lay your hands on him;
remember the battle—you will not do it again!
Behold, the hope of a man is false;
he is laid low even at the sight of him
Who can open the doors of his face?
Around his teeth is terror.
His back is made of rows of shields...
His sneezings flash forth light,
and his eyes are like the eyelids of the dawn.
Out of his mouth go flaming torches;
sparks of fire leap forth.
Out of his nostrils comes forth smoke,
as from a boiling pot and burning rushes.
His breath kindles coals,
and a flame comes forth from his mouth.
He makes the deep boil like a pot;
he makes the sea like a pot of ointment.
Behind him he leaves a shining wake;
one would think the deep to be white-haired.
On earth there is not his like,
a creature without fear.
He sees everything that is high;
he is king over all the sons of pride."

The illustration of the leviathan is used in Job to subdue human pride, to remind mankind that since we don't even have control over these gigantic creatures, what right do we have to think we have any control over the *author* of those creatures (and all creation)? That's why God adds in verse 10 that *"No one is so fierce that he dares to stir him up. Who then is he who can stand before me?"* God is using this image of a lizard titan to humble Job, and us. It should also bring to mind what the head of the monster studying Monarch tells a government official in *Godzilla: King of the Monsters* (2019).

Admiral Stenz: **This alpha predator of yours, doctor, do you really think he has a chance?**

Dr. Serizawa: *The arrogance of men is thinking nature is in our control, and not the other way around.*

It makes me tremble just a little bit, to realize how this inspired but unspecified creature in scripture aligns with the enduring image of Godzilla. Intentional or not, call it collective unconscious if you will, I think the 70-year persistence of this character is partly owed to the fact that it tapped into this biblical imagery. In the original film, even man's greatest weapon yet—a nuclear explosion—only served to agitate and awaken its wrath.

"Godzilla was baptized in the fire of the H-bomb and survived. What could kill it now?" - Dr. Yamane, *Gojira* (1954)

Now, any good theologian will interject that mankind was given a mandate in Genesis to subdue creation, to have dominion over the earth. However, because of the fall of man—because of sin—this mission has become toil for us, arduous and even dangerous. Even creatures of the world are set against us. That's a product of our sin, and so Godzilla mirrors that leviathan-crushing reminder of the curse, the price of sin, and our helpless state apart from intervention.

"…we human beings are weak creatures."
  - Dr. Serizawa, *Gojira (1954)*

"…it's gonna send us back to the Stone Age! You have no idea what's coming." - Joe Brody, *Godzilla (2014)*

Now, any good Godzilla fan will remind us that the films where the King himself brings curse and devastation pale in number with the movies where he acts as a form of protector… sometimes for Tokyo, sometimes for the world ecosystem, and sometimes with a seeming general care of humankind. So… what is he then? Even in the 2014 Legendary film, opinions differed:

Vivienne Graham: *A god, for all intents and purposes.*

Ford Brody: *A monster.*

It turns out Godzilla's Americanized name was aptly formed as well. This "god-reptile" serves as a narrative hybrid; in some instances he's a harsh reminder of the curse, while in other incarnations he's a bit like God himself, overseeing a world in which he is King and everything is subject to his rule. As discussed in the 2019 American film:

Senator Williams: *So, you'd want to make Godzilla our pet.*

Dr. Serizawa: *No. We will be his.*

In the 60s and 70s Toho films, Japan belonged to Godzilla… though he lived on Monster Island, condescending to seek and save Tokyo from aliens and smog monsters (and sometimes even from themselves). The Legendary films have expanded his territory to the entire planet; enemies and monsters rise up, like Ghidorah or the other titans, and Godzilla emerges to smack them down. At the same time, when men grow in their hubris and seek to replace him with a Mechagodzilla—a graven image, if you will—he'll rise to eradicate their "idol" and bring judgment on the counterfeiters.

We also see believers in these films, protagonists who trust in the big guy like a god… even when he's not as "tame" as humans would like him to be. He's a "wild lion" much like Aslan is described in C.S. Lewis' Chronicles of Narnia.

"Course he isn't safe. But he's good. He's the King, I tell you."
- Mr. Beaver, *The Lion, The Witch and the Wardrobe*

"Godzilla saved us. You were there with Mom. You saw it. How could you doubt him?" - Madison Russell, *Godzilla vs. Kong*

As for the "allies with an adversarial relationship" Godzilla has developed with Kong in recent films, well… let's just say the furry guy needs to know his place. You might see something off here in terms of godly parallels when Godzilla seems to attack Kong seemingly unprovoked, but look closer. There's only one King! Kong has a subservient role here; he gets the killing blow in their first shared movie only because Godzilla literally bequeaths him the power, breathing energy into his battle axe (which is made of a Godzilla scale/plate). We then get to see Kong play out a Moses metaphor in *Godzilla x Kong: The New Empire* as he frees his fellow apes from a hellish slavery, leading them into the promised land of the Hollow Earth. Yet he can't do this by his own power, can he? He must ascend and solicit help from the king.

Speaking of Moses, remember when God sent him on a mission in Exodus 4, then showed up along the way and tried to kill him? (Go read it, it's a trip.) I'm just saying, Godzilla expecting Kong to respect territory and approach correctly—and his harsh response when this isn't done—is less out of line with God than many modern Christians might think. Uzzah (who touched the Ark of the Covenant with good intention) would definitely agree. Christians rest in the grace of Jesus, but our God is a titan-sized powerhouse who is terrifying to all outside that grace. He has also brought earth-shaking and fiery discipline to his chosen people throughout biblical history, so in terms of parallels there may be as much Godzilla as Superman when crafting a fictional portrait.

If we expand the big lizard metaphors to a franchise that resurrected a year after Godzilla, the *Jurassic World* movies weigh us down with similarly humbling messages. Even the titles alone tell a story. Think about it; the first three movies were about a Jurassic *Park*. Foolish humans played with DNA and brought large, extinct animals back that they ultimately couldn't control. Still, the humiliating and sometimes lethal lessons were predominantly learned on a couple of islands safe from the rest of the populated globe. In the new trilogy, the 2015 title is aptly expanded to Jurassic *World*. True, the first film takes place on an isolated park again, but this time greed and human folly lead to a global problem. Is it the dinosaurs' world now? You bet Jurassic is.

The second film evokes a broken world of biblical proportion with the title *Fallen Kingdom*. We might think this refers to the destruction of Isla Nublar by a volcanic eruption midway through the film, but when a young girl opens a Dino-sized Pandora's Box in Act Three our world is inundated with competitors for—as the third film tells us—*Dominion*. The folly of man literally rains down on characters in that film as a biblically sized plague of fire and locusts. And while it seems some co-existence may be possible, reflections are made on how big and old they are, and by comparison how small and fleeting we are. Seeing the giant aquatic Mosasaur in the final moments of the brings us right back to that leviathan in Job.

"...this is Godzilla's world. We just live in it." - Chief Warrant Officer Barnes, *Godzilla: King of the Monsters*

The major takeaway when watching movies like this is that the world is not ours: we may not be subject to dinosaurs, titans or Kongs—no Godzilla holds dominion over us—but we do answer to a King (of the Monsters, and everything else) and this reminds us to have a humble posture in terms of the world and our place in it. Not only is this world not our own, according to scripture *I am not my own*. I belong to God. It's *God's world; we just live in it.*

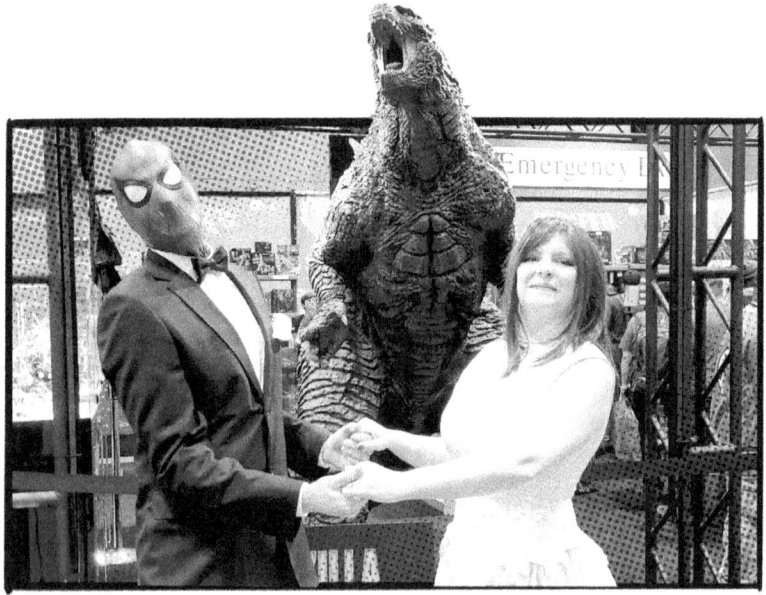

I can't be sure, but I think he's giving us his blessing.

Other horrors have emerged and franchised in the MARVEL-Us and MONSTER-Us Era, however, from which no godlike parallels can (or ought to) be drawn. One franchise in particular is worth discussing, as the monsters aren't just metaphors but come close to biblical realities. Truly monstrous…

Scene 4: If You Wan Something Done Right…

"Whatever you do, don't stop praying." - Sister Oana, *The Nun*

I devoted a half-chapter in the original Cinemagogue book to the value and use of horror and supernatural films, but that was published the release of *The Conjuring* in 2013, a horror movie directed by James Wan that practically makes my case for me in one sentence! I managed to add that quote to the 2023 Director's Cut edition of the book, but the quote is worth repeating here:

> *"The devil exists. God exists. And for us, as people, our very destiny hinges upon which one we elect to follow."* - Ed Warren, *The Conjuring*

Not the kind of direct admonition you'd ever expect to get from *Godzilla vs. Kong*, *Star Wars: The Force Awakens* or even *Avengers: Infinity War*, is it? I'm the first to admit that—despite all the teaching and examples of how to draw theological ideas from film and narrative—knowing how to see the parallels doesn't necessarily build an easy bridge to casual conversation. Some people may watch *Man of Steel* and want to remain in the realm of comic books instead of considering how Jor-El mirrors the God of the Bible. However, when a movie blatantly depicts a biblical concept in a story, dealing with God or demons through a Christian lens, it's a lot easier to spark a conversation with something as simple as *"so, what do YOU think about that?"*

James Wan, by all accounts, is not a professing Christian… yet he's built the highest grossing horror franchise of all time around not only biblically-sourced ideas of demons, but a real-life Christian couple and stories of their experiences with the occult. *The Conjuring* movies are based loosely on real-life paranormal investigators Ed and Lorraine Warren (and their concepts of possession and exorcism are loosely based as well). But at the end of the day, it still haunts our imaginations with the notion that there is more beyond the material world… something most Hollywood films rarely do. This franchise begs us to consider, and perhaps tremble, that there is a war going on beyond what we normally see.

> *"The court accepts the existence of God every time a witness swears to tell the truth. I think it's about time they accept the existence of the Devil."* - Ed Warren, *The Conjuring: The Devil Made Me Do It*

The three *Conjuring* films have anchored the franchise, concluding with a fourth in 2025, and have spun off the *Annabelle* and *The Nun* series as well from characters and concepts introduced in the core films. There are certainly attributes of demons that aren't expressly biblical, with the doll Annabelle being the most obvious; there's no biblical basis for demons attaching themselves to objects. At the same time, the scriptures give us very little detail about the workings of demons, so I'm not against some creative license with fiction. What's been great about Wan's universe is the place of centrality held by the church, and those who profess Christian faith.

Ed Warren: *Have your children been baptized?*

Roger Perron: *Uh, no. We never got around to that. We're not really a church going family.*

Ed Warren: *Well, you may want to rethink that...*

For decades, horror films had been systematically removing the aspect of Christian faith and/or biblical imagery as a defense against evil. Crosses no longer repel vampires; demons dispatch priests with dismissive attitudes and mock the effectiveness of prayer or the church. Wan's franchise not only brought this iconography back, but put it front and center. Of course, Hollywood films typically see everything *Christian* through a *Catholic* lens, so we rarely see a Protestant flavor of the faith. But even I have to admit—from a theatrical perspective—cathedrals, vestments, and Catholic icons lend themselves to more interesting cinematography. It's not personal.

Now, these stories also portray ideas about demon-infused objects that aren't biblically based; there are mistaken ideas about holy water and other objects being imbued with godly power. Still, the necessity of prayer, the authority and power of Christ, and other biblical realities are shown in a way that is more reverent than most other genres of film. Simply having positive, faithful, even heroic Christian characters runs counter to the typical movie trend of believers as bigots and bad guys, hypocrites or mean-spirited legalists.

It might also surprise some Christians that the first two films featuring the Warrens were written by Christian screenwriters (Chad and Carey Hayes). When you see atheist forums complaining about

The Conjuring universe films with terms like "preachy", "propaganda" and "militantly Christian" a Jesus follower might consider they're worth a look. Horror is often considered controversial subject matter for Christians, even though we see what might be considered a jump-scare in our Bible:

> *"Amid thoughts from visions of the night,*
>   *when deep sleep falls on men,*
> *dread came upon me, and trembling,*
>   *which made all my bones shake.*
> *A spirit glided past my face;*
>   *the hair of my flesh stood up."*
>   - Eliphaz, Job 4:13-15

In the Old Testament we find that "goat demons" are being worshipped in Leviticus, and King Saul is vexed by a harmful spirit in 1 Samuel. Most people think of "Legion" and Jesus' encounter with those demons in the gospels, although Paul also casts an evil spirit out a girl in the Book of Acts. All that to say, these are things Christians believe are real and at work in the world, then and now. Excluding them from storytelling—out of fear, or disdain for scary movies and the genre—indirectly removes them from art that should be reflecting life. It thus communicates that they aren't a part of reality, which isn't the message Christians should want.

> *"Look, I've only been with the company for a couple of weeks, but I gotta tell you... these things are REAL! Since I've joined these men, I have seen sh— that'll turn you white!"*
>   - Winston Zeddemore, *Ghostbusters*

Now, considering all the things these stories get wrong about demons, not to mention all the other fictional conjuring that doesn't put things in a biblical framework such as haunted houses, ghosts, werewolves and a bevy of nightmarish monsters, one could argue this confuses more than it helps. But I disagree: these tales still foster conversation about the afterlife, what happens when we die, and what enemies might be lurking "behind the veil". Yes, scripture indicates that human spirits don't linger and haunt the living. Freddy Krueger would never be able to inhabit teen dreams. Toxic waste won't reanimate the dead. But by the same token... gamma radiation doesn't give people hulking strength. A DeLorean can't time travel. Thanos isn't real; there are no Infinity Stones. John Wick would never survive his four-film gauntlet (especially that fall from the roof). Fast cars won't take down a submarine in the arctic, no matter how furious they are.

If we're willing to deviate from reality for a multitude of material world fictions, we can allow for some fictional deviations within the spiritual world. The only extreme caution I would have would be in any depiction of God himself... which is why it's nice he doesn't turn up in a lot of horror fiction.

The *Conjuring* universe hasn't been alone in this resurgence of ministers and Christians facing demons and monsters, with atheists and agnostics caught in the middle. The success of James Wan's shared world surely fueled Netflix's decision to fund the semi-shared universe guided by horror auteur Mike Flanagan. The Roman Catholic-turned-atheist infuses a lot of religious musing into his work, particularly the angelic/vampiric series *Midnight Mass.* While not necessarily painting Christians or the priest in the story in a rosy light, it features a nuanced and anguished exploration of faith and doubt, conversations between atheists and believers, and the struggle for meaning and hope of transcendence. I've seen a lot of lapsed Catholics say the story spoke to them, which tells me there are rich conversations for Christians to have with that demographic.

Even Flanagan's extremely graphic and bloody adaptation of Edgar Allen Poe's work, *The Fall of the House of Usher*, offers a shocking commentary on deviancy and depravity, with the creeping dread of a real judgment from beyond for deeds done in darkness. Flanagan also directed the second entry in the *Ouija* film series, *Origin of Evil*. These films don't glorify toying with the occult, but rather emphasize why everyone should steer clear. The 2022 chiller *Talk to Me* doubles down on this danger and cautions against opening oneself to spirits.

Director Scott Derrickson, a professing Christians who worked on Marvel movies like Doctor Strange, also gave us a horror entry with his film *The Black Phone*. The 70s-based serial killer story surprises us with a supernatural twist and a spiritual look at prayer and God's providence. Meanwhile, Russell Crowe put on the white collar to fight against demonic forces in *The Pope's Exorcist,* based on the real-life Reverend Gabriele Amorth. More recently, *Late Night with the Devil* deals directly with disbelief as a talk show host decides to stage a live show on October 31st with mediums and an allegedly possessed girl, alongside skeptics and supernatural debunkers who are in for a surprise.

As I was writing this chapter, a not-so-scary afterlife entry rose from the grave, in keeping with this era's franchise formula. Studios have been digging like crazy to unearth intellectual properties they might breathe life back into, and thus we find ourselves facing *Beetlejuice Beetlejuice*. True to form, Jenna Ortega's new character provides us with another skeptic forced to accept the reality of the afterlife (this time including hell) and all the while Michael Keaton shows us he's still the ghost with the most. (Based on box office success, we'll probably be saying his name three times in theaters a few years down the road.)

Similarly, after an ill-conceived reboot sucked the life out of the *Ghostbusters* in 2016, the spirit-catching franchise was released from that trap five years later with *Ghostbusters: Afterlife*. Yet again, characters were forced to reconcile the reality of the spiritual world, as well as reconciling relationships (and saving the world).

Speaking of reviving ancient intellectual property, there were classic films other than *Beetlejuice* and *Ghostbusters* that were mined from decades past in the hope of cashing in on the MARVEL-Us formula. Not all these attempts worked, but a few stood out as memorable milestones that marveled without need of capes. *Mad Max: Fury Road* and *Top Gun: Maverick* were shining examples of shocking success, both financially and critically. One of my favorite 21st century directors, Denis Villeneuve, gave us the acclaimed science fiction masterpiece that is now my favorite film of all time: *Blade Runner 2049*. Perhaps I'll cover these in a future book, but for now, let's talk about some of the misfires…

Scene 5: **Mad Dash - Franchise Road**

Many felt the follow-up to *The Lord of the Rings* trilogy should have been titled *The Hobbit: An Unexpected Letdown.* The *Pirates of the Caribbean* franchise seemed to slowly sink. *Harry Potter* soared, but *Fantastic Beasts* fizzled. Speaking of beasts, the *Transformers* tried to reshape itself and rise for a new generation… with mixed results. The *Terminator* said "I'm back" but few gave it the time of day. The *Alien* franchise tried to bring new fire with *Prometheus* in 2012 but struggled for years to truly break out until *Romulus* in 2023. The *Predator* fumbled a few times but finally made a comeback because someone decided to *Prey.*

The franchise wars have had misfires, casualties, and walking wounded alongside the decade of success that the MCU and others enjoyed. Perhaps the hardest one to watch was the fate of my fictional friend *Indiana Jones*; despite a mountain of Mouse money piled high to haphazardly change his destiny, few bothered to dial him up. Something was wrong… something treasured was absent, and something else had been swapped in to replace it. Remember when a younger Indiana Jones tried to swap a priceless idol for a bag of sand? That didn't go so well, and Hollywood has arrogantly made the same mistake; now their ideology/idolatry threatens even the most lucrative and loved cinematic universes, including the MCU. If there's hope for franchises—and the movie industry in general—the powers that be need to embark on their own adventure, a quest to reclaim what's been lost and once again become raiders of a lost art.

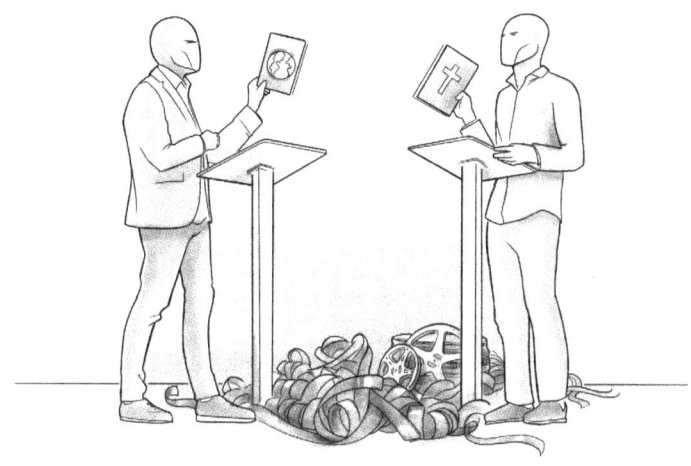

Act 8: **A Tale of Two Pulpits**

or

"the universal dangers of monologuing"

Scene 1: **In Which I Blame Myself**

"Movies are the modern day pulpit..." - James Harleman, *Cinemagogue: Reclaiming Entertainment and Navigating Narrative for the Myths and Metaphors they were Meant to be*

Stop me if you've heard this story… in 2001, I started a ministry in the basement of my church called Film and Theology. I wanted to teach Christians how to think biblically and spiritually about movies and how—indirectly baked into the narrative—there are themes and ideas that communicate subtle messages, even truths, about life and faith, our fear of meaninglessness and our inherent aspiration for transcendence. That ministry eventually moved upstairs, then moved online, and others started listening. Other like-minded Christians also created similar ministries, and a fresh form of film and television engagement began to grow globally. By 2015 successful podcasts like Popcorn Theology had sprung up, inspired by early ventures like mine but taking everything to the next level: a "marvelous era" in its own right.

Oddly enough, this all kind of synchronizes with what we've seen in the 21st century in terms of the evolution of superhero movies. I think of the minister who mentored me in 1998 as kind of like *Blade*, which came out the same year. He was the first pastor who paved the way, showing me that movies were much more than I realized. My basement ministry in 2001 then kind of made me like *Spider-man*—or perhaps just one of the *X-Men*—as these experimental forays into mindful movie consumption in the 2000s blossomed into expanded, amazing Christian conversations in the 2010s, aided by the advent of social media and diverse forums, chats, Facebook groups and more. Believers more broadly began to see and speak about film in a different light, abandoning nonsense phrases like *"I just watch movies for entertainment"* and seeing the power inherent in the medium, to shape minds and inculcate ideas.

The problem was… someone else was listening too.

Like Skynet in *The Terminator*, or Ultron in *The Avengers*, Hollywood became self-aware. I joked about this in the prologue of this book, with the AMC theater speech by Nicole Kidman, but that was simply one expression of a darker self-realization that transpired in the 2010s. As Christians more fully embraced the reality that secular tales have messages woven in by gifted storytelling tailors, the rest of the world also saw this in part, sparking similar conversation. Cinephile sites have sprung up cataloguing tropes, repeated themes, the hero's journey and more (though typically sidelining or omitting the more spiritual angles and Christian correlations). Naturally, this led to a whole new generation of aspiring actors, screenwriters, directors and more entering the industry with a different perspective on the power of narrative.

"A man has an idea. The idea attracts others. The idea expands. The idea becomes the institution." - Top Dollar, *The Crow*

Power corrupts, as they say, and it seems narrative power corrupts narratively. The emerging problem we've seen is that this current crop of "creatives" aren't deft tailors of tales; they've exchanged the narrative looms for story anvils, beating messages into their movies with all the subtlety of blacksmith hammers. They've become… well, frankly, they've become *us*.

Now, when I say that they've become *us*, I'm not just referring to mindfully consuming or creating; when I say *us*, I mean Christian storytelling. And by Christian storytelling, I mean *bad* storytelling. I know some will object here, and yes… I could certainly cite some great examples of good Christian stories. But for years, Christians have had the monopoly on preachiness in our narratives. We've earned the reputation. I tried to clarify in my first book that storytelling is a pulpit in one sense, but ultimately the art form demands that it not function that way overtly. That kills the magic.

How fun would a magic show be if the magician explained how each trick was done as they did it? Not very: even if you're clever enough to sort it out later, the amazement is from not comprehending it in the moment. This is also how great stories unfold; there may be lessons to be learned, or ideas to take away… but these lessons are best when they're thoughts that percolate and linger long after the initial story washes over you. Conversely, making a movie that's simply an excuse for an ideological excursus cheapens the medium, with characters monologuing and *telling* us what to think rather than acting and behaving in situations that *show* us how they think. Although characters in movies certainly make speeches, the general idea in storytelling is "show, don't tell"; this gets complicated and nuanced in application, certainly; there are natural times in movies for characters to monologue, addressing their friends, their team, their classroom, etc. That's why storytelling is an *art*. Not everyone with a message to convey can simply throw a story veneer over their sermon and fool everyone.

Sadly, as well-meaning Christians have fumbled the ball with myriad movies over the years in this manner, the Hollywood landscape in the last decade has become littered with secular sermonizers, the industry infiltrated by hacktivists with a message to hammer home but lacking the storytelling passion or prowess to pull it off. Worst of all, they've taken established and beloved franchises that already had shape and form, ripped off their skins like Buffalo Bill in *The Silence of the Lambs,* and thrown them over their agenda… dancing around and hoping we wouldn't notice the difference (or that they'd effectively murdered the source). Movies have truly become the "modern day pulpits" without pretense.

Now to be clear, I'm not prideful enough to believe my first book and ministry actually moved so far upstream as to influence Hollywood (there would still be a perverse arrogance there in terms of my reach and impact). But whatever the cause of the zeitgeist, the sacred and secular operation of examining, diagnosing and even dissecting narrative has become popular, and alongside that: some insiders, like indelicate story surgeons, have started stitching all sorts of glaring agendas together with all the artfulness of Dr. Heiter in *The Human Centipede*.

Scene 2: **Mickey Mouse, Antichrist?**

"Who's to say the rules must stay the same forevermore?
Whoever made them had to change the rules that came before.
So make your own way, Show the beauty within.
When you follow your heart, There's no heart you can't win."
   - Cinderella, *Cinderella II: Dreams Come True*

"The heart is deceitful above all things and beyond cure…"
   - Jeremiah 17:9

"The word of our God stands forever…" - Isaiah 40:8

I grew up watching *The Wonderful World of Disney,* and there are lots of classic cartoons and movies to enjoy, provided the messages are filtered. It's not that there haven't been problems in the past, all the way back to Jiminy Cricket's promise that wishing on a star will bring us everything our heart desires. Thankfully I had loving parents, weekly Sunday school, and private school education to push back on flawed narratives. Disney, Marvel, Lucasfilm, DC, Universal, 20th Century Fox… all had unique flavors and ideas to sift and sort properly, redeeming some and rejecting others.

But then…

Disney acquired the Muppets in 2004. Mickey strolled into Pixar in 2006 with an offer they couldn't refuse. Donald Duck waddled away with Marvel's ownership in 2009, and George Lucas handed his keys to the Magic Kingdom in 2012. Finally, 20th Century Fox decided that the 21st Century would be controlled by Disney as well. One by one, the House of Mouse swallowed up everything it could in the MARVEL-Us Era, amassing a massive conglomerate composed of multiple divisions, united under one roof with a swelling set of homogenized ideologies and agendas.

> *"And I saw a beast coming out of the sea. It had 10 horns and seven heads, with ten crowns on its horns, and on each head a blasphemous name... given a mouth to utter proud words and blasphemies and to exercise its authority... Then I saw the beast and the kings of the earth and their armies gathered together to wage war... they also worshipped the beast and asked, "Who is like this beast? Who can wage war against it?"* - from Revelation, chapters 13 and 19

I'm having a bit of fun here... or am I?

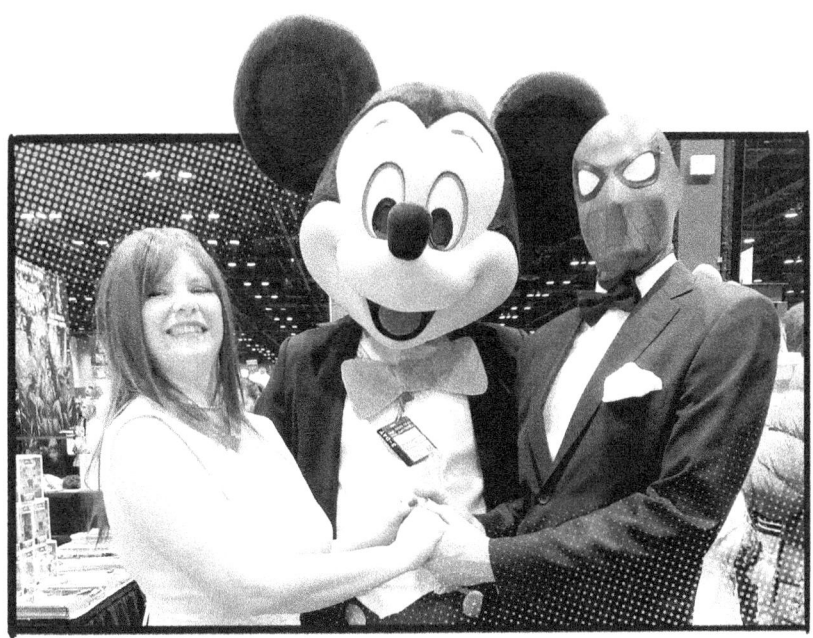

I, for one, welcome our new rodent overlord...

We always think of the beast, the dragon, and other imagery in Revelation as emerging through government and power as we've previously understood things to be. Some have imagined these might also be represented by powerful corporations instead of governments... so why not entertainment conglomerates? Should we be just as wary of a company that has a monopoly on media, not to mention people's hearts and happiness? A company that literally calls themselves a special "kingdom" and declares their parks to be the "happiest places on earth"? Heaven on earth?

I know self-professed Dis-nerds who live for their next visit, their next fix, the next movie... it's the very definition of worship. And that kind of attraction and devotion can easily cause a conformation to whatever worldview they express.

> *"It's time to see what I can do,*
> *to test the limits and break through.*
> *No right, no wrong, no rules for me—I'm free!*
> *Let it go, let it go..."* - Elsa, *Frozen*

This chillingly effective film came out right after I published my first book and took the world by snowstorm: amazing box office and —from one angle—a great story one could learn from. Unfortunately, it suffered from Disney's "Middle-Movie-Music Syndrome", a malady that misdirected people in *The Lion King* and definitely deviated people from essential narrative beats in Elsa's journey. The actual point of the film's narrative seems to have been kidnapped by culture—or marketing—and muddled midway in both movies.

Kids left Simba's story singing the very catchy *"Hakuna Matata"* tune when, in fact, that song was the distracting "idle phase" and malaise the lion cub needed to shake off, to finally face his fears and take the reins of responsibility (which he does at the film's end). Similarly, a frustrated Elsa in *Frozen* mocks self-control and seeking to be good, casting off all restraint and singing her song of liberation... and what happens next? She leaves a massive trail of chilling, ignorant destruction in her wake, and nearly causes the death of her sister... and the entire kingdom! (How's that selfish, narcissistic freedom working out for you?) Elsa makes everything worse until the film's real protagonist—her sister Anna—becomes an instrument of salvation.

And yet… people the world over were embracing this mid-movie melody as if it were a new life proverb. Sidebar: every earnest parent should consider what they're lauding alongside their soon-to-be-Elsa's-age daughters (and boys, let's be equitable here). I'm sure we're all anxiously awaiting the day our kids say "F— all y'all, I'm out of here… and I don't need your ethics, values, morals, Jesus or any of that crap. I'm free." Right?

On one hand, it's bizarre how people seem to prop up the message of this song as laudable when it isn't even consistent with the narrative. The hero is Anna, not Elsa, seeking to alter her sister's course (which is leading her sibling to become a villain). Elsa's song boldly declares how she's never going back (yet she does). *Spoiler alert:* she reconciles and resumes her role (which certainly means some rules are back too). And, of course, the narrative's REAL ne'er-do-wells are punished for their schemes (hey, what happened to *"no right, no wrong, no rules for me?"* Did that only apply to Elsa?). Right and wrong are still being administrated… happily ever after. In other words: the power ballad everyone's singing gets nowhere near providing a solution. It's a song about *license*, not *liberty*.

> *"Do you not know… you are servants of the one whom you obey: either of sin, which leads to death, or of obedience, which leads to righteousness? But thanks be to God, that you who were once servants of sin have become obedient from the heart to the standard of teaching to which you were committed, and… have become servants of righteousness."* - Romans 6:16-18

Elsa's anthem, unchecked, is about lawlessness that leads to more lawlessness, even death. Stop trying to be good? Stop desiring perfection? On the contrary: Christian love—the kind of sacrificial love Anna clearly demonstrates to her sister in the film—doesn't leave us with the advice to *"let it go"*. We aren't called to self-determined freedom; we're called to sacrificial service… to live and show love toward God and others. To imitate Christ's perfection. We aren't called to "follow our heart", we're called to be *obedient to the heart of righteousness*. And one primary fruit of that is self-control.

Clearly, the anthem that emerges in the middle of the film is the ranting of a confused young adult reveling in a *sense* of newfound freedom, which turns out to be more destructive than the strictures she faced before. Worst of all—and possibly intentional—is that, while the film's narrative reverses Elsa's decision to let it all go, the misguided mid-movie song resurfaces as the credits roll, and we're all encouraged to sing along! The big, Academy Award-winning musical number's lyrics clearly cracked under the events of the third act... yet apparently few were paying attention. Belting out *"Let it Go"* makes about as much sense as the snow man Olaf's Ode to summer in the film: **we're glorying in something that actually reduces and destroys us.** In Olaf's case that's what makes his song hilarious and ironic – but with Elsa's song people miss the point.

Thanks to the Kingdom of Mouse, this song would go on to become a cultural anthem for the next decade, for "letting it go" and "coming out" in terms of sexual identity, gender identity, and all sorts of unbiblical lifestyle choices and vice. Let your freak flags fly! The movie also heralded an increasing boldness and even brazen obviousness in terms of messaging within Disney's other acquisitions (like Star Wars and Marvel). Some films and series have gotten so blunt that it almost renders the concepts in Cinemagogue useless! After all, who needs to "sift the narrative" and surface the themes when characters basically explain them to the camera? *"I represent X, and you should believe X."* Thanks, Captain Obvious.

Scene 3: **Can't Stop the (Virtue) Signal, Mal**

"You sly dog! You got me monologuing!"
- Syndrome, *The Incredibles*

Back in the 1980s, the "moral majority" was a right-wing political organization founded by Jerry Falwell. The term would stick in a general way culturally, often as a pejorative for those pesky Christians complaining about the lack of prayer in schools, the lack of morality in government and in media: movies, music, television and more. Rock music was evil, horror movies had demons living in the film stock, etc. This group was often mocked culturally and told they shouldn't be impinging on free speech or pushing their ideologies and agendas. Even many Christians in America called them legalists or extreme in their policing, but predominantly the pushback came from non-Christians and the political left.

Debating the merits or extremes of that moral majority isn't the point of this book, but what is fascinating is that over the last decade —in an increasingly secular culture—the children of those who used to complain the loudest have evolved into a new "moral" majority, a secular moralism easily as legalistic and perhaps more caustic than the religious group their parents vilified decades prior. Things have flipped; if this were *Stranger Things*, we might see our present state as living in the Upside Down. This militant, modern morality in the media has affected storytelling, creators, actors, fandom and more, in an escalating expectation of virtue signaling. It's the modern equivalent of everyone culturally expected to be standing in church on Sunday in suits and ties, singing the same hymn together. And if you step out of line, expect to be excommunicated.

Have some good things come from aspects of secular moralism in Hollywood? Certainly… perverts and criminals like Harvey Weinstein have been taken out of play, Diddy parties have been canceled, and other long-term abuses the entertainment industry kept swept under the carpet have been cleaned up to a degree. But in the same way Christian reforms were often accompanied by overreactions, false accusations, witch hunts and more, the industry has erred even more greatly because they aren't rooted to morality's true Vine.

The Scarlet Twitter

With no physical church to engage in anything resembling biblical discipline, this new legalism is largely lived out on social media. One need only look up the cases of James Gunn and Chris Pratt to see a pattern familiar to the Christian. There's a rebuke… then a call to repentance… then shunning, followed by an apology. The apology is judged and dissected, and—depending on the rants of what is likely a vocal minority—the person is back "in" or not. Historically, studios (like Disney, the soon-to-be-only studio) have waited and seen how the public on social media view these pariahs, content to let their career rise or fall on majority public opinion.

Lately, however, we see them opening or closing the gates based not on what the masses will think but rather their own gospel. This Hollywood "bible" has been revealed over the last decade to include several different books, though the title is simply "The Religion of Identity Politics". In this bible we find books like 1st and 2nd Feminism, The Parade of Pride, White Fragility, and the Revelation of Representation. On these rocks Hollywood has built their church… and I think the MARVEL-Us Era is—in part—to blame.

Scene 4: **Crisis of Infinite Births**

"Everyone comes to Zootopia thinking they can be anything they want. Well you can't. You can only be what you are. Sly fox. Dumb bunny." - Nick Wilde, *Zootopia*

As the pictures in this book make fairly obvious, my wife and I began dabbling in cosplay; we'd frequently go all out for Halloween, but in 2011 we decided to go to Seattle's Emerald City Comic Con dressed as Marvel's characters Iron Fist and The Black Cat. Our entry into cosplay culture was rapidly accelerated when we attended a costume competition that was poorly administrated. Seattle's comic convention was owned locally then, and I happened to know the owner; I mentioned the show's shortcomings and he basically told me to put up or shut up; that's how Kat and I found ourselves with a side gig running cosplay contests. When Emerald City was purchased by a larger company, we found ourselves administrating New York Comic Con, Chicago's C2E2, and more— plus Rose City Comic Con in Portland—until a little pandemic shut everything down for a few years. We hosted as The Clock King and Catwoman; another year I was Lex Luthor. I hosted one event as Uatu the Watcher that wound up in an episode of SyFy's *Heroes of Cosplay* (blink and you'll miss me). Those were interesting times.

After the pandemic, we were asked about returning… but frankly, the landscape had changed. What had been for years a tolerant culture—live and let live—was rapidly becoming a demanding and militant culture: conform or be cancelled! Say the wrong thing, use the wrong pronoun, give someone what they think is a wrong look, and you're obviously a misogynist homophobic hate-filled bigot. We enjoyed our time, but the culture had shifted.

(To be fair, there are plenty of comic book aficionados and cosplay enthusiasts that are kind, courteous, classically tolerant and a joy to engage with. I suspect they represent the majority, but a militant minority has grown and gained enough influence and power enough to effectively control the culture…something I hope changes in the future.)

Cosplayers (most of them not competitive and in the actual contests, but simply dressing up and attending the conventions) are an interesting subculture. Beyond the simple desire to dress like a fantasy character they love, there is often an investment in their character—down to the details—with a hero worship that goes beyond admiration. They want you to see them as the character… they want to get it right, they want to—for a time—*become* and *inhabit* that character. They want to be someone else. Sometimes this extends to changing themselves, but sometimes it's also altering the character to some degree; for example, gender-bending a character has become popular. Gender-bent Robin, a gender-swapped Princess Leia… cosplayers don't let something like biology stop them from becoming the character they want to be. They don't have to be Batgirl; they can be a gender-bent Batman. In other words, they can be anyone and anything they want to be, or the character can be anyone or anything they want them to be: it's a fierce self-determination, and in cosplay culture it has lately become accompanied by demands for affirmation.

As you might expect, a disproportionate percentage of LGBTQ+ persons inhabit comic con and cosplay subculture, and I believe there's a parallel and reinforcement in this culture in terms of fantasy and reality. Video games and role-playing culture have also fed this mindset; if a female D&D player can be a male barbarian, and a man can get obsessed with playing a video game as a stunning (and brave) female character, why can't they become or embody these personas in real life? Is your fantasy character your preferred person? Why not bend reality to match?

"Your scientists were so preoccupied with whether or not they could, they didn't stop to think if they should." - Ian Malcolm, *Jurassic Park: The Lost World*

Admittedly, even I didn't see this connection at first. You might naturally push back with *"What? So… this means every guy playing Tomb Raider and enjoying his video game time more than real life is going to start thinking he wants a sex change?"* Of course not, but in a culture already confused in other areas of sexuality and gender, we probably haven't considered the potential pitfalls of identity investment and exchange regarding fantasy characters and how it may be impacting an up-and-coming generation. We can debate which comes first in these circumstances—a deviant lifestyle drawn to that kind of fantasy subculture, or the immersion in media that might psychologically entice one toward deviation—but I suspect it's both/and. The subculture draws a high percentage of LGBTQ+ persons and, in turn, they trumpet and advocate for their lifestyle in those fandoms in ways that encourages experimentation and emulation, tempting and leading others down the path.

We also see how comics and comic book movies have evolved to accommodate and reinforce the *"anyone can be anything"* mantra. At one of the cosplay competitions we ran, one of the contestants was a "Lady Loki". Turns out Marvel did this in the comics even before the female variant in the Disney+ *Loki* series. Whether it's fans bending these characters to fit their own image, or comic writers fueling those desires—or their own—everyone can have whatever shape of a character they want. This brings us back to notions of "head canon": this is *my* Loki. In *my* universe, this is who the *character* is, and this is who *I* am. We believe we define our reality and identity.

In 2011, I had no problem with Miles Morales as Spider-man… in the comics it occurred in an "Ultimate" Marvel universe—an alternate reality where Peter Parker died—so the original tale seemed story driven. However, while the movie *Enter the Spider-verse* was an admittedly hilarious film, the final lines don't really make sense when you think about it. Nor are they helpful when it comes to this false narrative of identity. Miles, talking to the audience, tells us:

"Anyone can wear the mask. You can wear the mask. If you didn't know that before, I hope you do now. Cuz I'm Spiderman. And I'm not the only one. Not by a long shot."

I can almost hear Oprah handing them out like new cars: *you get a Spider-man! You get a Spider-man! You get a Spider-man!* I mean sure, I'd love to put on the mask (I even did for a photo shoot with the wife) but guess what? I can't be Spider-man. I can't even be Batman: I'd just be that imitator in *The Dark Knight* wearing hockey pads.

"Sticking feathers up your butt does not make you a chicken!"
- Tyler Durden, *Fight Club*

Peter Parker and Miles Morales were uniquely chosen—by providence or fate—to be bitten by a rare, radioactive spider. I don't have powers, the audience he's talking to doesn't have powers, and even the vast majority of the people in his own fictional universe aren't going to be bit by a special spider any time soon… so no: not just "anyone" can wear the mask. Certain people with certain attributes and providential opportunities are able to fill that role. This is where comics and comic book films have joined the modern mantras of our culture—and poured gasoline on it thanks to their global exposure—with a desire to eradicate all roles and distinctions, many of them God-given (like male and female).

"When I was a kid, I thought Zootopia was this perfect place where everyone got along and 'anyone could be anything'. Turns out, real life's a little bit more complicated than a slogan on a bumper sticker. Real life is messy. We all have limitations."
- Judy Hopps, Zootopia

Probably in the same way everyone missed the point of *Frozen*, a lot probably walked away missing a key point of 2016's *Zootopia*. Early in the film, Nick Wilde states the obvious truth: *Everyone* cannot be *anything*. He points out he's a fox and Judy is a bunny, but he deviously muddies the water by adding adjectives: *sly* fox, *dumb* bunny. By film's end, we see that Judy (and Nick) aren't defined by those adjectives. She's not dumb—but guess what? She's still a freakin' bunny! Wearing a fox suit, or even getting surgical alteration, wouldn't change that. That's why she concludes by saying we all have limitations.

So no, a *girl* can't be Spider-*man*. And Spider-man can't be a girl. But guess what ladies? There's Spider-Woman. Black Widow. Scarlett Witch. Let's not forget Wonder-Woman, Batgirl, etc. And we don't need Spider-trans. We don't need the Stunning Spider. He has web fluid; he's not gender fluid. Forcing characters like Spider-man and others to accommodate every gender, race, color and creed destroys any uniqueness the character has on a trendy altar of representation. Just substitute "Spider-man" for "special" in this classic quote from *The Incredibles*:

Helen: ***Everyone's*** ~~***special***~~ ***[Spider-man], Dash.***

Dash: ***Which is another way of saying no-one is.***

Bending characters in these bizarre and misguided attempts at inclusion has also given rise to a toxic state of naval-gazing I call…

Scene 5: **Over-realized Representation**

Now believe me, I get it. Lieutenant Uhura on the bridge of the starship Enterprise was a monumental step forward and a very positive form of representation. Years later, Benjamin Sisko would be the Commander of Deep Space Nine. Captain Janeway would take the helm of the Voyager. Star Trek, in many commendable ways, paved the way for healthy cultural progress in the 20th century, bringing America more in line with actual, biblical values of equality. As a concept, "representation" is laudable, but the term today has mutated into something narcissistic and self-defeating.

Going back to my mythical Hollywood "bible", I don't think I'd have a problem with the book of 1st Feminism. Some very positive things were changed and shaped in the 20th century in terms of the rights and treatment of women, many of those with ripples to this day. The second book, however (or what I believe is more accurately described as fourth-wave feminism) is a mean-spirited, man-hating, petty distortion reduced to admittedly "micro" issues being elevated to "aggression". Like the sly fox Nick Wilde, they "add the adjective" but in this case it's to masculinity—*toxic* masculinity—and then they never mention anything positive about masculinity, keeping the two bound together.

In similar fashion, much of the racial tension remaining in this country is fueled by the political left in an exploitative way that shames children for the sins of their forefathers; they've literally borrowed religious ideology, making black slavery in America the "original sin" for which all "white" Americans must forever sit in shame and guilt for, performing a Catholic-style penance and sitting in cultural Purgatory for an indefinite future. For a movie tie-in here, go watch Matt Walsh's *Am I Racist?* for more. But I digress…

When I was eight or nine, I watched *The Wizard of Oz*. I didn't enjoy the movie, however… in fact I couldn't. I just felt a disconnect. I looked at this young girl Dorothy and couldn't see myself. As a boy, I couldn't relate to a female character. I didn't feel represented, so… *NO! I'm totally kidding.* I loved it. I enjoyed the movie enough to dive in and read the entire Oz book series by L. Frank Baum. I even love the *Return to Oz* movie with Fairuza Balk. It didn't matter a wit that the main character was a girl! I identified with her as a *person*. As a *human*. I related to her journey and with her character. Some aspects were intriguing because she looked, thought and acted *differently* than me. In fact, empathizing with someone who distinctly wasn't like me (but looked like my female classmates) may have made me nicer to the girls at school.

What are we WATCHING for?

Modern representation is rooted in the idea that anyone can be everything, so there must be some version of everything that looks *just like me!* Gay Superman, Black Superman, race-swapped Scooby Doo characters, rainbow-colored cultures in every corner of Tolkien's Middle Earth… the list goes on and on, all in the name of making sure everyone sees *themselves*. Because that's what it's all about, right? Me. I'm the center. Show me… *me*. Make me everything. It's affected the creative process to where so much time is spent on productions getting the perceived need for representation right that the rest of the creative process—especially the narrative—suffers. And it's self-defeating when it comes to what good storytelling should actually be doing.

Storytelling, at its best, should be taking us into a tale where we *experience the other*; the protagonist may or may not have qualities we relate to (and if we do, it should be the content of their character, not the color of their skin). Christians are chastised again and again with the reality that we aren't Jesus. We're not even King David. We are not the center of the story. It's *not about you*.

Representation can be helpful in certain seasons we've already discussed, such as the back half of the last century with the women's and civil rights movements, but at some point today this just becomes narcissistic pandering for all of us. We don't want to experience the other; we just want another mirror. The hero is us.

One of my first, favorite comic books as a kid was Marvel's Power Man and Iron Fist (most people today know Power Man simply as Luke Cage). Now, I can accept I may have partially identified with Danny Rand because he was white, but he was also slight. I was nowhere near Luke Cage's brawny build. I was also shy as a youth, more like Danny than the brash Luke. But both of their upbringings were utterly different than mine. Danny was disciplined. Luke was street-smart. I didn't see myself as either of them so much as I was intrigued *by* them. At the end of the day my interest was not that Luke or Danny represented *me*. I was a cowardly kid; they weren't scared of anything. They were also adults, not children; I wasn't looking at myself, but someone older.

In other words, the best stories will primarily allow us to experience the other… looking for the aspirational aspects that make us want to be *less* like ourselves and *more* like the virtues we see in characters that are truly written as heroes: to see someone worthy of imitation, yet reminded that we'll never be that central character. I'll never be Superman, but I can be *like* Superman. The goal of the Christian isn't to *be* Christ, it's to be *like* Christ. Since the former would be idolatry, perhaps we should similarly stop trying to have our superhero icons represent us, and rather try to be representations of them where applicable.

And the reality is, I (and my generation) grew up with a multi-colored media experience that reached parity decades ago. As we've already established, the MARVEL-Us era grew out of the successful *Blade* films. Any actual student of film and television can see the evidence for themselves, from strong female characters to people of all colors and cultures. The cancel-culture clamor for more representation has indeed gotten tiresome, and not just for me… we're finally starting to see the fallout from Hollywood banging that gong, especially over the last five years.

This may be part of what killed the MARVEL-Us Era…

Scene 6: **It's Just Not Twerking Anymore**

"She's got help." - Okoye, *Avengers: Endgame*

It was an unnecessary and forced visual moment that made no sense in terms of the climactic battle with Thanos' forces; male and female combatants (and living plants) were all scattered across the landscape engaged in various altercations. Then—with no audibly conveyed plan in advance—all the women for no known reason simply disengaged from their distinct battlefronts at the same time (abandoning their male comrades) to converge on the indestructible Captain Marvel, who honestly didn't need their help anyway. It got some easy cheers (but nothing close to Captain America wielding Thor's hammer) for a "grrrrrl"-power moment that was unnecessary, and didn't emerge from anything natural in the narrative. Could they have saved that idea for a future storyline where a plausible reason might have made it poignant? Certainly. Instead, it was done for one reason only: *checking a box*. A box that fed-up critics have started calling *The Message*. Others call it *woke*.

Contrast that *Endgame* moment of awkward intersectionality with the Avengers assembling in the first film… or better yet: when they all leap into battle at the beginning of *Age of Ultron*. Like *"she's got help"* they're all obviously posed shots, like something right out of a comics cover or cartoon theme song. Yet in two of them the maneuver is derived from the narrative; nothing seems forced. And in those images we see men and women, thunder gods and green monsters, people representing not one segregated intersection but rather a world of differences, coming together in unity not born of biology but ideals and shared mission. That's the vision of shared "help" we should be looking for, culturally and biblically: not forced distinctions the Bible says shouldn't define us, or divide us.

And thus, what many hoped was a blip with the awkward *Captain Marvel* movie became more and more the Marvel motif: Mock, reduce and replace male characters (as if somehow that elevates women). Race swap other characters. And for anyone saying "but they're just following the comics" it's true: the comics have been adhering to the secular bible longer than the movies, and *sales have been in decline for years*. The books with new characters rarely last long, and invariably the legacy characters get resurrected.

It wasn't just the Marvel head of the Mouse-beast that started checking boxes and evangelizing their new identity politics gospel, either; although I cut Rey some slack that many Star Wars fans won't (and even defend choices made with Luke Skywalker) after a couple seasons of *The Mandalorian* the trajectory became more obvious with each new Star Wars iteration. Beloved characters like Obi-wan Kenobi were nerfed and sidelined so "diverse" characters in his show could enjoy more screen time, capability and competency. With the DEI disaster that was *The Acolyte*, lifelong and casual fans have been abandoning the franchise.

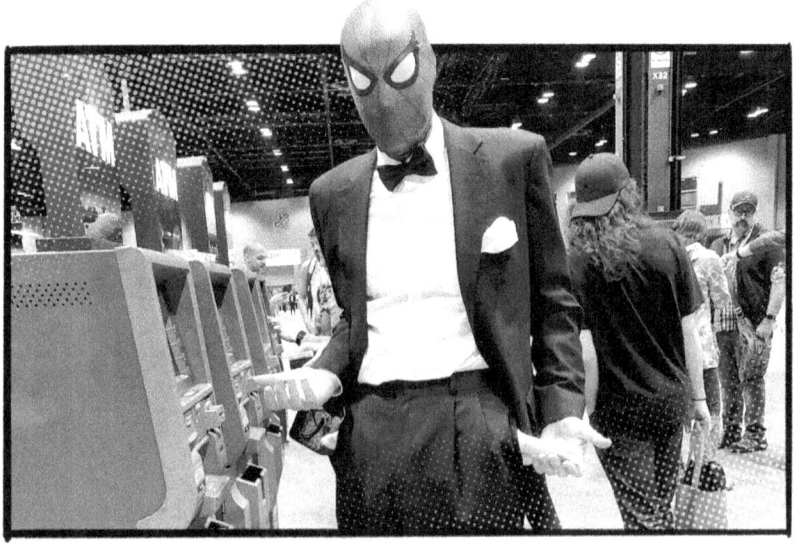

What do you mean, the account's overdrawn?

The last few years haven't been kind to Disney. Their animated films—*Strange World, Elemental, Wish*—underperformed or outright bombed; the new *Indiana Jones* died on the table. Pixar's *Lightyear* also suffered, and back at Marvel the budget-inflated and story-incoherent *She-Hulk* couldn't shake it (although she tried, too hard). Captain Marvel's second movie, bolstered by two other heroes hoping to salvage actress Brie Larson's already critiqued attitude and acting, became the worst-performing MCU film. Something was wrong… and while terms like "superhero fatigue" and "franchise fatigue have been bandied about and certainly have *some* merit, it's not just that. Several properties that bombed above weren't superhero movies or established franchises. The overarching issue was an expressed fatigue with Disney's blatant, incessant sermonizing through story. If not for the double-punch of the successful Pixar's *Inside Out 2* and Marvel's *Deadpool and Wolverine*, Disney in 2024 might have been renamed The Tragic Kingdom.

The Mouse isn't alone in its folly, however: a ton of television networks, as well as Apple, Amazon, Netflix, and others are equally guilty… and in various sectors they're feeling the financial crunch. In the same way the world—and some Christians—have largely ignored Christian movies and television for heavy-handed storytelling crimes, there's now a seeming cultural repudiation of this current secular preaching; people are voting with their wallets and viewing habits.

In my first book I emphasized the value in engaging secular narrative for discussion and encouraged Christians—even young believers—to engage more. But the way things were headed since then? With youth already facing two strikes of indoctrination by public schools and social media, the third strike of modern movie catechism might have been something I began cautioning against, or even suggesting a strategic withdrawal. I planned to end this book on a much darker note, warning parents that the more overt messaging is going to have a detrimental effect on younger minds.

However, as we see both the pop culture and political landscape experiencing a seismic shift in 2024, I find myself relatively calm… and definitely curious… about where things are headed from here.

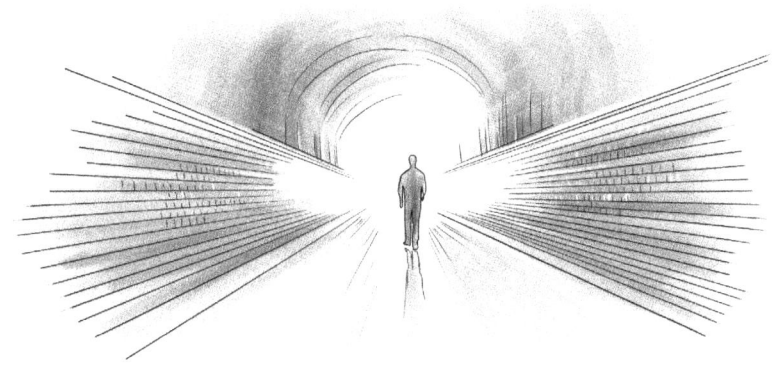

Epilogue: "**S**" **is for Hope**

or

"a light at the end of the multiverse tunnel"

Scene 1: **The Dog Days Are(n't) Over**

*"**Krypto… home. Take me home.**"* - Superman, *Superman*

As this book was in its final edit, the teaser trailer for the 2025 James Gunn directed *Superman* debuted around the world. A haggard, caped Clark Kent lies in a bleak snowy landscape, bleeding and wheezing, whistling for his trusty super canine companion to come and take him home. One might liken this to the state of not just the DC franchise, but Marvel's broken crown as well, or even Hollywood's ailing box office. Time will tell, but the movie teaser has all the elements of an apology and a promise. Are they picking up their battered, sermonizing bodies and returning "home"?

What do we hear in the film trailer? New instruments, but John Williams' classic score. What do we see? A boy and his dog, a man and his father. A farm in middle America. A girl not posturing like a boss, but protected by a super man. A loving embrace and a kiss between—gasp!—a man and a woman. There is no whiff of modern mantras here, no forced messaging. We're teased with a return to fundamentals, and not just of the Superman character, but perhaps the classic values of a culture once more closely connected to Christian ideals. We even see people throwing rocks at Superman in the trailer, decrying the boy scout... much like we've already seen people squealing about how studios seem to be pivoting away from all the identity politics and giving in to conservative complaints. I know I'm reading a lot into a two-minute movie ad, but I hope it heralds a course correction for the industry... even if it's not for the right reasons.

"If there's a steady paycheck in it, I'll believe anything you say."
- Winston Zeddemore, *Ghostbusters*

I never expected Hollywood to grow a moral backbone. If the post-pandemic, message-infected cinema is going to recover I don't expect it will be because they collectively repent and turn to Jesus. The entertainment community isn't likely to abandon their mostly liberal leanings or secular worldviews... but pressure from the people who buy the tickets and popcorn, who pay for the streaming services and post thoughtful reviews, may at least make them retreat from worshipping their ideologies to embrace their old, familiar, and favorite idol: *Mammon*. And frankly, I'm okay with that.

"Bread is made for laughter, and wine gladdens life, and money answers everything." - Ecclesiastes 10:19

The politically charged decade that coincided with the MARVEL-Us Era definitely impacted and shaped the entertainment industry. As people became more polarized culturally, this bled into everything from late night talk shows to major motion pictures. Entertainers and storytellers became more brazen in bashing those they disagreed with through their craft. Instead of sliding in ideas as subtext, they just blurted them out in the text itself, ultimately alienating as much as 50% of their audiences. Perhaps more. This has culminated in an ailing industry on life support. The same messaging and attitudes in the political arena have also yielded a fierce repudiation of the left in the 2024 election. From the entertainment industry to the ballot box, the people have spoken: tone down the radical messaging or we're done with you.

"With everything that's happening... people might just need a little old-fashioned." - Phil Coulson, *The Avengers*

A look at the 2024 box office reveals that movies steering clear of the messaging—the Hollywood bible—have not only fared better but profited greatly. On top of *Inside Out 2* and *Deadpool and Wolverine* there was *Twisters, Despicable Me 4, Beetlejuice Beetlejuice, Godzilla x Kong* and *even Bad Boys: Ride or Die. Dune: Part Two* also did well (with an admittedly feminist spin that needlessly changes Chani's character) but predominantly all the successes are those that put "The Message" back on the shelf. Also notice: all the above movies are franchises. "Franchise fatigue" evidently isn't the problem, unless we're talking about poorly-handled franchises co-opted by the modern secular gospel. Franchises aren't dead, and I doubt superhero franchises are either. I'm not sure they'll enjoy the same headliner status they did last decade, but I'm hoping James Gunn will stick to storytelling basics and steer DC along a better path. Don't let me down, my namesake!

As for Disney? I'd like to think they've learned their lessons, but Star Wars still seems to be suffering a lack of direction and a washed-up leader who won't leave. And Marvel? The 2025 slate looks lukewarm at best, and banking on Robert Downey Jr. to save them by "Doom-ing" them in the coming Avengers movies is a gamble I'm curious to see play out. I wish them well: I'd love to see what's next for Spider-man, to see Peter Quill return, and I'm cautiously optimistic for *Daredevil: Born Again*. Presently, Disney's reputation is on the same level as the "worst Wolverine" that Deadpool first meets in the bar during their cinematic team-up... but remember: as we saw in that story, this doesn't mean things can't be redeemed.

Jumping universes, Yoda once told Luke Skywalker that *"once you start down the dark path, forever will it dominate your destiny."* However, we later see Vader (and Kylo Ren) reject that path and redeem themselves before the end. So there's still a chance the House of Mouse can clean their castle, grabbing the preachy activists masquerading as creatives and tossing them out like Vader hurled the cackling Emperor Palpatine, returning Walt's wonderland to its former glory.

Scene 2: **An Attitude of Gratitude**

"Everybody wants a happy ending. Right? But it doesn't always roll that way. Maybe this time." - Tony Stark, *Avengers: Endgame*

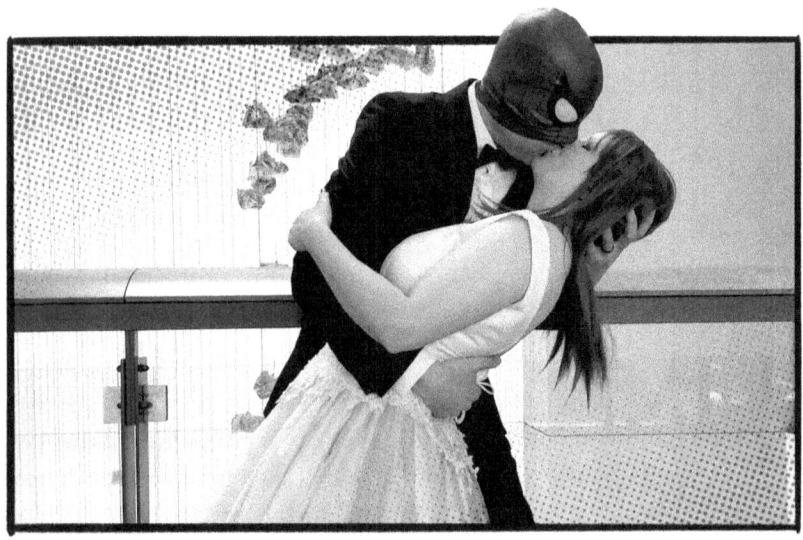

One more day, brand new day… nothing's breaking up this marriage baby.

I saved the most critical parts of the book for the last chapter, but lest I leave a dour—or sour—taste in anyone's mouth, let's make sure you know where I stand at the (potential) end of the MARVEL-Us era. As I turned 50 in 2023, and since spent some time meditating on the half-century of life God's given me under the sun, I find myself concerned in some ways but not jaded. I'm frustrated with the last five years, but hopeful. And not only hopeful, but grateful.

"I'm hoping if you play this back, it's in celebration. I hope families are reunited, I hope we get it back and something like a normal version of the planet has been restored, if there ever was such a thing." - Tony Stark

Cinema has been around for less than 150 years. Most of human civilization has never had the luxury of such grandiose fiction and fantasy on display. How spoiled we are! Even if the entertainment industry fell apart and things were never the same again, the sheer number of movies I love and enjoy rewatching are almost more numerous than the days I have left to watch them. Perhaps our attitude should be better than looking at Hollywood and asking, *"what have you done for me lately?"* Scheduling watch parties of old films, coordinating group outings to see new films, and finding times to stage film and theology conversations is an almost overwhelming juggling act. So many movies, so little time! Woe is me, indeed. Let's all complain about how our cups runneth over…

When you think about it, five years was the length of "the blip" between *Avengers: Infinity War* and *Endgame*. With signs of things turning around in Hollywood, perhaps we'll look back at 2019-2023 as "the dip" in cinematic storytelling; perhaps we're in the moviegoing endgame now, and a hulking Hollywood will snap its fingers and bring back the creativity that has lost its luster.

"If you told me ten years ago that we weren't alone, let alone, you know, to this extent, I mean, I wouldn't have been surprised, but come on… This time travel thing we're gonna try and pull off tomorrow, it's got me scratching my head about the survivability of it all." - Tony

I was thinking about all the time-hopping the Avengers did in the final film of the Infinity Saga. Then I made it personal… if you time traveled back to that young, four-year old James Harleman, watching the premiere of *The Incredible Hulk* TV show in 1977 with his dad, and told him what to expect from the 21st century in terms of superhero storytelling, that kid would have just stared—eyes wide and mouth open—in stunned disbelief.

If you sent another intrepid hero hurtling back to 1983—shortly after *Return of the Jedi*—and told ten-year-old James about all the Star Wars comics, books, prequels, sequels and series that were to come, both good and bad… I don't think my brain would have been able to process it.

If someone from the future popped back to my high school years and told me how many Batman movies (and actors) we'd have after Michael Keaton—and the global mainstream appeal of comic book heroes—I would have scowled and flipped them off with a dismissive "whatever". This is a niche subculture, man, there's no future where everyone on the planet knows who "Iron Man" is.

Flash forward then to James in 1998, excited about his revitalized faith, and tell him he'll spend the next quarter-century of his life not just talking about Jesus, but seeing all his favorite childhood fictions fully realized in film? But wait, there's more: tell him he'll be given a mission to mindfully consume, converse, and correlate all these fictional favorites to the true story he's come to love the most? My head probably would have exploded.

"Then again that's the hero gig. Part of the journey is the end. What am I even tripping for? Everything's gonna workout exactly the way it's supposed to."

Indeed Tony, the overall theme of this book, and the last 25 years, should be one of celebration. What more can I say but to borrow the final words of Iron Man in *Avengers: Endgame* and direct the sentiment instead to God:

"I love you 3000."

And in the immortal words of Stan Lee:

"Excelsior, true believer."

Roll Credits...

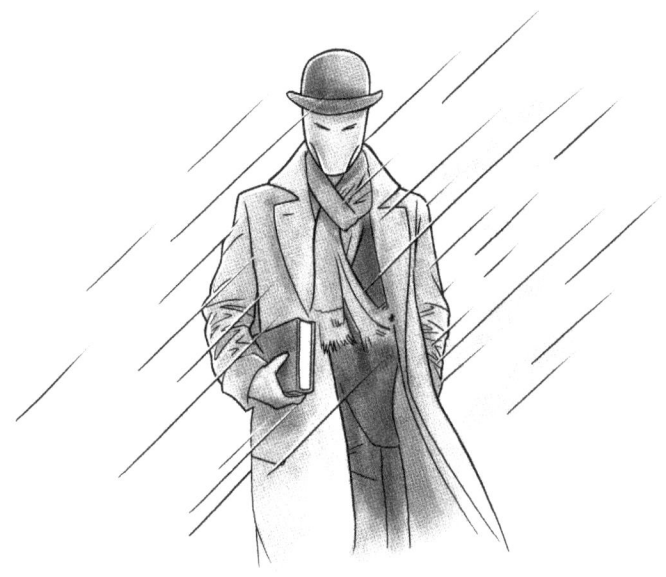

Post-Credits Scene: **Like Tears in Rain**

or

"all those moments will be lost in time"

Scene 1: **Like Cells, Interlinked**

Deckard: *We could keep at this, or we could get a drink.*

K: *I'll take the drink.*

Okay, I tried to let this go. *Save this for another book*, I said… but then again, it was the MARVEL-Us Era that paved the way for a sequel to my once-favorite film: *Blade Runner*. If not for the franchise frenzy and intellectual property mining that occurred, it may never have happened. And did I even *want* it to happen? I approached this movie with great trepidation. Different director. So many things that could go wrong. I never felt the original movie *needed* a sequel, and we've seen sequels sully people's favorite franchises for cash-grabs and worse. So…

"Is it the same now, as then? …all these years, drunk on the memory of its perfection." - Niander Wallace, *Blade Runner 2049*

BLADE RUNNER 2049: Our Place in the Story

"…because you've never seen a miracle." - Sapper Morton

The film opens with a man—well, technically an artificial human replicant—willing to die because he's seen something that gives him transcendent hope. His killer, Ryan Gosling's Officer K, is our protagonist: a synthetic man eking out a living in a world that has a use for him, but also disdain. We follow K on a journey of self-discovery that will lift him to the highest hope of the hero's journey, then summarily dash those dreams, replacing them with a cloud of confusion before bringing him a moment clarity at the film's end.

I've talked about the North and South Poles of storytelling—the *Life Transcendent* story and *Life Under the Sun*—and in the first Cinemagogue book I raised the curious case of movies like *The Dark Knight*: some of the greatest films manage to walk a tightrope line between the two poles and leave viewers with some internal struggle. This movie may be the most stunning case of this tension I've ever encountered, which is part of what makes it the top of my list. As mentioned earlier, the sequel to my favorite film is now my new favorite film of all time. Certainly the sublime direction by Denis Villeneuve contributes to this, accompanied by a superb score by Hans Zimmer. Original *Blade Runner* screenwriter Hampton Fancher's fingerprints are all over this follow-up, and Oscar-worthy performances by Gosling, Ana de Armas, Sylvia Hoeks, Jared Leto and Harrison Ford don't hurt either. Still, it's the biblical nuances of *hero* and *humbling* that make all the difference, coalescing into a narrative rarely captured so perfectly in storytelling.

Are We *Matter*, or *Do* We Matter?

"Mere data makes a man. A and C and T and G.
The alphabet of you." - JOI

Blade Runner's original story was less about actual Artificial Intelligence and more a metaphor for racism, or a caste system: treating a certain class of people as less than human. Expendable. Harrison Ford's character, Rick Deckard, tangled with replicant Roy Batty, who also opined on the fleeting nature of life… how we're here, then gone, with all our experiences and memories snuffed out and ultimately lost, amounting to nothing. Again, it's not just a replicant's lament; it's the ultimate question plaguing the mind of mankind. Is this all there is? Is there a deeper meaning? Are we part of something greater? Do we have a soul that goes on after death?

Lieutenant Joshi: *You've been getting on fine without one.*

K: *What's that, madame?*

Lieutenant Joshi: *A soul.*

This theme is continued in the sequel with K, who's been living life under the dismal sun of 2049, assuming like many an atheist or agnostic in the world that this hardscrabble material existence is probably all there is; life is hard, then we expire. He's going through the motions, trying to find joy—or JOI—where he can. This humdrum view of the world is disrupted, however, when he finds the corpse of a pregnant woman… and it's Rachel. It's a *replicant*.

Birth of a miracle child

"…Rachel was barren… God remembered Rachel, and God listened to her and opened her womb." - Genesis 29:30-32

Niander Wallace recites this verse (and speaks of angels, the Kingdom of Heaven, and more) establishing a biblical resonance that can't be ignored. A womb that shouldn't be able to conceive or give birth has done so, creating a child whose existence may tear down the status quo. K's boss sees the child as a threat to their way of life, not unlike King Herod, who saw the birth of Jesus as a threat and reacted similarly. She tells K this child "breaks the world," that it will tear down a wall between kind: Ephesians 2 similarly says Jesus *"has broken down in his flesh the dividing wall of hostility"*. Clearly people see this development as either monster or messiah. The underground replicants have their own designs on what the child will be, and what the revolution should look like. Wallace doesn't necessarily want the child dead, but wants to harness and control its power. (Side note: the "ruler" of this world is blind.)

There are obvious similarities here with the virgin birth and the biblical coming of Messiah: people either wanted Jesus dead, or to become a revolutionary leader as they saw fit… or else they simply

256

wanted to benefit personally from his power and have it advance *their* kingdom. The Christ also came in a way no one expected, escaped infanticide, and was raised to adulthood without anyone knowing who he really was, or what he would do. Naturally then, we learn that our protagonist turns out to be (drumroll please)...

...NOT the One

"I always told you. You're special." - JOI

This is, without question, one of the main reasons this movie has taken its place on top of the cinematic heap for me. Many times, and in many ways, I've lamented how so many Hollywood stories I love commingle the *convert* story with the *Christ* story. Neo discovers the truth of the Matrix, and then he is the destined savior. Same with *Avatar*, *Dark City*, and so many hero's journey stories; Blade Runner 2049 dares to chart a different path. This is one of the few times I've ever seen a person awakened, transformed, converted—he saw the miracle—and then have the humbling experience of realizing he's not the story's promised savior.

"You imagined it was you? Oh, you did. You did! We all wish it was us." - Freysa

K's life is rocked with the reality of the miracle child, then the notion that he might be that child, and then the discombobulating third shock dispels that notion; the movie maintains the reality of a bigger story, but shifts K left of center. Our protagonist isn't the main character; in fact, we don't even see that ultimate story play out. When father and daughter are reunited at film's end, we're left with a million questions and our imagination regarding what she will do, or become. K's tale is just an intimate portrait, an "average Joe's" chapter in a much larger meganarrative. K struggles to emotionally recalibrate in light of this revelation, to decide what part he's going to play in the story.

"For what we proclaim is not ourselves, but Jesus Christ as Lord, with ourselves as your servants for Jesus' sake."
- 2 Corinthians 4:5

A Christian's job, after being changed by the reality of the incarnation, is to *point* to the narrative's true hero, to *serve* that pivotal figure. And in some cases—like K—to even lay down our lives for our Savior's cause. K isn't a parallel for Jesus… he's more like Rahab, who helped the two Israelite spies escape in Joshua chapter two. Or perhaps he's like Stephen, the first Christian martyr who appears in just two chapters of the book of Acts. Both K and Stephen's lives ended in blood, staring up into the heavens…

> *"But Stephen, full of the Holy Spirit, looked up to heaven and saw the glory of God, and Jesus standing at the right hand of God."* - Acts 7:55

The question is, what does K see? Do we watch him breathe his last, the soft snow falling on his cheeks, in some miserable life under the sun? Or do we feel a sense of life transcendent here? Or perhaps *love* transcendent?

The Nature of Love

"I know what's real." - Rick Deckard

If the first film dealt with what it means to be human, the other major theme in this sequel is love: what is it? Does it even exist? Do we just fool ourselves? Is it subjective? If it is real, what does it look like? How do we receive love, and how do we give it?

It's no coincidence that two supporting characters are called LUV and JOI. In the first film, we explored love between a human and a replicant; our takeaway in that story was that it was supposed to be real. This movie takes a good amount of time depicting the relationship between K and JOI: making us root for them, hope for them, despair when her transmitter is crushed. But this all becomes emotionally suspect when the JOI advertisement hologram calls K *"a good Joe."* JOI was everything he needed her to be, but was it real? Was it love? Maybe not. Wallace's JOI A.I. just gave K everything she was *designed* to give him. She even overlays herself with a prostitute so she can "be with him", (which clearly isn't real). With the advent of AI in the 2020s, this discussion is timelier and more topical than we may have anticipated. Contrast K and JOI's relationship with Deckard's rejection of the Rachel copy; Deckard can't be bribed because he isn't self-deceived. He isn't tempted by manufactured joy.

"Sometimes to love someone, you gotta be a stranger." - Deckard

This is one of the few pieces of wisdom Deckard shares with K (after they stop hitting each other). It's an odd line, but Deckard has given up his life—even knowing his daughter—to engineer the plan to keep her safe. Every day he didn't seek her out was a sacrifice. It's not love as we normally picture it, but it's a deep love nonetheless.

In John 15 Jesus said, *"Greater love has no one than this, that someone lay down his life for his friends"*. We also know that we weren't friends with God when he did this for us; we were sinners, we were estranged from God. He knew us, but we were strangers to him. We didn't even ask for it… but he did it anyway. He chose to die for us, to call us friends. To love us sacrificially.

Standing beneath the false JOI on a dark street, K realizes what love is. The JOI offered by Wallace—the world—was not truly love. He's accepted that he's not the miracle child; his memories are fake. K's not related to Deckard; he and Ana are effectively strangers to him, and yet… K chooses to help them, to lay down his life for them, to rescue Deckard and reunite father and daughter (now that the offspring is presumed dead). Deckard asks K why he did this—*"what am I to you?"*—and I love that K simply smirks and doesn't repeat Deckard's line (that would have been banal). But the answer hangs in the chilled air: *he's loving the stranger.* It's a selfless, servant sacrifice, and in a small way imitates Christ.

"There's a little of every artist in their work." - Dr. Ana Stelline

The messianic Ana may be an enigma in this film, but in the end what we see K imitate is the servant love of our true Messiah. He finds meaning, purpose, and identity in this; he loses his life to find it. We're left wondering what he's thinking, and it's indeed subjective… but what I see is a sense of satisfaction, of true joy and sublime transcendence, as he stares up into heaven. He can truly rest, in peace. *Blade Runner 2049* defines that peace as finding our identity—and our humanity— in a story far greater than ourselves.

May we all find ours in the Greatest Story Ever Told.

'Nuff said.

"You're still here?"

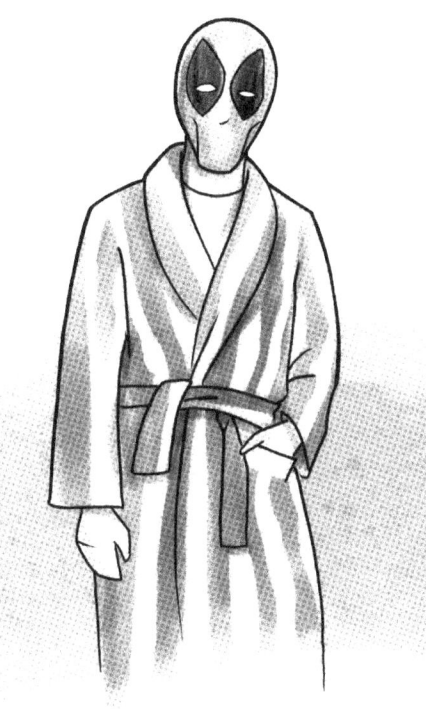

"It's over."

"Go home."

"GO!"

- Deadpool, *Deadpool*

www.ingramcontent.com/pod-product-compliance
Lightning Source LLC
Chambersburg PA
CBHW072132170526
45158CB00004BA/1339